Why are republics nowadays the most common form of political organisation, and the one most readily associated with modern democracy? In *The invention of the modern republic* a team of highly distinguished historians of ideas answers this question, and examines the origins of republican governments in America and Europe.

Although republican governments had existed in the West since classical antiquity, the modern national states of Europe took shape as large centralised monarchies. Until the late eighteenth century it was generally believed that republics could function only in small urban territories with considerable ethnical and political cohesion. This belief was reversed when the American colonies in 1776 and then France in 1792 became the first large republican states of the modern age. The contributions to this volume reflect on this transition, and explore how the republic was reinvented at the end of the eighteenth century as the ideal form of government for modern commercial states, with a large population and an independent and heterogeneous citizenry. The essays assess how republican institutions were adapted to the requirements of private property and modern commercial economies; and how developments in Italy and Germany were influenced by the American and French experiences. Given the renewed interest at present in the functioning and evolution of democratic institutions (especially in their relations with market economies) the issues discussed in *The invention of the modern republic* have a powerful contemporary resonance.

The invention of the modern republic

The invention of the modern republic

Edited by

Biancamaria Fontana

Professor of the History of Political Ideas,
University of Lausanne

CAMBRIDGE
UNIVERSITY PRESS

Published by the Press Syndicate of the University of Cambridge
The Pitt Building, Trumpington Street, Cambridge CB2 1RP
40 West 20th Street, New York, NY 10011–4211, USA
10 Stamford Road, Oakleigh, Melbourne 3166, Australia

© Cambridge University Press 1994

First published 1994

Printed in Great Britain at the University Press, Cambridge

A catalogue record for this book is available from the British Library

Library of Congress cataloguing in publication data applied for

ISBN 0 521 43088 7 hardback

CE

In Governments independent of the people, the rights and interests of the whole may be sacrificed to the views of the Government. In Republics, where people govern themselves, and where, of course, the majority govern, a danger to the minority arises from opportunities tempting a sacrifice of their rights to the interests, real or supposed, of the majority. No form of government, therefore, can be a perfect guard against the abuse of power. The recommendation of the republican form is, that the danger of abuse is less than in any other ...

James Madison to Thomas Ritchie, 18 Dec. 1825

Is it, then, our duty to see which of these not right forms of government is the least difficult to live with, though all are difficult ... ?

Plato, *Politicus*

Contents

x   Contents

Contributors

JOHN DUNN is Professor of Political Theory and Fellow of King's College, Cambridge.

BIANCAMARIA FONTANA is Professor of the History of Political Ideas at the University of Lausanne and member of the CREA (Centre de Recherche d'Epistémologie Appliquée), Paris.

FRANÇOIS FURET is Professor of History at the University of Chicago and President of the Centre Raymond Aron in Paris.

PATRICE GUENIFFEY is Maître de Recherche at the Ecole des Hautes Etudes en Sciences Sociales, Paris.

GEROLAMO IMBRUGLIA is Professore Associato at the University of Bari.

BERNARD MANIN is Professor of Politics at the University of Chicago, attached to the CNRS and member of the CREA, Paris.

WILFRIED NIPPEL is Professor of Ancient History at the Humboldt University of Berlin.

ANTHONY PAGDEN is Lecturer in History and Fellow of King's College, Cambridge.

PASQUALE PASQUINO is Researcher at the CNRS and member of the CREA, Paris.

PIERRE ROSANVALLON is Director of Research at the Ecole des Hautes Etudes en Sciences Sociales, Paris.

GARETH STEDMAN JONES is Reader in History and Fellow of King's College, Cambridge.

Acknowledgements

The essays collected in this volume were originally presented as contributions to a seminar on 'The Theory of Modern Republicanism' which met at King's College, Cambridge and at the Ecole Polytechnique in Paris in the course of the academic year 1989–90. This project was made possible by the support of a number of institutions: I wish to thank in particular Martin Hyland, Convenor of the King's College Research Centre, Jean Pierre Dupuy, director of Research of the CREA, François Furet, president of the Centre Raymond Aron, and Jean Khalfa for the French Cultural Delegation in Cambridge. Several scholars, whose work for different practical reasons does not appear in this book, contributed valuably to the research of the seminar: amongst others Laurence Cornu, Istvan Hont, Quentin Skinner, Michael Sonenscher and Richard Tuck. Finally, together with the other contributors, I am grateful to Richard Fisher of Cambridge University Press for undertaking the publication of these papers.

BIANCAMARIA FONTANA

Introduction: the invention of the modern republic

Biancamaria Fontana

This collective research on 'The Invention of the Modern Republic' was originally prompted by two quite different sets of events that featured very prominently on our television screens in 1989: on the one hand the lavish ceremonies and celebrations occasioned by the 200th anniversary of the French revolution of July 1789; on the other the gatherings, protests and demonstrations which marked the end of socialist regimes in the countries of eastern Europe. It was difficult for the historian to resist the feeling that these episodes were – at least imaginatively or symbolically – somewhat connected with one another; but it was hard to identify the link between them and hard not to re-echo the platitudes and facile enthusiasm of journalists and news reporters.

One did not need to be a sceptic at heart to be puzzled by the sight of Jessye Norman, draped in the French flag, hovering round the Arc de Triomphe singing the 'Marseillaise'. Was her performance intended to glorify liberty and universal values or to celebrate national pride? A blunder on the part of over-ambitious stage managers or just a new proof of the inexhaustible irony of history, of its infinite capacity to mix and pervert the symbols of the past? As for the cheering crowds in the squares of Berlin, Budapest and Prague, were they gathered there to applaud their liberation from foreign imperialism and domestic tyranny – as news reporters assured us – to voice renewed ethnic hostility, or to welcome the prospective delights of free-market society and consumerism – as the most censorious of western commentators were eager to suggest?[1]

Although these questions were potentially very complex to answer and involved tangled historical and political judgements, there was at least one element which they brought clearly into focus: 1989 was the year of the triumph of a particular political regime, a regime which had undergone its most dramatic historical tests at the time of the American and French revolutions, and which was now left to stand alone as a viable

---

[1] On the movement of 1989 in various east European countries see the testimonial by Timothy Garton Ash, *We the People: the revolution of 1989*, Harmondsworth, 1990.

model for modern industrial societies. This regime is still probably best described by the label of 'bourgeois liberal republic'. The formula was devised by its enemies rather than by its supporters at a time (the mid-nineteenth century) when its achievements seemed paltry when set against the high hopes of many for universal fraternity and justice; but it captures better than any other the specific character of this political form: the combination of 'limited' government – a government based upon popular representation and constitutional guarantees – and of a free-market economy – a society geared to the promotion of private property and individual interest.

The essays collected in this volume are an attempt to understand and clarify the nature of this political regime. They investigate its intellectual and practical presuppositions, the problems it addressed, its adaptation to a variety of national settings, its strength and its limitations. The use of the word 'republic' in this context may generate some ambiguity: it would be impossible, when reconstructing a line of reflection stretching over centuries, to establish neat breaks or unequivocal discontinuities in the language. It is sufficient to stress that what is attempted here is not a study of republican theory as such, or of the development of republican traditions from classical antiquity to post-revolutionary Europe, let alone an episodic history of republican experiences in the West.[2] It is, perhaps less ambitiously, a study of one particular type of 'republic' which was characterised precisely by its unorthodox and innovative rapport to the tradition of classical republicanism (see Nippel, Chapter 1 below): of one particular type, but a type with a future.

The model of the bourgeois liberal republic had its origins in two domains of political reflection which, strictly speaking, had very little to do with republicanism at all: they did not focus upon the city-state, civic identities and values or the rule of elective magistrates. The first of these domains was the elaboration of institutional strategies to limit the power of absolute sovereigns in large monarchical states. The establishment of a doctrine of division of powers, administrative delays and constitutional guarantees, combined with the sanction of popular resistance to abuse, prepared the way for that dramatic shift from the sovereignty of the monarch to the sovereignty of the nation which would become universally apparent after the ignominious failure of the flight of the French royal family to Varennes in 1791 (see Manin and Pasquino, Chapters 2 and 5 below). The second was the study of the conditions which favoured the development of rich commercial economies in extensive and heavily populated nations. By placing at the centre of their system the socio-

---

[2] For an essential bibliography of recent works on the history and development of republicanism see below, pp. 226–9.

economic reality of 'modern' civil society, the political economists stressed the association between wealth, security and the protection of individual property and activity from state interference.[3] In both cases the focus was upon the problems raised by the government of large states and centralised monarchies, while republican institutions were generally dismissed as a phenomenon of the past, associated with the small territories and relatively insular economies of the city-states of antiquity or of the Italian republics of the Renaissance (Imbruglia, Chapter 3 below).

The rebellion of the American colonies against the British crown in 1776 indicated for the first time the possibility of combining republican institutions and the mechanisms of limited government to guarantee the prosperity and security of a large national territory (Manin, Chapter 2 below). In France the difficulty of renewing the cumbersome and financially ruinous administrative machinery of the *ancien régime*, the bottled up resentment of aristocrats and bourgeois alike, combined with the political ineptitude of the royal family, brought about the sudden collapse of the monarchical regime, opening the way for a republican solution which only a few years before would have appeared wildly utopian (Gueniffey, Chapter 4 below). In France, as in America, the accent was not so much on elective as opposed to hereditary government – though election was generally regarded as preferable – but upon the limited, moderate character of the power that *any* government should be allowed to exercise.

Born of a theoretical and practical compromise in the aftermath of civil war and revolution, the bourgeois liberal republic predictably inherited a series of ambiguities and tensions which dominated its successive history. The demand for national sovereignty and the effective representation of popular will found itself at odds with the obstinate determination to protect property by restricting the electoral franchise and excluding non-proprietors from political decisions. The demand for political equality and abolition of privilege associated with the new conception of the sovereign nation clashed with that inequality of wealth and property which the political economists saw as the key requirement for the prosperity of modern commercial states.[4] More generally the preoccupation with human rights and the universalist moral ambitions born of the revolutionary experience were not easily reconciled with the essentially utilitarian vocation of the ideology of the market economy (Stedman Jones, Chapter 8 below).

---

[3] Istvan Hont and Michael Ignatieff, eds., *Wealth and virtue: political economy in the Scottish Enlightenment*, Cambridge, 1983.

[4] See my *Benjamin Constant and the post-revolutionary mind*, New Haven, Conn., and London, 1991, pp. 68–80.

In the American debates, as in the French Assembly, the new regime had proclaimed its vision of a future world in which commerce, exchange and the universal values of equality and liberty would bind together all nations, replacing the struggle of hostile empires with a peaceful league of free nations. If in America the establishment of national independence for a time concluded the fight against foreign powers, the new French republic soon found itself engaged in an extensive military struggle for its survival which rapidly turned from defensive war into a successful campaign of imperial conquest. Under the pretext of aiding patriots and revolutionaries against their 'tyrannical' sovereigns, republican France *de facto* imposed by the force of arms its own rule on neighbouring European nations (Pagden, Chapter 7 below). The vision of commerce as an agent of peace, cultural unification and political compromise clashed with the competitive instinct of expanding economies contending for markets and productive resources. Forced into the experience of war and conquest, revolutionary France rediscovered the civilising mission and nationalist ambitions of the ancient monarchy (Fontana, Chapter 6 below).

In the American federation, in spite of continuing domestic conflict, the new-born republic could at least readily identify its foundation with the conquest of national independence. In France the post-revolutionary regime found it difficult to produce a coherent account of its own origins, a reconstruction of the recent historical past which could be shared by all the forces which had contributed to its establishment. The allegiance to revolutionary values and the proud claim to have forged a new social and political order was not easily reconciled with the desire to heal the traumatic break that 1789 opened in the continuity of the national tradition. Caught between the conflicting demands of change and order, innovation and stability, religious heritage and enlightenment, national unity and party allegiance, the new France saw its history transformed into ideological warfare and an enduringly acrimonious clash of loyalties (Furet, Chapter 9 below).

In spite of these difficulties and tensions, the bourgeois liberal republic proved its truly Thermidorian vocation by a remarkable resilience, a great capacity for survival and adaptation. The extension of the electoral franchise to wider groups of the population, the attachment, however symbolical, to juridical forms and constitutional guarantees, the support of a relatively free public opinion, above all the lures of prosperity and social mobility, carried it through the storms of class conflict and violence (Rosanvallon, Chapter 10 below).

As John Dunn observes in the concluding essay of this volume (chapter 11), the endurance of this political model is the measure of the failure of other alternatives far more than it is an indication of decisive practical success. There have always been, there still are intolerable degrees of human misery and injustice hidden behind the glittering Thermidorian façade, with its easy promises of wealth, freedom and self-fulfilment. Yet the distance between promises and reality, however discouraging, has not proved quite as abysmal as it has been in the case of totalitarian regimes or socialist experiences. Certainly what has happened to the world economy in the last ten years or so makes it difficult to sustain the belief, shared by many good liberals in the aftermath of the second world war, that under the rule of modern democracy the brutality of capitalism in its early stages would finally turn into some new, more equitable, socially minded variety.[5] A political system which acknowledges its dependence – for justice, humanity and security – on the laws (or vagaries) of the world market does not sound *a priori* very enticing; but then all political systems today are dependent on such laws and take enormous risks whenever they choose to ignore this fact.[6] On the occasion of the celebrations of 14 July 1989 it was suggested that two hundred years after the revolution it was time that the bellicose words of the 'Marseillaise', with its references to fields drenched in blood and to ferocious soldiers, should be changed to something more suitable to the peaceful, leisurely disposition of the car- and armchair-bound citizenry of the present times. This embarrassment is symptomatic: the bourgeois liberal republic is not the kind of ideal one would instinctively wish to die for; yet there is plenty of evidence that today, without its shaky protection, we would be far more likely to be fighting for our lives.

The success of the bourgeois liberal republic is directly connected with the modesty of its ambitions. True, this system may educate its citizens to selfish individualism and immoderate greed; but it has given up the pretension that in any situation there will be just one possible common good, one perfect balance of powers, one just constitution, one ideal solution to our problems (Manin, Chapter 2 below). It has cured us of the taste for universal recipes and taught us that all political solutions must be the product of adjustment, mediation and compromise. The true heritage of the bourgeois liberal republic is not so much what it has achieved, but the chances it leaves open.

[5] Adam Przeworski, *Capitalism and social democracy*, Cambridge, 1985; Alain Bergounioux and Bernard Manin, *Le Régime social-démocrate*, Paris, 1989.
[6] John Dunn, ed., *The economic limits to modern politics*, Cambridge, 1990.

1 Ancient and modern republicanism: 'mixed constitution' and 'ephors'

Wilfried Nippel

An ancient historian who is asked to talk on ancient and modern republicanism faces, perhaps surprisingly, a fundamental problem: he does not know what ancient republicanism is at all. Ancient political theory in its heyday of creativeness during the fifth and fourth centuries BC is focused on republican city-states and their problems in maintaining liberty and stability. Existing monarchies are considered only as survivals from a remote past or as forms of government typical of semi-barbarian areas at the periphery of the Greek world or even as phenomena of oriental despotism. One-man rule could theoretically be considered legitimate only in cases where absolutely the best man should be in power.

City-states, indeed, lived under the threat of tyranny; tyranny was illegitimate domination *per definitionem*, irrespective of the ruler's actual conduct. The new Empire of the Macedonians and the states which succeeded it were not adequately discussed in political theory. In Rome, the establishment of freedom was associated with the expulsion of the kings, and later the Principate based its legitimacy on the alleged return to republican institutions and rules. Reflections upon 'the good monarch' in Hellenistic and Roman imperial times would try to persuade an absolute ruler to act with such self-restraint that people could still consider themselves as free citizens. Thus, since the city-state consisting of a self-governing citizen-body was considered the only legitimate form of political organisation, it is highly problematic to use 'republicanism' as a meaningful concept with respect to classical antiquity (at least in pre-Christian times).

The obvious way out of this dilemma is to adopt a retrospective approach and to define as ancient republicanism those elements of classical political theory which became an essential part of a modern republicanism that is defined by its opposition to legitimate types of monarchy.[1] The best known approach to identifying links between

---

[1] On the history of the term *res publica* and its derivatives from ancient to modern times see the important article by W. Mager, 'Republik', in O. Brunner *et al.*, eds., *Geschichtliche Grundbegriffe*, vol. 5, Stuttgart, 1984, pp. 549–651. For a short survey on 'republicanism'

ancient and modern republicanism is, of course, the theory of civic humanism or classical republicanism. This theory has seen a remarkable expansion during the past decades: from Hans Baron's revelation of its impact in early Renaissance Florence[2] through associating it with the myth of Venice,[3] the English debate on Machiavelli[4] or eighteenth-century radical Whiggism[5] to finally the masterly sketch of Pocock's 'Machiavellian Moment',[6] which connects ancient traditions and their Renaissance revival with the ideas of seventeenth- and eighteenth-century English republicans, American revolutionaries and theorists of the Scottish Enlightenment.

This is not the place to sum up these lively discussions and to weigh the approval and disagreement which Baron's and Pocock's works have provoked thus far.[7] I will simply discuss here some concepts which rank as essential elements of this classical republicanism. I shall argue that only sharper distinctions between certain variants of the ancient tradition will enable us to appreciate the divergent uses which were made of this reservoir of political ideas and to mark those turning-points in their history when the common ground with ancient political theory was in fact simply abandoned.

Pocock's view of classical republicanism implies a linkage between the Aristotelian ideal of active citizenship and the Polybian concept of mixed constitution.[8] In my opinion, this assumption is misleading. In his discussion of citizenship in the third book of *Politics*, Aristotle struggles with the great diversity in access to and use of civic rights to be found in the multitude of existing *poleis*. He stresses that the right to active

compare the article in D. Miller, ed., *The Blackwell Encyclopaedia of Political Thought*, Oxford, 1987, pp. 433–6.

[2] *The crisis of the early Italian Renaissance: civic humanism and republican liberty in the age of classicism and tyranny*, Princeton, N.J. (1955), rev. edn 1966. The concept can already be found in H. Baron, ed., *Leonardo Bruni Aretino. Humanistisch-philosophische Schriften*, Berlin, 1928, pp. xiff.

[3] Z. S. Fink, *The classical republicans*, 2nd edn, Evanston, Ill., 1962; Fink, 'King and doge: a chapter in Anglo-Venetian political and literary relations', *English Studies Today*, 4th ser., vol. 4 (1966), pp. 212–33.

[4] F. Raab, *The English face of Machiavelli. A changing interpretation 1500–1700*, London, 1964.

[5] C. Robbins, *The eighteenth-century Commonwealthman: studies in the transmission, development and circumstance of English liberal thought from the restoration of Charles II until the war with the Thirteen Colonies*, Cambridge, Mass., 1959.

[6] J. G. A. Pocock, *The Machiavellian moment. Florentine political thought and the Atlantic republican tradition*, Princeton, N.J., 1975.

[7] See for a short summary and references W. Nippel, 'Bürgerideal und Oligarchie. "Klassischer Republikanismus" aus althistorischer Sicht', in H. G. Koenigsberger, ed., *Republiken und Republikanismus im Europa der frühen Neuzeit*, Munich, 1988, pp. 1–18, esp. pp. 2f.

[8] *The Machiavellian moment*, pp. 66–80.

participation in all political decisions is the distinctive mark of citizenship only in the full democracy of the Athenian type (*Politics* 1275b, 5), whereas middle-of-the-road constitutions and moderate oligarchies use diverse techniques for graduating political rights with respect of a social elite and the bulk of the citizenry; whereby the latter should be granted not only legal security but also minimal political rights to ensure their loyalty to their home city.[9] The place that any constitution occupies within a continuous spectrum between full democracy and narrow oligarchy depends essentially on the distribution of political rights through the indigenous population.

Aristotle's reflections upon an allegedly more stable mixture of democracy and oligarchy concentrate either on the appropriate restriction of the franchise by means of the census or on devices to influence the actual exercise of political rights; hence the idea that the democratic provision of political pay should be combined with a rule to fine rich people who failed to take over political functions, or the idea of combining the principles of selecting by lot and voting by ballot with respect to political office.[10] The underlying assumption (shared by all critics of Athenian democracy since the late fifth century)[11] is that democracy does not simply imply political equality of all citizens, but designates the domination of only a part (though the great majority) of the citizenry, i.e. the rule of the masses or the poor.

Aristotle presumes that the body of active citizens thus constituted, which in any event would be smaller than it was in full democracy, would occupy the different political bodies in almost the same way; i.e. he does not consider that different political bodies would represent in any way different social groups. But the constitutional problem as such is thought of in terms of the respective claims of social classes; justice and common weal are considered as the result of counterbalancing their demands for social honour and material rewards; it is not understood as a problem between individuals and the state.

This is also true of a quite different version of the mixed constitution model which was developed to describe the unique Spartan constitution and its extraordinary stability over centuries. The Spartan system consisted of two hereditary kings who were the military commanders, the council (*gerousia*) formed by twenty-eight men over sixty appointed for life, five ephors elected annually, and finally the assembly of all Spartans.

---

[9] For a more detailed discussion see Nippel, 'Bürgerideal und Oligarchie', pp. 4–7.

[10] *Politics* IV,9, 1294a, 30 to b 13; see W. Nippel, *Mischverfassungstheorie und Verfassungsrealität in Antike und Früher Neuzeit*, Stuttgart, 1980, pp. 52–63.

[11] The pseudo-Xenophontian tract on the Constitution of the Athenians is especially revealing; compare Nippel, *Mischverfassungstheorie*, pp. 35f. and *ibid.*, pp. 43ff. on further discussions on the notion of democracy.

In diverse passages of Plato and Aristotle the idea is ventilated that Sparta thus made up a constitution which mixed monarchy, aristocracy and democracy; and more specifically that its stability was due to the mutual control between its governmental bodies, especially between the kings (always jealous of each other) on the one side and the ephors on the other side.[12]

Polybius was the first to elaborate a detailed model of a mixed constitution with a system of checks and balances amongst governmental bodies. He applied it not only to Sparta, whose decline in the mean time he ignored (6,10), but also to the Roman republic (6,11–18).[13] Whereas the Spartan constitution was described as the work of the great legislator Lycurgus, the Roman constitution was seen as the product of a long development full of internal conflicts, which however had led to an equilibrium within Roman society that enabled the Romans to undertake a successful policy of expansion.

I will not go into the details of Polybius's analysis of the Spartan and especially the Roman constitution or of his 'cycle of constitutions' (6,3–9). I wish only to stress those points which are of importance for the following discussion.

First, in the Polybian model almost no consideration was given to the role of an active citizenry.

Second, the concept of checks and balances derived from observations upon Spartan and Roman constitutional reality; it tried to account for a distribution of power which had developed historically and could be seen as a social compromise between nobility and people; it was not based on normative ideas of a necessary differentiation of governmental functions.

Third, the model of the mixed constitution allowed the accommodation within a republican framework of quasi-monarchical powers – such as strong executive magistrates – not as an alien element, but as a factor of stability.

Fourth, the model of the mixed constitution revealed by implication an understanding of democratic institutions which differed sharply from the common view that direct participation in decision-making was the hallmark of democracy. In the context of the theory of mixed constitution the Spartan ephors and the Roman tribunes, elected magistrates, were seen as acting on behalf of the people. The theoretical difficulty in the relationship between the people and what are supposed to be the people's magistrates is revealed by the fact that different accounts of the Spartan constitution which identified it as mixed ignore either the ephors (as did

[12] See Nippel, *Mischverfassungstheorie*, pp. 124–36.
[13] *Ibid.*, pp. 142–53.

Polybius) or the assembly of the people when identifying the democratic element in the constitution.[14]

I shall add some remarks on the ambivalent character of ephors and tribunes which are necessary for a comprehensive understanding of their future role in political theory. In historical times the ephors were the actual governors of the Spartan state. Access to this office was in practice open to ordinary citizens rather than monopolised by a relatively closed political elite. Having absolute power over the citizens, the ephors themselves were not subject to control and accountability. Thus in the fourth century the assessment of the ephorate as a democratic institution was contrasted by the opposed view which saw it as an almost 'tyrannical' body.[15] The evaluation of the ephors' relationship with the kings was also ambiguous. Tensions between the ephors and (one of) the kings, who were a living contradiction of the egalitarian spirit of the Spartan social and political order, were notorious. The ephors were thought to represent the community of Spartans against the kings; thus they exchanged monthly oaths with the kings: the kings swore to observe the laws of the community, the ephors not to encroach on their powers.[16] The ephors were not considered part of the original Lycurgan constitution and they were not mentioned in the so-called Great Rhetra.[17] They were thought of as a later institution especially created to 'bridle' the kings so that in Sparta, as the great exception in Greece, kingship could survive.[18] A most important version of this explanation reads that king Theopompus was responsible for the establishment of the ephorate. Being reproached by his wife for having reduced the inheritance of his descendants he replied that on the contrary he had taken the necessary steps to preserve it in full.[19]

Like the ephorate, the Roman tribunate could also be understood, as in Cicero, as an institution intended to curb the power of the consulate (*De legibus* 3,16; *De re publica* 2,58). A more relevant point is the relationship between the tribunate and the *plebs* itself. On the one hand one could say that the tribunes were obliged to act according to the people's wishes as Polybius (6,16,5) said.[20] But on the other hand only the tribunes could provide a formalised and binding expression of the people's will. Furthermore, each individual tribune was free to stop the deliberations of the people by means of his veto.

That is why Cicero, even in relation to the Struggle of the Orders and

[14] Aristotle, Politics 1265b 35ff.; 1270b 5ff.'; 1294b 13ff.
[15] Plato, *Laws*, 712d; Xenophon, *Constitution of the Lacedaemonians* 8,4.
[16] Xenophon, *Constitution of the Lacedaemonians* 15,7.
[17] Plutarch, *Lycurgus* 6.
[18] Plato, *Laws* 692a.
[19] Aristotle, *Politics* 1313a 26ff.; Plutarch, *Lycurgus* 7,2; Valerius Maximus 4,1, ext.8.
[20] Cf. Cicero, *De oratore* 2,167; Plutarch, *Tiberius Gracchus* 15,2ff.

the disturbances of the late republic, came to a qualified acceptance of the tribunate's usefulness: as an institution which symbolised liberty the tribunate served at the same time to keep the people's will under reasonable control (*De legibus* 3,23–6).

As symbols of liberty, tribunate and *provocatio* were often mentioned in one breath.[21] *Provocatio* meant the Roman citizen's right to an ordinary trial instead of being subject to summary jurisdiction by magistrates. Its absolute validity came under discussion during those crises of the late republic which escalated into armed conflicts. Advocates of the established order claimed that in such cases the responsible magistrates, in agreement with the senate, were authorised to override the law in order to save the republic as a whole.[22] This claim was expressed by the so-called *senatus consultum ultimum*, which was formally passed for the first time in 121, and could be rendered with the formula *salus populi suprema lex*.[23] Following the crushing of Tiberius Gracchus and his followers in 133 by the private initiative of senators against the will of the responsible magistrate[24] there was, however, a school which argued that the proclaimed rights of senate and magistrates could not exclude altogether any ordinary citizen's right to take all necessary means to save the state. If the magistrates failed to do their duty nobody should question the citizen's natural right to use force against force.[25] Thus, the conflicts on the validity of *provocatio* during states of emergency simultaneously shaped ideas of reason of state and of citizens' legitimate self-help which were even thought of as complementary. During the early principate, the reason of state aspect was further developed with recourse to the category of *utilitas publica*.[26] I should add that, as a rule, Stoic or Roman legal thought did not register any contradiction between natural law and positive law or between *iustitia* and *utilitas*. Conceptions of higher-ranking law were not supposed to limit the validity of the established law.[27]

As for the further history of these concepts it is helpful to single out those aspects which illuminate the flexible use which could be made of the ancient tradition. During the Florentine Renaissance, resorting to the tradition of mixed constitution meant discussing the proper extension of

[21] Livy, 3,45,8; Cicero, *In Verrem actio secunda* 5,163.
[22] See W. Nippel, *Aufruhr und 'Polizei' in der römischen Republik*, Stuttgart, 1988, pp. 79ff.
[23] Cicero, *Pro Sestio* 33; *De domo sua* 94; *De legibus* 3,8.
[24] Valerius Maximus 3,2,17.
[25] Cicero, *Pro Sestio* 91f.; *Pro Milone* 8f.; *Orationes Philippicae* 3,3; 5,1; 11,28; 14,17; *Ad familiares* 11,7,2; cf. J. Bleicken, *Lex publica. Gesetz und Recht in der römischen Republik*, Berlin, 1975, pp. 486f,. 502f.
[26] Tacitus, *Annales* 4,38,1; 14,44,4; *Historiae*, 2,5,13.
[27] Cf. G. Watson, 'The natural law and stoicism', in A. A. Long, ed., *Problems in Stoicism*, London, 1971, pp. 216–38; M. L. Colish, *The Stoic tradition from antiquity to the early middle ages*, vol. 1, Leiden, 1985, pp. 88f., 364, 389.

political rights within the citizenry as well as the most effective arrangements of governmental institutions.[28] With respect to the latter point, Venice, with its political stability guaranteed by a complicated structure of government, was seen as the embodiment of a Spartan type of mixed constitution. During the discussions of the late fifteenth and early sixteenth centuries, the supporters of oligarchical government advocated the imitation of the Venetian model, which was partly achieved by the establishment of the *gonfaloniere* for life in 1502; they agreed however with the partisans of popular government on the importance of the Great Council – as a symbol of *libertà*, the maintenance of which would help to block claims for broader participation.[29]

The myth of Venice originated in Florence before it became part of Venetian self-praise from the later sixteenth century.[30] The equation of the ephors with the Council of Ten, which Contarini had proposed, proved problematic in the later centuries when Venice's glory began to fade: authors critical of the Ten's role as instruments of internal security and state inquisition recalled the ephors' notoriety as quasi-tyrannical magistrates.[31]

The great exception amongst the admirers of Venice was, of course, Machiavelli. Though he started the *Discorsi* with reference to Polybius's cycle of constitutions, he offered an original interpretation of Roman

[28] Cf. N. Rubinstein, 'Politics and constitution in Florence at the end of the fifteenth century', in E. F. Jacob, ed., *Italian Renaissance Studies*, London, 1960, pp. 148–63; F. Gilbert, 'Florentine political assumptions in the period of Savonarola and Soderini', *Journal of the Warburg & Courtauld Institutes*, vol. 20 (1957), pp. 187–214; Gilbert, 'The Venetian constitution in Florentine political thought', in N. Rubinstein, ed., *Florentine studies*, London, 1968, pp. 463–500; R. Pecchioli, 'Il "mito" di Venezia e la crisi fiorentina intorno al 1500', *Studi Storici*, vol. 3 (1962), pp. 451–92; Pocock, *Machiavellian moment*, Part II.

[29] Savonarola, 'Trattato terzio. Della instituzione e modo del governo civile', in *Opere*, vol. 11, ed. by L. Firpo, Rome, 1965, p. 474; Guicciardini, *Ricordi* nos. 21, 38 (quoted from F. Guicciardini, *Selected Writings*, ed. by C. and M. Grayson, London, 1965, pp. 10f., 15); Jean Bodin, *Six livres de la République* (1583), reprint Aalen, 1961, Book, II, ch. 1; cf. R. V. Albertini, *Das florentinische Staatsbewußtsein im Übergang von der Republik zum Prinzipat*, Bern, 1955, pp. 102, 124, 127f., 154; F. Gilbert, *Machiavelli and Guicciardini*, Princeton, N. J., 1965, pp. 85ff.; Pocock, *Machiavellian moment*, pp. 128f., 142f., 146, 278f.; Q. Skinner, *The foundations of modern political thought*, vol. 1, Cambridge, 1978, pp. 159f.

[30] Cf. R. de Mattei, 'La teoria dello "stato misto" nel dottrinarismo del seicento', *Rivista di studi politici internazionali*, vol. 15 (1948), pp. 406–36; F. Gaeta, 'Alcune considerazioni sul mito di Venezia', *Bibliothèque d'Humanisme et Renaissance*, vol. 23 (1961), pp. 58–75; M. Gilmore, 'Myth and reality in Venetian political theory', in J. R. Hale, ed., *Renaissance Venice*, London, 1973, pp. 431–44; W. Bouwsma, 'Venice and the political education of Europe', *ibid.*, pp. 445–66; R. Finlay, *Politics in Renaissance Venice*, London, 1980, pp. 27ff.; E. Muir, *Civic ritual in Renaissance Venice*, Princeton, N.J., 1980, pp. 13ff.; E. O. G. Haitsma Mulier, *The Myth of Venice and Dutch republican thought in the seventeenth century*, Assen, 1980.

[31] See E. Rawson, *The Spartan tradition in European thought*, Oxford, 1969, pp. 148ff.

republican history. The liberty of the citizens was achieved by the regulated conflict between nobility and people; the balance between both was guaranteed by the tribunes who served as *guardia di libertà*. In other systems, like Sparta and Venice, this function would lie with the nobility. That allowed for greater and longer-lasting stability but had to be paid for by renouncing a policy of military conquest. Expansion had to be based on an armed citizenry that could never be absolutely pacified (*Discorsi* I, 2–5). In the case of the Roman republic the conflict between nobility and people proved advantageous for the common weal as long as the people were content with being protected by the tribunes against encroachments from the nobility. But when the people themselves wanted a share not only of political honours but also of the nobility's property, as happened with the Gracchan agrarian law, the tribunate was no longer adequate to control the populace, and the destruction of the republic ensued (*Discorsi* I, 39).[32]

Outside the republican context the tradition of ephors and tribunes gained special importance, sometimes as part of arguments in favour of the mixed constitution, sometimes as a notion of its own.[33] Between the fourteenth century (e.g. Marsilius with respect to France under Philip the Fair)[34] and the seventeenth century (e.g. the constitutional debates and conflicts in Sweden)[35] it was applied in a great number of contexts in which the relation between crown and estates was at stake; and *mutatis mutandis* it was relevant to the conciliarist theory as well. In particular the version concerning king Theopompus was used to assert that certain demands of the estates were in the true interest of the crown itself. One of its early examples concerned the rights and functions of the *Justicia major* of Aragon[36] which were often quoted, from Bodin, Beza and Hotman[37] to late-seventeenth-century authors like Neville and Moyle.[38]

The idea of bridling the crown acquired great force in the writings of sixteenth-century monarchomachs who equated not only the assemblies

---

[32] Cf. G. Bock, 'Civil discord in Machiavelli's *Istorie fiorentine*', in G. Bock, Q. Skinner and M. Viroli, eds., *Machiavelli and republicanism*, Cambridge, 1990, pp. 181–201, esp. pp. 191ff.

[33] See for references Rawson, *Spartan tradition, passim*; P. Catalano, *Tribunato e resistenza*, Turin, 1971.

[34] *Defensor pacis*, ed. by R. Scholz, Hanover, 1933, Book I, ch. 8.

[35] See N. Runeby, *Monarchia mixta*, Stockholm, 1962, pp. 544ff; German summary of the book written in Swedish: 'Notizen über eine verhinderte Republik', in Koenigsberger, ed., *Republiken und Republikanismus*, pp. 273–84.

[36] See R. E. Giesey, *If not, not: the oath of the Aragonese and the legendary laws of Sobrarbe*, Princeton, N.J., 1968.

[37] See Giesey, *If not, not*, pp. 21ff.

[38] H. Neville, *Plato Redivivus* (*c.* 1681); W. Moyle, *An essay upon the constitution of the Roman government* (*c.* 1699), both in C. Robbins, ed., *Two English republican tracts*, Cambridge, 1969, pp. 187, 243.

of the estates but also different kinds of inferior magistrates with the ephors. The idea that resistance by the estates or other magistrates was justified, provided they had an indisputably legal position like Spartan ephors or Roman tribunes, was approved by Calvin, if with some hesitation.[39] The argument was also used by other Reformers like Butzer[40] or even Luther and Melanchthon who, however, identified the ephors with the electors of the Holy Roman Empire.[41] And the so-called 'Confessions' of the (Lutheran) Magdeburg citizens and magistrates in 1548 proved most influential in spreading the idea of the inferior magistrates' competence.[42]

The model of the ephors was especially attractive for the Scottish and English monarchomachs of the late 1550s in the conflict with Catholic sovereigns,[43] and for Huguenot authors after the St Bartholomew's day massacre.[44] It supported the claim that resistance to an allegedly tyrannical monarch would uphold the monarchy itself – as in the example of Theopompus.[45] It also allowed the interpretation of the respective coro-

[39] *Institutio Christianae religionis*, IV,20,31; *Corpus reformatorum* XXX,1116; compare Bodin, *République*, Book II, ch. 5.

[40] See H. Baron, 'Calvinist republicanism and its historical roots', *Church History*, vol. 8 (1939), pp. 30–42.

[41] See C. G. Shoenberger, 'Luther and the justifiability of resistance to legitimate authority', *Journal of the History of Ideas*, vol. 40 (1979), pp. 3–20.

[42] See R. M. Kingdon, 'The first expression of Theodore Beza's political ideas', *Archiv für Reformationsgeschichte*, vol. 46 (1955), pp. 88–100; I. Höß, 'Zur Genesis der Widerstandslehre Bezas', *ibid*. vol. 54 (1963), pp. 198–214; Skinner, *Foundations of modern political thought*, vol. 2, pp. 207ff.; E. Hildebrandt, 'The Magdeburg *Bekenntnis* as a possible link between German and English resistance theories in the sixteenth century', *Archiv für Reformationsgeschichte*, vol. 71 (1980), pp. 227–53.

[43] See W. S. Hudson, *John Ponet (1516?–1556). Advocate of limited monarchy*, Chicago, Ill., 1942; J. H. M. Salmon, *The French religious wars in English political thought*, Oxford, 1959, ch. 2; M. Walzer, 'Revolutionary ideology: the case of the Marian exiles', *American Political Science Review*, vol. 57 (1963), pp. 643–54; B. Peardon, 'The politics of polemic: John Ponet's *Short Treatise of Politic Power* and contemporary circumstance 1553–1556', *Journal of British Studies*, vol. 22 (1982), pp. 35–49; J. E. A. Dawson, 'Revolutionary conclusions: the case of the Marian exiles', *History of Political Thought*, vol. 11 (1990), pp. 257–72.

[44] See R. E. Giesey, 'When and why Hotman wrote the *Francogallia*', *Bibliothèque d'Humanisme et de Renaissance*, vol. 29 (1967), pp. 581–611; Giesey, 'The monarchomach triumvirs: Hotman, Beza and Mornay', *ibid.*, vol. 32 (1970), p. 41–56.

[45] Philippe du Plessis Mornay (?), *Vindiciae contra tyrannos* (1579), ch. 3 (quoted from the German translation in J. Dennert, ed., *Beza, Brutus, Hotman. Calvinistische Monarchomachen*, Cologne, 1968, p. 126); Hotman, *Francogallia* (ed. by R. E. Giesey and J. H. M. Salmon, Cambridge, 1972), ch. 12, p. 312; compare ch. 1, p. 155; ch. 12, p. 304; ch. 26, p. 480. And compare Milton, *A defence of the people of England*, ch. 4, in Milton, *Political writings*, ed. by M. Dzelzainis, Cambridge, 1991, p. 130. In 1580 the estates of the Low Countries, who invited the Duke of Anjou to rule (instead of Philip II), quoted the Theopompus story to persuade the Duke to accept the estates' rights; they failed, however. See G. Griffiths, 'Humanists and representative government in the sixteenth century: Bodin, Marnix and the invitation to the Duke of Anjou to become ruler of the

nation oath as a sort of contract comparable to the exchange of oaths between kings and ephors in Sparta;[46] in this way the idea of the ephors could be combined with learned arguments from the positive law of the land: Hotman's *Francogallia* is the obvious example. This sort of reasoning helped to avoid recourse to the *causa religionis*, i.e. one did not claim a right of resistance because of the monarch's 'wrong' confession.[47] The application of the ephors model not only to estate assemblies but also to various minor magistrates implied, on the one hand, that one endorsed an alternative procedure in case the estates were not convened by the crown, and on the other hand that one avoided the final consequence of the justification of tyrannicide by private citizens.

However, not all authors were prepared to rule out this last resort. Especially the Marian exiles were dramatically confronted with the fact that the return to idolatry (as they understood it) had been accomplished by act of parliament and that there were virtually no other institutions which could prevent it. This is why, for example, Ponet or Goodman did not exclude the recourse to self-help against a tyrannical ruler and based this on a sort of natural right which could be used in case the magistrates failed to do their duty.[48] This had a strong resemblance to the Ciceronian argument that under extreme circumstances even the *privatus* was entitled to take the initiative to save the state. (Later Catholic monarchomachs, who in general took over the arguments of their Protestant predecessors, found it easy to justify tyrannicide by making excommunication the necessary precondition.)[49]

The ideas of indivisible sovereignty and of reason of state were developed in response to the experience of religious wars. These doctrines included the refutation of the models of mixed constitution and of the ephors as instruments of lawful resistance. Bodin made considerable efforts to demonstrate from historical evidence that the alleged examples of mixed constitutions – Sparta, Rome, Venice, France (as labelled by Seyssel), the Holy Roman Empire – as well as the supposed function of

Low Countries', in *Representative institutions in theory and practice*, Brussels, 1970, pp. 61–83.

[46] Hotman, ch. 19, p. 402; Théodore de Bèze, *Du droit des magistrats*, ed. by R. M. Kingdon, Geneva, 1970, ch. 6, p. 28.

[47] Cf. E. Wolgast, 'Die Religionsfrage als Problem des Widerstandsrechts im 16. Jahrhundert', *Sitzungsberichte der Heidelberger Akademie der Wissenschaften, Phil.-Hist. Klasse*, no. 9, 1980.

[48] John Poynet (Ponet), *A short treatise of politike power* (1556); Christopher Goodman, *How superior powers be obeyed* (Geneva, 1558) (both reprinted as facsimiles, Amsterdam, 1972). Compare the references to Goodman and Ponet in Milton's 'Tenure of kings and magistrates', in *Political writings*, ed. Dzelzainis, pp. 41f.

[49] For a survey of monarchomach theories compare P. Mesnard, *L'Essor de la philosophie politique au XVIe siècle*, Paris, 1969, pp. 309ff.

the ephors could not stand;[50] a line of argumentation subsequently adopted by Filmer.[51] Bodin in particular took seriously the complexity of the historical evidence even if in the end he trimmed it in accordance with those conclusions which his preconceptions demanded.

In contrast to Bodin, the proponents of reason of state followed Lipsius's lead in quoting repeatedly out of context Cicero's, Seneca's and Tacitus's key sentences on *salus populi* and *utilitas publica*.[52]

The ambivalence of all these concepts which made them available for purely partisan purposes was again apparent during the English revolution. During the first four decades of the seventeenth century several minor and major constitutional conflicts between both Stuart kings and their parliaments were fought in terms of juridical controversies. This type of discourse focused on the real meaning of the Common Law; there was therefore no demand for talking about mixed constitutions or ephors. *Salus populi* and reason of state were, however, several times referred to in court and parliamentary proceedings on behalf of the crown's prerogative.[53] However, the question whether such arguments would constitute a legal title to override the law was never settled.

From 1641, when the conflict between king and Commons escalated into an open struggle for sovereignty, mixed constitution and ephors became key subjects in the propaganda 'war of manifestoes'. Mixed constitution could become a serious issue as parliament for the first time

[50] 'Methodus ad facilem historiarum cognitionem', ch. 6, in *Œuvres philosophiques*, vol. 1, ed. by P. Mesnard, Paris, 1951, pp. 174f.; *République*, Book II, ch. 1.

[51] 'The anarchy of a limited or mixed monarchy' (1648); 'Observations upon Aristotles politiques touching forms of government' (1652), in P. Laslett, ed., *Patriarcha and other political works of Sir Robert Filmer*, Oxford, 1949, and now in J. P. Sommerville, ed, *Filmer, Patriarcha and other writings*, Cambridge, 1991.

[52] Justus Lipsius, *Politicorum sive civilis doctrinae libri sex*, Leiden, 1589. On Lipsius as the key figure of Neostoicism see G. Oestreich, *Neostoicism and the early modern state*, Cambridge, 1982; Oestreich, *Antiker Geist und moderner Staat bei Justus Lipsius*, Göttingen, 1989; T. G. Corbett, 'The cult of Lipsius: a leading source of early modern Spanish statecraft', *Journal of the History of Ideas*, vol. 36 (1975), pp. 139–52. Quotations from Tacitus (and Seneca) often served as substitute for references to Machiavelli's *Principe* (banned by the Index) but Tacitus contained also a potential of anti-absolutist thought which was exposed during the seventeenth century; cf. P. Burke, 'Tacitism', in T. A. Dorey, ed., *Tacitus*, London, 1969, pp. 149–71; C. Schellhase, *Tacitus in Renaissance political thought*, Chicago, Ill., 1976; J. H. M. Salmon, 'Cicero and Tacitus in sixteenth-century France', *American Historical Review*, vol. 85 (1980), pp. 307–31; Salmon, 'Stoicism and Roman example: Seneca and Tacitus in Jacobean England', *Journal of the History of Ideas*, vol. 50 (1989), pp. 199–226; A. T. Bradford, 'Stuart absolutism and the "Utility" of Tacitus', *Huntington Library Quarterly*, vol. 46 (1983), pp. 127–55; B. Worden, 'Classical republicanism and the Puritan revolution', in *History and imagination. Essays in honour of H. Trevor-Roper*, London, 1981, pp. 182–200; M. Stolleis, *Arcana Imperii und Ratio Status*, Göttingen, 1980.

[53] See D. S. Berkowitz, 'Reason of state in England and the Petition of Right 1603–1629', in R. Schnur, ed., *Staatsräson. Studien zur Geschichte eines politischen Begriffs*, Berlin, 1975, pp. 165–212.

acquired the right to meet on a regular basis. It was in particular a declaration of the crown, namely the king's answer to the parliament's Nineteen Propositions, published in June 1642, which popularised the idea that the English constitution was a mixture of 'absolute monarchy, aristocracy and democracy' which by the 'experience and wisdome of your ancestors' had been moulded 'as to give this kingdome ... the conveniences of all three ... as long as the balance hangs even between the three estates'. The king declared that he could not make any more concessions to parliament without destroying 'the ancient, equal, happy, wellpoised and never enough commended Constitution of the Government of this Kingdom' and without being himself made a duke of Venice and the kingdom a republic.[54]

This remarkable application of Polybian theory to the English constitution implied the following important points:

> First, the mixed constitution was declared to be the product of a historical development, thus avoiding the question of its origins and its legal consequences.

> Second, the declaration adopted the intrinsic logic of the system which demanded that every part should accept certain rules of the game and therefore be prepared to compromise.

> Third, it declared the House of Lords to be an indispensable element in maintaining the proper balance between king and Commons, i.e. its existence was legitimated by its function, not by the nobility's vested privileges.

> Fourth, it made clear that only harmony amongst king, Lords and Commons would maintain the social order; that otherwise the masses would gain the upper hand and anarchy would prevail.

The king's declaration, which had been drafted by his newly appointed ministers Falkland and Culpepper, was a sharp, but two-edged propaganda weapon: on the one hand, by promoting the image of a constitutional monarch and warning against social revolution, it made considerable impact on the better classes and helped the isolated king to win support; on the other hand, by talking about 'three estates' it put the king

---

[54] The text is printed in J. Rushworth, ed., *Historical collections ...*, London, 1659–1701, reprint Farnborough, 1969, vol. 3,1, pp. 725–35; the relevant sections of this work can be found in J. P. Kenyon, ed., *The Stuart constitution. Documents and commentary*, Cambridge, 1966, pp. 21–3, or in A. Sharp, ed., *Political ideas of the English civil wars 1641–1649*, London, 1983, pp. 40–3. Cf. C. C. Weston, *English constitutional theory and the House of Lords 1556–1832*, London, 1965, pp. 23ff.; Pocock, *Machiavellian moment*, pp. 361ff; Nippel, *Mischverfassungstheorie*, pp. 258ff; J. Sanderson, 'The *Answer to the Nineteen Propositions* revisited', *Political Studies*, vol. 32 (1984), pp. 627–36.

on the same level as the houses of parliament and, by implication, endorsed the fact that the bishops were no longer regarded as constituting one of the three estates.[55]

The theory of mixed constitution or mixed monarchy was immediately taken up by writers on the royalist as well as on the parliamentarian side. They could not, however, overcome the theoretical problem, sharply analysed by Philip Hunton, that mixed monarchy implied joint sovereignty, which, under the prevailing circumstances, necessarily led to a situation of constitutional deadlock for which no legal solution was available.[56]

Hunton's outstanding analysis (which also demonstrated that a joint legislative power could be combined with a subordinate executive power entrusted to the monarch) was far beyond the reach of contemporary pamphleteers. Most of them wanted to pay lip-service to the mixed monarchy idea yet at the same time to advocate the Commons' actual claims. Therefore they resorted to auxiliary arguments, especially the reformulation of the 'ephors' and the 'reason of state' doctrines. Henry Parker, champion of parliamentary supremacy, argued in 1642 that the English solution to endow parliament with the competence to override the king's prerogative was a much better one than the ephors or tribunes model. The latter would work effectively only if the people rebelled; the ensuing civil war would probably lead to a new tyranny. Representation of the people's will by parliament would avoid these fateful consequences.[57]

The more the conflict intensified, the more that radical versions of the 'ephors' doctrine were likely to be employed. As the king was put to trial, reference was made to the tradition that Spartan ephors had sometimes impeached kings and in one case, i.e. that of the reformer king Agis in 241, had even achieved an execution. This argument was used by the court's Lord President to counter the king's challenge of the proceedings' validity[58] and it was employed – together with the whole stock of traditional

---

[55] See C. C. Weston, 'Concepts of estates in Stuart political thought', in *Studies presented to the Intern. Commission for the History of Representative and Parliamentary Institutions*, vol. 39, Brussels, 1970, pp. 85–130; C. C. Weston and J. R. Greenberg, *Subjects and sovereigns*, Cambridge, 1981.

[56] *A treatise of monarchy* (1643); *A vindication of the treatise of monarchy* (1644). Excerpts are printed in Sharp, ed., *Political ideas*, pp. 153–61. Compare Nippel, *Mischverfassungstheorie*, pp. 269ff.; J. H. Franklin, *John Locke and the theory of sovereignty*, Cambridge, 1978, ch. 2.; J. Sanderson, 'Philip Hunton's "Appeasement": moderation and extremism in the English civil war', *History of Political Thought*, vol. 3 (1982), 447–61.

[57] H. Parker, *Observations upon some of His Majesties late answers and expresses* (1642), quoted from Sharp, ed., *Political ideas*, pp. 141f. Compare Filmer's reply, 'The anarchy ...', in Sommerville, ed., *Filmer*, pp. 165f.

[58] Quoted from Sharp, ed., *Political ideas*, p. 52.

justifications for tyrannicide – in Milton's defence of the king's trial and execution.[59]

Furthermore, pamphleteers defending the Commons made use of the argument that *salus populi* or *utilitas publica* would in an emergency allow them to ignore the royal veto, to take over functions of the crown or later even to abolish the House of Lords as 'useless' and the office of the king as 'dangerous to the liberty, safety, and public interest of the people'.[60] Alternatively, the 'fundamental laws' of the realm were appealed to, both to support the Commons' claim to sovereignty and to charge the king with their breach.[61] These assertions were understood as expressing 'Paramount Law', but this was only a tautological formulation of the necessity to override existing law under certain circumstances. The theoretical weakness of all these constructions was that they fell short of constituting a hierarchy of laws. They did not differentiate between a constitutional law-giver, who decided the shape of government, and the role of a parliament which could only avail itself of competences entrusted to it by such a founding act.[62]

Naturally, even if such an idea had been developed, the Commons would not have welcomed it. The Leveller idea of founding a new order by an 'Agreement of the people' contained *in nuce* such a distinction between constituting act and constituted powers whereby the representatives of the people were barred from interfering with such rights as liberty of religion and conscience. But the Leveller concept was totally unacceptable to the sitting Members, who indeed wanted to make their own tenure as well as that of the ruling class at large perpetual.

The lack of an indisputably legitimate law-giver was the congenital defect of the Cromwellian attempts to achieve a lasting settlement. The parliaments convened by the Lord Protector were not prepared to remain without reservations within the framework provided by the so-called 'Instrument of Government' and the 'Humble Petition and Advice' respectively.

The constitutional regulations themselves revealed strong tendencies to

---

[59] *A defence of the people of England*, ch. 8, in Milton, *Political writings* (ed. Dzelzainis), p. 200.

[60] Parker, *Observations*, quoted from Sharp, ed., *Political ideas*, p. 137; Robert Austin, *allegiance not impeached*, (1644), pp. 43ff.; *Act for the abolishing the kingly office* (1649), in Kenyon, ed., *Stuart constitution*, p. 340. And see J. A. W. Gunn, *Politics and the public interest in the seventeenth century*, London, 1969, ch. 1; R. Ruck, *Natural rights theories. Their origin and development*, Cambridge, 1979, ch. 7.

[61] See Nippel, *Mischverfassungstheorie*, pp. 246–9 for references.

[62] The development of this idea is surveyed by M. P. Thompson, 'The history of fundamental law in political thought from the French wars of religion to the American revolution', *American Historical Review*, vol. 91 (1986), pp. 1103–28.

return to the ancient constitution based on 'three estates'[63] although the possibility of making Cromwell king had at last been dropped. The disputes about the competences of a second chamber, however, strengthened the widespread belief that only a House of Lords would be strong and independent enough to constitute a element of balance between the monarch or quasi-monarch and the popular chamber.

During the Cromwellian era, James Harrington set out to develop the model of a republic which should create an 'immortal commonwealth'.[64] Harrington's *Oceana*, with its mixture of originality, erudition and eccentricity, is of course a rewarding subject in its own right. Furthermore, Harrington is of special interest for our discussion since Pocock had made him the very key figure in the transmission of ideas from antiquity to eighteenth-century Anglo-American political theory. But at least with respect to the mixed constitution this interpretation obscures fundamental differences with respect to the ancient theories of mixed constitution as well as to the seventeenth-century English adaptation of this figure of speech.

Just a few remarks on the governmental structure of 'the Commonwealth of Oceana' must suffice: it consists of a two-chamber legislative and a great number of councils and committees which form the executive branch. The senate, elected on the basis of a census franchise, would represent the 'natural aristocracy' which existed in any given society, whereas the other chamber would be the popular assembly. The senate was to present bills, whereas the popular assembly should decide on those proposals without foregoing discussions and without any alterations. The strict separation of debating and resolving should effect such an interweaving of 'wisdom' and 'interest' as to guarantee the common weal. Public offices were to be filled by complicated and indirect procedures which would combine balloting and selection by lot. All public posts, those of local government included, would be subject to rotation, short terms of office, restrictions on multiple terms, and overlapping periods of tenure. Members of governmental offices and councils were to be recruited from the senate; their depending on that body and changing in composition every year put the executive bodies in a subordinate position.

Thus, Harrington skilfully 'ransacked ... the archives of ancient pru-

---

[63] *Humble Petition and Advice* (1657), in Kenyon, ed., *Stuart constitution*, p. 353.
[64] During his examination after his imprisonment in 1661 Harrington declared that the decisive impulse had been the controversial discussion in the army leadership as to whether Cromwell should assume the kingship. 'Upon this some sober men came to me and told me: if any man in England could show what a commonwealth was, it was myself. Upon this persuasion I wrote; and after I had written, Oliver never answered his officers as he had done before ...': in *The political works of James Harrington*, ed. by J. G. A. Pocock, Cambridge, 1977, p. 859.

dence', as he himself put it,[65] and made use of the variety of institutions and devices which were developed in ancient Israel, Sparta, Rome and Venice[66] to prescribe those arrangements that would enable a 'government of laws and not of men'.

Harrington's understanding of 'government of law' – the formula goes back to Livy (2,1,1) – amounts to a quasi-automatic production of commonweal by means of institutional arrangements which would leave no space for particular interests. Citizens have to function as part of this complicated machinery. Sentences like the following are unequivocal: 'The spirit of the people is no wise to be trusted with their liberty, but by stated laws or orders; so the trust is not in the spirit of the people, but in the frame of those orders.' Or: 'In a commonwealth rightly ordered they [the people] can have no other motion than according unto the orders of their commonwealth'; and finally: 'Give us good orders and they will make us good men.'[67] *Pace* Pocock this is quite different from an active participation of virtuous citizens.[68] The attempt of excluding from public life any pursuit of particular interests also forms a great contrast with a mixed constitution which in one way or the other was thought to neutralise conflicting interests of social groups and/or office-holders by way of channelling and balancing their interaction.

If one looked for an ancient model for *Oceana* (in addition to the most important Venetian example) Plato's late work, the *Laws*, would be the obvious choice: a social and political system founded by a law-giver who tried to create a stable order by prescribing all its details.

The idea of a law-giver after the example of Lycurgus and Solon is a key element in Harrington's thought.[69] It shows that he differentiated clearly the exercise of sovereign power at the act of constituting[70] from the working of the established order. But Harrington's solution was merely a version of the Platonic one that an enlightened ruler should use his power to establish a stable order in which afterwards there would be no place left for him. Harrington's law-giver, the Lord Archon, was to be assisted by a 'Council of Legislators' who would 'labour in the mines of ancient

---

[65] *Works*, ed. Pocock, p. 208.
[66] Compare Algernon Sidney's reminiscence in a conversation during his Paris exile: 'the design of the English [republicans] had been, to make a Republic on the model of that of the Hebrews, before they had their Kings, and on that of Sparta, of Rome, and of Venice, taking from each what was best, to make a perfect composition'; quoted from J. Scott, *Algernon Sidney and the English republic, 1623–1677*, Cambridge, 1988, p. 15.
[67] *Works*, ed. Pocock, pp. 737, 738, 205.
[68] Compare J. C. Davis, *Utopia and the ideal society. A study of English utopian writing 1516–1700*, Cambridge, 1981, pp. 209, 239.
[69] See S. Etzold, '"A commonwealth made at once". Der Gedanke der Gründung in James Harrington's *Oceana*', Dissertation, University of Cologne, 1987.
[70] *Works*, ed. Pocock, p. 207.

prudence',[71] becoming experts on one of the ancient city republics or one of the relevant modern republics, Venice, Switzerland and Holland; and by a 'Council of Prytans' who were to hear suggestions or remonstrances by private persons and would at their own discretion inform the 'Council of Legislators'. Harrington makes it quite clear that this was just to create an illusion of the people's participation: 'This was that which made the people (who were neither safely to be admitted unto, nor conveniently to be excluded from the framing of their commonwealth) very believe when it came forth that it was no other than whereof they themselves had been the makers.'[72] This could not solve the problem of the legitimacy of the law-giver. Harrington begged the question by presenting his work as the authoritative record of a foundation which had already taken place. This demonstrates the difficulty of persuading Cromwell to assume the role of an English Lycurgus or Timoleon.[73] Harrington used these examples to paint the picture of a law-giver who after the act of foundation deliberately resigned from power – the Spartan case – and of a tyrannicide turned tyrant who then justified his domination by changing into law-giver – the Sicilian case.

Yet Harrington was convinced that a return to the ancient constitution with king, Lords and Commons was impossible. This is why he should not be equated with the mainstream of English authors who following the civil war thought that a mixed constitution in England was just this. Harrington based his judgement on a historical analysis which interpreted English history within the context of the universal history of the West. In his view, a feudal monarchy needed the economic and military support of a landed aristocracy. Since the reign of the Tudors the people, i.e. the middle classes, had won the upper hand with respect to ownership in land. Thus a monarchy based on a hereditary nobility had become historically obsolete. A republic would need an agrarian law that put an upper limit on the acquisition of real estates to stabilise the original distribution of landed property. Harrington's idea of balance means an affinity between the distribution of landed property and the governmental superstructure.[74]

Harrington's assessment of the agrarian question in antiquity gives also the basis for his respective judgements of ephors and tribunes: whereas

---

[71] *Ibid.*

[72] *Ibid.*, p. 209; cf. W. Steinmetz, 'Utopie oder Staatsplanung? – James Harringtons *Oceana* von 1656', in K. L. Bermann and H. U. Seeber, eds., *Literarische Utopien von Morus bis zur Gegenwart*, Königstein, 1983, pp. 59–72, esp. pp. 67f.

[73] *Works*, ed. Pocock, pp. 357f.

[74] Harrington's novel interpretation of the balance idea caused embarrassment with contemporaries who were used to thinking in terms of the constitutional balance between the 'three estates'; cf. Scott, *Algernon Sidney and the English republic*, pp. 16, 40f.

the Spartan magistrates could fulfil their functions thanks to the stable distribution of land, the lack of an adequate agrarian law in Rome was responsible for the failure of the tribunes to stabilise the republic.[75] (Evaluation of the historical role of ephors and tribunes with respect to agrarian laws which had started with Machiavelli was to be continued by later authors: it is sufficient to mention that Vico blamed both institutions for not defending the popular interest in the land, Babeuf claimed legitimacy for his redistribution programme by invoking the Gracchi, and Niebuhr was happy to detect that the tribunes' agrarian laws by no means meant a violation of private property.)[76]

To come back to the ephors model in constitutional debates: this model enjoyed an extraordinary popularity in the late 1650s. The failure of the Cromwellian Protectorate in 1659 and the re-emergence of the Rump brought about an almost inevitable restoration of monarchy and nobility.[77] Republicans of every kind, defenders of the good old cause of the Rump parliament, theocratically-minded puritans or even millenarianists, and, last, but not least, Harrington and his intellectual followers – they all agreed that just maintaining the Rump's regime without any restrictions placed upon it could not be a sensible alternative. The Rump's unchecked domination after 1648 had been experienced by a great majority of people as collective tyranny. The point later made by a royalist author, 'If the Commons are sovereign, who will be tribunes of the people to check them?',[78] had to be taken seriously even by ardent republicans.

This is why in the years 1658–60 the idea was ventilated that a council on the model of the ephors should be set up which might control parliament in two respects: on the one hand by checking encroachments on the fundamental rights of the people like liberty of conscience, and on the other by preventing a future parliament from overthrowing the republican constitution by voting a restoration of the monarchy.[79] (The dissenting voice was Milton's: he favoured the Rump's regime and argued that ephors or tribunes were either ineffective or too powerful, as the

[75] *Works*, ed. Pocock, pp. 277ff.
[76] See A. Heuß, *Barthold Georg Niebuhrs wissenschaftliche Anfänge. Untersuchungen und Mitteilungen über die Kopenhagener Manuskripte und zur europäischen Tradition der lex agraria (loi agraire)*, Göttingen, 1981. Vico: *Scienza nuova*, 1744, Book II, §§592, 668.
[77] See A. Woolrych, 'Last quests for a settlement, 1657–1660', in G. E. Aylmer, ed., *The Interregnum*, London, 1972, pp. 183–204.
[78] Quoted from C. Roberts, *The growth of responsible government in Stuart England*, London, 1966, p. 151.
[79] According to E. Ludlow (*Memoirs*, ed. by C. H. Firth, Oxford, 1894, vol. 2, pp. 98f.) it was 'proposed that there might be joined to the popular assembly, a select number of men in the nature of the Lacedemonian Ephori, who should have a negative in things, wherein the essentials of government should be concerned, such as the exclusion of a single person, touching liberty of conscience, and other things to the last importance to the State'.

ancient examples showed.)[80] In the context of this debate, Harrington found an extraordinary response since in his shorter published works following the *Oceana* he reduced his comprehensive theory of republicanism to those practical devices which were in accord with current views.[81] He propagated his ideas on bicameralism and rotation, and associated them with the doctrine of the ephors[82] and defended the historical adequacy of Calvinist versions of this theory, which had been attacked by champions of monarchical absolutism during the first civil war.[83]

Such considerations on the historical institutions notwithstanding, the true importance of the debate on ephors and tribunes during the Interregnum lies in the fact that they were now considered as metaphors for instruments of control which a law-giver should institute to ensure that certain individual rights should be respected unreservedly even by the representatives of the people.

In theoretical terms the Interregnum debates mark the breach with ancient republicanism. For the first time a constitution was considered as Paramount or Fundamental Law which was no longer a merely rhetorical figure or thought of in terms of a contract between ruler and nation. It was on the contrary a body of law which was not subject to alterations by a simple legislative act and which served simultaneously to preserve the distribution of governmental functions according to the law-giver's arrangements as well as to protect the individuals' rights from encroachments by the legislative. True, we must wait until the debates of the American and French revolutions to find mature conceptions of the foundation acts which could claim legitimacy, the distinction of the *pouvoir constituant* from the *pouvoirs constitués*,[84] the elaboration of a canon of

---

[80] *The ready and easie way to establish a free commonwealth*; quoted from H. Erskine-Hill and G. Storey, eds., *Revolutionary prose of the English civil war*, Cambridge, 1983, p. 217.

[81] See J. G. A. Pocock, 'James Harrington and the good old cause', *Journal of British Studies*, vol. 10, no. 1 (1970), pp. 30–48; I. Roots, 'The tactics of the Commonwealthmen in Richard Cromwell's parliament', in *Puritans and revolutionaries. Essays in seventeenth-century history presented to Christopher Hill*, Oxford, 1978, pp. 283–309; J. Cotton, 'The Harringtonian "Party" (1659–1660), and Harrington's political thought', *History of Political Thought*, vol. 1 (1980), pp. 51–67.

[82] 'Pour enclouer le canon', *Works*, ed. Pocock, pp. 728–33.

[83] 'The stumbling block of disobedience and rebellion' (1658), in *Works*, ed. Pocock, pp. 567–77, a reply to a tract of the same title by P. Heylyn.

[84] See *The Federalist*, no. 63 (Everyman's Library Edition, 1965, p. 324) on the consequences for the role of the people and its representatives:

> Lastly, in Sparta we meet with the Ephori, and in Rome with the Tribunes; two bodies, small indeed in numbers, but annually elected by the whole body of the people, and considered as the representatives of the people, almost in their plenipotentiary capacity ... From these facts ... it is clear that the principle of representation was neither unknown to the ancients nor wholly overlooked in their political constitutions. The true distinction between these and the American governments lies

fundamental and civil rights. And only then was it acknowledged that democracy meant representation, instead of direct participation, and that democracy itself should no longer be understood as a particularistic but as a universalist concept.[85] But the debates of the 1650s paved the way for this sort of constitutionalist theorising.[86]

That in practice the English had shrunk from such a constructive constitutionalism and had returned to their tradition of a balance between the 'three estates' in parliament was best expressed by the promotion of the mixed constitution to the generally accepted model of the eighteenth-century constitution.[87] This model now symbolised the sovereignty of the king-in-parliament which in practice meant the domination of the natural rulers, insulated against pressures from below. Their claim that they would respect fundamental rights even if there were no legal limits for parliamentary acts was based on the assertion that the mutual checks and balances between king, Lords and Commons would be a sufficient guarantee of the mixed sovereign's self-restraint. Consequently there was no need for the proposals of a stricter separation of the legislative and executive branches of government which had been ventilated since the mid-seventeenth century.[88] The model of the mixed constitution implied an appropriate picture of the type of parliamentary government which developed during the eighteenth century; its theoretical weakness was, however, that it could not accommodate the feature of judiciary independence.

Checks and balances could again be separated from the association with estates and social classes and be understood as a purely technical device available for a constitutional law-giver who saw in overlapping competences a better guarantee for keeping constituted powers within their proper channel than a strict separation of powers: such at least was the American solution.

A quite different line of modern constitutional theory developed along

in the total exclusion of the people, in their collective capacity, from any share in the latter, and not in the total exclusion of the representatives of the people from the administration of the former.

[85] See G. Stourzh, 'Vom Aristotelischen zum liberalen Verfassungsbegriff', in F. Engel-Janosi et al., eds., Fürst, Bürger, Mensch, Vienna, 1975, pp. 97–122.
[86] The development of John Adams's political thought is especially illuminating with respect to the tension between the old and the new understanding of democracy; see P. Nolte, 'Aristotelische Tradition und Amerikanische Revolution', Der Staat, vol. 27 (1988), pp. 209–32.
[87] See Nippel, Mischverfassungstheorie, pp. 303ff.; H. T. Dickinson, Liberty and property. Political ideology in eighteenth-century England, London, 1977, passim.
[88] For the separation of powers doctrine compare W. B. Gwyn, The meaning of the separation of powers. An analysis of the doctrine from its origins to the adoption in the United States Constitution, New Orleans, La., 1965; M. J. C. Vile, Constitutionalism and the separation of powers, Oxford, 1967.

the idea of juridical mechanisms to preserve the constitutional order. Again, this could be associated with the ephors idea. In some aspects it may be traced back to Althusius who had developed the ephors doctrine into a generalised model which set up *ephori* of various ranks to control the *summus magistratus*.[89] Similar ideas appeared later, for example in Rousseau (*Contrat social* IV,5; *Lettres écrites de la montagne* IX) and Fichte[90] who both spoke of tribunes and ephors who should keep the supreme power in accordance with the general will, an idea that was also discussed in the French constitutional debates in 1793.[91] Ephors and tribunes were now understood as institutions quite different from the historical ones, especially as they were neither supposed to defend particular interests nor to participate in legislative and executive matters but solely to function as a sort of constitutional court that would take action only if the constitutional order was in danger. Nineteenth- and twentieth-century constitutional theory discussed a variety of solutions to the role of 'guardians of the constitution' which quite often were associated with the ephors and tribunes imagery.[92]

In this discussion I have tried to follow some components of so-called classical republicanism from their ancient origins to modern applications. In spite of all deficiencies and blind spots which such an attempt necessarily entails, it should be clear that the use which could be made of ancient constitutional concepts in later times was at least partly due to the ambiguity of the ancient tradition; hence it could even outlast fundamental discontinuities and innovations in political theory, fissures which current interpretations of classical republicanism are often inclined to underestimate.

---

[89] *Politica Methodice Digesta* (1610), ed. by C. J. Friedrick, Cambridge, Mass., 1932. See already Leonardo Bruni's comparison of institutions which serve as a sort of guardian of the constitution: the heads of the *Parte Guelfa* in Florence, the Roman censors, the Athenian Areopagus, and the Spartan Ephors: 'Laudatio Florentinae urbis', in H. Baron, ed., *From Petrarch to Leonardo Bruni*, Chicago, Ill., 1968, pp. 261f.

[90] 'Grundlagen des Naturrechts', in *Johann Gottlieb Fichte Gesamtausgabe*, vol. 3, *Werke 1794–1796*, ed. by R. Lauth and H. Jacob, Stuttgart and Bad Cannstadt, 1966, pp. 448ff.

[91] See Catalano, *Tribunato e resistenza*, p. 35.

[92] See C. Schmitt, *Der Hüter der Verfassung*, Tübingen, 1931, pp. 1–11.

2 Checks, balances and boundaries: the separation of powers in the constitutional debate of 1787

Bernard Manin

At times the constitutional debate of 1787 came close to an exegesis of Montesquieu's theories. Madison indeed engaged in a brief commentary of *The Spirit of the Laws* to refute the claim that the constitution violated the principle of the separation of powers. 'The oracle who is always consulted and cited on this subject', Madison wrote, 'is the celebrated Montesquieu ... Let us endeavor in the first place to ascertain his meaning on this point.'[1] The slightly sarcastic reference to the 'oracle' on the question betrayed a certain impatience. Madison nevertheless considered that the invocation of the famous name by his opponents carried sufficient weight with the public to warrant a documented rebuttal. In a subsequent *Federalist Paper* Hamilton reiterated that the constitution did not transgress the maxim understood in its 'true meaning'.[2] The Anti-Federalists, for their part, invoked repeatedly Montesquieu's axiom. Many of their pamphlets quoted *The Spirit of the Laws* verbatim: 'when the legislative and executive powers are united in the same person or in the same body of magistrates, there can be no liberty, because apprehensions may arise, lest the same monarch or senate should enact tyrannical laws, to execute them in a tyrannical manner'.[3]

I am grateful to my friend and colleague Jan Goldstein who kindly corrected the writing style of this essay.

[1] Madison, *Federalist 47*, in A. Hamilton, J. Madison and J. Jay, *The Federalist papers (1787–1788)*, ed. by C. Rossiter, New York, 1961, p. 301. Hereafter references to the *Federalist papers* will mention only the number of the paper and the page in the edition by Rossiter.

[2] Hamilton, *Federalist 66*, p. 401.

[3] Centinel, Letter II, in H. J. Storing, ed., *The complete Anti-Federalist*, 7 vols., vol. II, 7, 50, Chicago, Ill., 1981. (Hereafter references to Anti-Federalist writings and speeches will be denoted as: *Storing*, followed by the three numbers of Storing's classification, the Roman number indicating the volume.) See also: A Federal Republican, *Storing*, III, 6, 23; 'The address and reasons of dissent of the Minority of the Convention of Pennsylvania', *Storing*, III, 11, 44; William Penn, *Storing*, III, 12, 13; Brutus (of Virginia), *Storing*, V, 15, 1; Cincinnatus, *Storing*, VI, 1, 32 (Cincinnatus even cited Montesquieu in French). The foregoing list includes only the passages where the famous phrase of *The Spirit of the Laws* (Book XI, ch. 6) is cited verbatim. But in a multitude of other utterances Anti-Federalist writers just invoked Montesquieu and his axiom. Unfortunately, the most recent and otherwise excellent English translation of *The Spirit of the Laws* (ed. and transl. by A. M.

Thus there is no doubt that the ratification of the constitution generated an argument over the separation of powers. Yet it seems difficult to
define precisely what was in contention on this matter. Numerous studies
have analysed the Federalist conception of the separation of powers and
of checks and balances in isolation. The main difficulty, however, is to
characterise exactly the Anti-Federalist position. To be sure, the Anti-
Federalists were not a homogeneous group, nor did they have a unified
leadership. Their constitutional views did not find an expression as
coherent and articulate as the *Federalist Papers*. However, despite the
heterogeneity of the opponents of the constitution, historians have succeeded in discerning the main thrust of their arguments on various points,
such as the adequate size of a republican government, the importance of a
bill of rights or the requisite characteristics of good representation.
Concerning their opinions on the separation of powers and the principle
of checks and balances, historical analyses have been notably less successful. Accounts of the Anti-Federalist position vary. The only point on
which there seems to be some agreement is that the Anti-Federalists
lacked definite and firm views on these issues.

I.   The Anti-Federalists' predicament: a historiographical survey

Historians typically use the vocabulary of perplexity, awkwardness and
lack of coherence to describe the attitudes of the Anti-Federalists toward
the separation of powers. Gordon Wood for example claims that the
Anti-Federalists invoked the separation of powers in opposition to the
constitution, because in 1787 Montesquieu's axiom had become part of
the constitutional language of the day. By that time, the maxim had
gained such a wide acceptance that it was 'perhaps inevitable' that the
Anti-Federalists had recourse to it.[4] Moreover, Wood argues, in the
ratification debate the Anti-Federalists had to address a question that was

Cohler, B. C. Miller and H. S. Stone, Cambridge, 1989) is not entirely accurate in its
rendering of the last segment of Montesquieu's crucial sentence. It reads as follows: when
legislative power is united with executive power, 'one can fear that the same monarch or
senate that makes tyrannical laws will execute them tyrannically' (p. 157). Now the French
text is: 'ou peut craindre que le même monarque ou le même sénat ne fasse des lois
tyranniques *pour* les exécuter tyranniquement' (my emphasis). Montesquieu's wording
brings out the dimension of intentionality: if the branch which exercises the legislative
power is also vested with the executive power, there is a risk ('one can fear') that it will
enact tyrannical laws *in order to* or *with a view to* execute them tyrannically. The risk of
tyranny results from the intentions or temptations that the combination of the two
functions might generate in the body which exercises them. The element of intentionality
which is missed by the contemporary English edition was correctly rendered by the
Anti-Federalists' translations.

[4] G. S. Wood, *The creation of the American republic 1776–1787*, Chapel Hill, N.C., 1969,
p. 549.

not the one they would have liked: should America have a national republic or a confederated system? The outcome of the Philadelphia Convention forced them instead to discuss the structure and powers of a national government. Once the question was posed in this way, the Anti-Federalists were 'compelled' to argue on Federalist terms. The situation led them in particular to resort to 'those mechanical Enlightenment terms most agreeable to the thought of the Federalists: the division and balancing of political power'.[5] According to Wood, the Federalists were in a better position than their adversaries to use that language because of the 'peculiar way' they had come to view governmental power. The Federalists indeed broke away from the classical Whig doctrine that the popular branch of the legislature (the lower house) was the privileged or even the exclusive representative of the people. They considered instead every branch of the government as equal agents of the people. They could then easily argue that the principal differentiation between the departments of government should reside in their functions: the executive, legislative and judicial functions posited by the doctrine of the separation of powers.[6] Because the Federalists regarded all the branches as equal, they could claim that *each* should be *equally* protected from possible interferences by the others, and not primarily the popular branch of the legislature. There was, Wood argues, a rather natural match between the Federalists' general conception of government and the doctrine of the separation of powers that enabled them 'to wield it with a comprehensiveness and effectiveness that left their opponents bewildered'.[7] Aside from bewilderment, however, the substance of the Anti-Federalist position concerning the separation of powers remains unclear in this account.

A somewhat different picture emerges from M. J. C. Vile's classical book on the separation of powers and from H. Storing's essay on Anti-Federalist thought.[8] The account offered by these studies rests on a differentiation between two constitutional principles that Wood's interpretation does not separate: the theory of the functional separation of powers and the principle of checks and balances. In essence the argument is that while the Anti-Federalists 'fully' accepted the former, they 'became uneasy' when the Federalists advocated the latter.[9] On this interpretation,

[5] Wood, *The creation of the American republic*, p. 548.
[6] *Ibid.*, p. 598.
[7] *Ibid.*, p. 549.
[8] See M. J. C. Vile, *Constitutionalism and the separation of powers*, Oxford, 1967, pp. 12–36, 153–60; H. Storing, 'What the Anti-Federalists were for', *Storing*, I, ch. 7, pp. 53–63. Although Vile's book did not contain a detailed study of the Anti-Federalist position, one can consider that it laid the groundwork for the interpretation later developed by Storing. Storing explicitly acknowledges his indebtedness to Vile in a footnote of his introductory essay ('What the Anti-Federalists were for', *Storing*, I, p. 95, note 19).
[9] Storing, 'What the Anti-Federalists were for', *Storing*, I, pp. 60, 62.

perplexity still characterises the position of the Anti-Federalists, but it has a more limited and circumscribed object.

One can indeed distinguish, as Vile propounds, between the pure theory of the separation of powers and the doctrine of checks and balances. In its 'pure' or 'stark' form, the theory of the separation of powers states that: (1) the government should be divided into three branches performing legislative, executive and judicial functions; (2) each branch should be confined to the exercise of its own function and not allowed to encroach upon the functions of other branches; (3) the persons who compose the three departments should be distinct, no individual being allowed to be at the same time a member of more than one branch.[10] Thus, the pure theory of the separation of powers can be characterised as a theory of functional separation and specialisation. The doctrine of checks and balances on the other hand makes by itself no reference to the three functions of government; it only asserts that political power should be distributed among various governmental bodies so that any one is prevented from abusing its power by the others.[11] The latter doctrine represents a development of the theory of the mixed constitution whose origins can be traced to Aristotle and Polybius.[12] In America John Adams promoted the idea of a mixed or balanced government in his *Defence of the Constitutions of Government of the United States of America* (1787). The theorists of the mixed constitution held that to prevent abuses of power, the various governmental bodies should be capable of actively resisting and counterbalancing each other. In addition, the traditional doctrine of balanced government prescribed that the different branches of the government should represent distinct social forces. The modern conception of checks and balances, however, did not retain the latter aspect. It only borrowed from the ancient doctrine the formal model of active checks and counterbalances. Thus, on the principle of checks and bal-

---

[10] Vile, *Constitutionalism and the separation of powers*, pp. 12–13. The question here is not whether or not Montesquieu himself advocated this pure version of the theory of the separation of powers. The fact is that for decades if not centuries, most legal experts and political actors (with the notable exception of the American Federalists) believed and proclaimed that he did. C. Eisenmann has definitively established that Montesquieu did not put forward a theory of functional specialisation in two important studies (relatively unknown in the English speaking world). See C. Eisenmann, 'L'Esprit des lois et la séparation des pouvoirs', in *Mélanges Carré de Malberg*, Paris, 1933; 'La Pensée constitutionnelle de Montesquieu', in *Recueil Sirey du Bicentennaire de l'Esprit des Lois: la pensée politique et constitutionnelle de Montesquieu*, Paris, 1952. These two articles have been reprinted in *Cahiers de Philosophie Politique de l'Université de Reims*, Brussels, 1985.

[11] See Vile, *Constitutionalism and the separation of powers*, pp. 18–36.

[12] See in particular, Aristotle, *Politics*, IV, 1293b 31 to 1294b 39; Polybius, *The Histories*, VI, ch. 10, 1–14, and chs. 11–18. On the different theories of the mixed constitution see the remarkable work by W. Nippel, *Mischverfassungstheorie und Verfassungsrealität in Antike und früher Neuzeit*, Stuttgart, 1980.

ances, one branch of the government may be authorised to exercise some active influence on another in order to resist and counteract its power. The pure theory of the separation of powers, by contrast, prohibits as undue intereference any influence of one of the functionally defined departments over another: in this case, the checks are merely passive (or negative). The two doctrines, then, are clearly different. Constitutional theory usually regards the American constitution as combining a qualified version of each. The constitution rests on a modified form of the functional separation of powers insofar as the three branches of the government (the President, the Congress and the Courts) are primarily (but not exclusively) defined by their functions, which are thus exercised by separate agencies. On the other hand, the constitution establishes a system of checks and balances among these branches by granting them some measure of active influence over each other: the President can influence the Congress through his veto power, one branch of the Congress (the Senate) can control the President in the exercise of his powers of appointment and of treaty making, the judiciary can actively check the Congress through judicial review.[13] Moreover, there is virtually no functional differentiation between the Senate and the House of Representatives and the relations between the two chambers come close to a pure balance of power.[14]

On Vile's account, the Federalists introduced the principle of checks and balances into the proposed constitution, because the crisis which followed the revolution of 1776 had convinced them that the pure principle of the separation of powers was insufficient. Indeed, in the wake of the independence the principle in its pure form had been emphatically extolled as an 'essential precaution in favor of liberty'. It had been written into virtually all the state constitutions.[15] In spite of these proclamations, however, the state legislatures had meddled in every type of governmental business, including that in principle reserved to the judiciary. Moreover, some legislatures had enacted laws which a segment of the population at

[13] Vile, *Constitutionalism and the separation of powers*, pp. 156–7.
[14] *Ibid.*, pp. 141, 156.
[15] The Massachusetts Declaration of Rights, to mention only one example, stated (Art. XXX):

> In the government of this Commonwealth, the legislative department shall never exercise the executive and judicial powers, or either of them. The executive shall never exercise the legislative and judicial powers, or either of them. The judicial shall never exercise the legislative and executive powers, or either of them: to the end it may be a government of laws and not of men.

Cited in P. B. Kurland and R. Lerner (eds), *The Founders' constitution*, 5 vols., Chicago, Ill., 1987, vol. 1, pp. 13–14. Vile admits, however, that most state constitutions did not conform fully to the pure principle of the separation of powers insofar as they established bicameral legislatures, except in Pennsylvania and Vermont (*Constitutionalism and the separation of powers*, p. 141).

least regarded as the very embodiment of arbitrariness and injustice (debt relief legislation, for example).[16] Thus in 1787 it was possible to argue that the pure separation of powers had demonstrated in practice its inability to limit effectively the powers of the legislatures. The Federalists could plausibly claim that additional precautions had to be taken to keep all branches of government, and particularly the legislature, within bounds. The Anti-Federalists, Vile argues, did not approve these additional precautions, but their attack 'lacked coherence and a clear alternative set of principles'.[17] They had reservations about checks and balances, but the pure separation of powers no longer appeared as a viable alternative. Even though they might have favoured the latter doctrine with respect to the state governments, they could not propose a similar system for the federal government. For, in 1787 it was quite clear that such an arrangement would most probably lead to an extremely powerful central legislature, which they did not want, because of their attachment to the liberties of the individual states.

Yet Vile does not explain why the Anti-Federalists attacked the principle of checks and balances. In his more recent study Storing offers two answers. First, he argues, the Anti-Federalists opposed the balanced system provided by the constitution on the ground of its complexity. In their opinion, such a complex government hindered democratic accountability: the people would never be able to locate precisely the source of mismanagement or abuse. The opponents of the constitution on the contrary regarded responsibility to the people as the cornerstone of republican government. They identified responsible government with simple government.[18] The difficulty, however, is to grasp what they meant by simple government. Storing does not discern any precise answer to that question in the Anti-Federalist literature. He wonders indeed why the Anti-Federalists spent most of their time criticising the checks and balances provided by the constitution 'rather than taking a firm stand for simple and responsible government'. His hypothesis is that the conditions for simple government did not exist any way for the general government. Moreover, Storing argues, the Anti-Federalists had no model to draw

---

[16] Vile, *Constitutionalism and the separation of powers*, pp. 133–47. Wood also notes the great discrepancy between the emphatic affirmations of the need to separate the several governmental departments and the actual practice the state governments followed. He argues that when the revolutionaries in 1776 spoke of the separation of powers, they were primarily thinking of insulating the legislature from executive manipulation; they did not have in mind the protection of the other branches against legislative interference (*The creation of the American republic*, pp. 151–7).

[17] Vile, *Constitutionalism and the separation of powers*, p. 157.

[18] See in particular Storing, 'What the Anti-Federalists were for', *Storing*, I, pp. 55–6; see also Kurland and Lerner, eds., *The Founders' constitution*, vol. 1, pp. 336–8 (introductory remarks to the chapter entitled 'Balanced government').

upon: neither in theory nor in practice had the case for simple government been squarely put.[19] This, however, amounts to claiming that the opponents of the constitution did not know exactly what they wanted, at least for the federal government. The problem is further complicated by the fact that the Anti-Federalists did not advocate pure majority rule at the federal level. An omnipotent and omnicompetent federal government, periodically called to account for its actions through elections, would have obviously constituted a simple and responsible government. To be sure, there was a strand of radical populism in Anti-Federalist thought. The fact is, however, that the Anti-Federalists did not propose pure and simple majority rule for the federal government. As Storing points out, they, too, feared oppressive *federal* majorities, if to a lesser degree than the Federalists and for different reasons.[20] This is in particular why they insisted that the constitution should include a bill of rights. It is also because they acknowledged the threat posed by tyrannical majorities that they favoured the general principle of dividing political power, both among federal and state governments, and among the three functional branches of the federal government. Storing notes that they 'typically criticized the constitution because there was too little separation [of powers], not too much, and too few checks, not too many'.[21] How, then, could the Anti-Federalists advocate at the same time simplicity and differentiation in the constitutional structure? How did they reconcile their demand for responsible government and their adherence to the principle of the division of power? Were they just perplexed and confused?

On Storing's interpretation, the Anti-Federalists had also another motive for objecting to the system of checks and balances proposed by the Federalists. The only way in which they could think of a balanced government was 'in traditional terms of a government composed of representatives of social orders – either the fixed orders of a mature Britain or the natural orders of a youthful America'.[22] Now, as mentioned above, the checks and balances provided by the constitution precisely departed from the traditional model of the mixed government to the extent that they were not intended to embody distinct social forces. All the departments of the government were to be emanations of the people as a whole. Indeed the disembodiment of government from the society constitutes one of the major features of the historical process which reached its culmination in 1787.[23]

[19] Storing, 'What the Anti-Federalists were for', *Storing*, I, pp. 56–7.
[20] *Ibid.*, pp. 39–40.
[21] *Ibid.*, p. 55.
[22] *Ibid.*, p. 63.
[23] Wood, *The creation of the American republic, passim.*

The common interpretation that the Anti-Federalists felt uneasy and perplexed about the separation of powers and the related question of balanced government runs, however, into one major difficulty. It cannot account for the emphasis that the Anti-Federalists placed on these issues. Now a simple but massive fact attracts attention: the sheer quantity of references to the separation of powers in Anti-Federalist writings. The Anti-Federalists did more than 'accept' the principle of the separation of powers; they actively and emphatically promoted it. Montesquieu's maxim might have objectively played into the hands of their adversaries. Yet their own perception must have been different. Why would they have raised that question, if they felt that they had no definite views on it and no alternative to offer? In a debate where the objective is to win, political actors usually do not bring up issues that perplex them, nor do they put forward arguments that they themselves find weak. Rather, they are eager to present what *they* consider as the best possible case. With the benefit of hindsight, the historian is inclined to think that the losing side must have had a particularly weak case. That might be true *sub specie aeternitatis*, but such a perspective necessarily misses the actors' own understanding of what they were doing. If it is highly unlikely that the Anti-Federalists considered their arguments about the separation of powers to be as confused as contemporary accounts claimed they were, some closer study of their objections and propositions is in order. The notion of the Anti-Federalists' predicament might after all reflect the historian's predicament concerning their views.

The present study, it must be noted, is by no means an attempt to explain *why* the Anti-Federalists were defeated in the ratification debate. First, the debate did not revolve only, nor even primarily, around the separation of powers; it bore on many other questions that were probably more important in the minds of the actors. Second, it would be extremely simplistic and naive to assume that the ratification of the proposed constitution was only or predominantly a matter of ideas and theories. Social, economic and organisational factors played a crucial role in the victory of the Federalists. The fact is, however, that the structure of the situation forced the actors to argue. And argue they did. The point here is only to understand what they were saying.

II.   The Anti-Federalist case

To elucidate the Anti-Federalists' conception of the separation of powers, one must look at the precise contexts in which they mentioned Montesquieu's axiom. First and foremost, they invoked it in their objections to the proposed Senate. The Senate, they pointed out, was vested with legislative functions, but also with executive functions since it shared with the President the power of appointment and the power of making treaties.[24] Moreover, insofar as the Senate was to try impeachments, it would exercise judicial functions.[25] Thus the Minority of the Pennsylvania Convention complained that the constitution presented

the undue mixture of the powers of government; the same body possessing legislative, executive, and judicial powers ... Such various, extensive and important powers combined in one body of men are inconsistent with all freedom; the celebrated Montesquieu tells us that when the legislative and executive powers are united in the same person or in the same body of magistrates, there can be no liberty ...[26]

The Pennsylvania Minority then cited the famous statement of *The Spirit of the Laws*. In another Anti-Federalist pamphlet Centinel made the following observation regarding the powers of the Senate: 'This mixture of the legislative and executive moreover highly tends to corruption. The chief improvement in government, in modern times, has been the compleat separation of the great distinctions of power; placing the legislative in different hands from those which hold the executive; and again severing the judicial part from the ordinary administrative.' Centinel, too, supported his claim by a verbatim quotation of Montesquieu.[27] An impressive number of Anti-Federalist writers insisted over and over again that the powers granted to the Senate transgressed the principle of the separation of powers.[28]

By comparison, pamphlets or speeches where they criticised the Senate for failing to embody social forces appear relatively rare. To be sure, this line of argument was not altogether absent. Thus the Federal Farmer, though admitting that in the absence of a nobility a second chamber representing the aristocratic element of the society was impossible in the United States, thought nevertheless that the two legislative branches

---

[24] The constitution stipulated that the president 'shall have Power, by and with the Advice and Consent of the Senate, to make treaties ... he shall nominate, and by and with the Advice and Consent of the Senate, shall appoint Ambassadors, other public Ministers and Consuls, Judges of the Supreme Court, and all other officers of the United States, whose appointments are not herein otherwise provided for, and which shall be established by law ... ' (Art. II, sec. 2, cl. 2).

[25] 'The senate shall have the sole power to try all impeachments.' (Art. I, sec. 3, cl. 6).

[26] 'The Address and Reasons of the Minority of the Convention of Pennsylvania ... ', *Storing*, III, 11, 42–4.

[27] Centinel, Letter II, *Storing*, II, 7, 50.

[28] See (in addition to the texts mentioned in note 3, which mostly relate to the powers of the Senate) G. Mason, 'Objections to the Government formed by the Convention', *Storing*, II, 2, 7–8; Cato, Letter V, *Storing*, II, 6, 35; The Federal Farmer, Letter III, *Storing*, II, 8, 30; Brutus, Essay XVI, *Storing*, II, 9, 202–4; Letter of R. H. Lee to the Virginia Gazette, *Storing*, V, 6, 1; Address by a Plebeian, *Storing*, VI, 11, 16; Notes of the speeches given by George Clinton before the New York State Ratifying Convention, *Storing*, VI, 13, 32.

ought to have represented really different social forces. He deplored 'the partitions' between the two chambers provided by the constitution, noting that they would be 'merely those of the building in which they sit: there will not be found in them any of those genuine balances and checks, among the real different interests, and efforts of the several classes of men in the community we aim at'.[29] Consequently, the Federal Farmer proposed that particular qualifications be required for both the electors and the elected in the case of the Senate. Like most other Anti-Federalists, he expressed reservations about the participation of the Senate in the power of making treaties (even though he confessed that he could not find any alternative solution), and definitely opposed its participation in the power of appointment (in this case he suggested the establishment of an 'executive council' to assist the President).[30] Patrick Henry, too, objected to the constitution on the ground that the different branches of government did not reflect real and deeply rooted social interests. In his view such institutions would be too weak and artificial to effectively check one another. 'To me', he wrote, 'it appears that there is no check in that government. The President, Senators and Representatives all immediately, or mediately, are the choice of the people. Tell me not of checks on paper; tell me of checks founded on self-love.'[31] Henry even praised the English government, which although it was not republican contained at least effective checks as the Lords and the Commons represented truly different social interests. The traditional model of the mixed constitution clearly inspired these objections. Other Anti-Federalists, however, strongly disagreed. Centinel, for example, vigorously criticised the form of balanced government advocated by John Adams. It was in the context of this critique that Centinel put forward the above mentioned argument that Adams's model of government would be much too complicated, thereby destroying all accountability in the rulers.[32] Thus, while there were disagreements among the Anti-Federalists about the desirability of a scheme of mixed government, the group was virtually unanimous in the objection that the proposed Senate unduly combined legislative, executive and judicial functions.

Moreover, even in the absence of higher qualifications for the Senators, most Anti-Federalists nonetheless considered the Senate as the 'aristocratic' part of the constitution. Some believed that the Senate would *de facto* be composed of the 'natural aristocracy' of the country as the system of

---

[29] The Federal Farmer, Essay XI, *Storing*, II, 8, 146.
[30] *Ibid.*, 147; Essay XIII, *Storing*, II, 7, 170–1.
[31] Patrick Henry, Speech of 9 June 1788, *Storing*, V, 16, 14.
[32] See Centinel, Letter I, *Storing*, II, 7, 9. The critique of Adams's scheme is in *Storing*, II, 7, 7–9.

indirect election would lead to the selection of the prominent and conspicuous Few.[33] Others in greater number claimed that the mode of designation of the Senators and the length of their term of office (six years) would create an aristocratic body in the sense that the Senate would be remote from the people and largely independent from them; this was for the Anti-Federalists the very definition of 'aristocracy'. Furthermore, they complained that the Senate would most probably become a 'permanent aristocracy', because the Senators would probably be re-elected several times.[34] Accordingly, some recommended a system of 'rotation' (term limits).[35] Others argued that the Senators should be subject to recall by the state legislatures which elected them.[36] Yet others suggested that the Senate should be elected directly by the people.[37] They all concurred, however, that the term of office of the Senators should be shortened.[38] They conceded that the terms of the Senators should be longer than those of the Representatives. They were thereby accepting, to use their own terminology, the 'aristocratic' character of the Senate, but not to the extent provided by the constitution. None of their alternative propositions aimed to secure a higher social status for the Senators. All these suggestions had one single and clear objective: to bring the Senate closer to the people. It does not seem, then, that regarding the composition of the Senate the Anti-Federalists' main complaint was that the senatorial aristocracy was a pure institutional construct and did not reflect a distinct social force. Rather, they objected that the Senate was *too* aristocratic, that is, too distant and independent from the people.

Yet more importantly, the Anti-Federalists protested that the aristocratic part of the constitution was too powerful. For the most part they did not oppose the institution of a second chamber.[39] They contended, however, that the constitution failed to establish a true balance in the legislature, because it granted too much power to the less popular branch. There could never be a real equilibrium between the two branches since

---

[33] Centinel, for example, spoke of the Senate in the following terms: 'the senate, who I suppose will be composed of the better sort, the *well born*, the *better sort*' (Centinel, Letter I, *Storing*, II, 7, 22; original emphasis).

[34] See, for example, Centinel, *Storing*, II, 7, 48; Brutus, *Storing*, II, 9, 200–4; A Columbian Patriot, *Storing*, IV, 28, 4; Impartial Examiner, *Storing*, V, 14, 33.

[35] Centinel, *Storing*, II, 7, 48.

[36] Luther Martin, *Storing*, II, 4, 42.

[37] Republicus, *Storing*, V, 13, 12.

[38] See, in addition to the authors mentioned in note 3, who all recommended shorter terms of office for the Senators, Luther Martin, *Storing*, II, 4, 42; John De Witt, *Storing*, IV, 12.

[39] In this case the notion of acceptance seems the most appropriate, because the Anti-Federalists did not positively argue in favour of a second chamber. They just did not object to it.

they were so unequally endowed.[40] For the opponents of the constitution the main cause of this dangerous imbalance within the legislature lay precisely in the fact that the Senate was granted some executive and judicial functions besides its normal and uncontested legislative role.

It does not seem, then, that the Anti-Federalists adopted the language of the separation of powers reluctantly and for the sole reason that the proponents of the constitution had cast the debate in these terms. In effect Montesquieu's maxim provided the Anti-Federalists with their preferred and most effective weapon against the Senate. As Madison recounted in 1789: 'Perhaps there was no argument urged with more success or more plausibly grounded against the Constitution, under which we are deliberating, than that found in the mingling of the Executive and Legislative branches of the Government in one body [the Senate].'[41]

One might conclude that the Anti-Federalists embraced the doctrine of the separation of powers only because they found it expedient for attacking a particular institution which they opposed for other reasons as well. Such a conclusion, however, would be misleading. In fact the Anti-Federalists had recourse to the famous doctrine against other provisions of the constitution. This suggests that they adhered to the maxim as a matter of general principle. The presidential veto did not arouse among the Anti-Federalists the same indignation as the powers of the Senate. Some did not object to the executive veto, the Federal Farmer for example. The Federal Farmer, however, presented the veto (and a few other provisions) as *exceptions* to an otherwise valid general principle. 'It is a good general rule', he wrote, 'that the legislative, executive, and judicial powers, ought to be kept distinct; but this like other general rules has its exceptions'.[42] Furthermore, various Anti-Federalist writers definitely censured the presidential veto on the ground that it violated the principle of the separation of powers.[43] William Penn, for example, declared that the 'division of power' ought to be one leading principle of free governments. After a literal citation of *The Spirit of the Laws*, he added:

[40] See John De Witt, *Storing*, IV, 3, 12–14. 'These considerations', De Witt wrote about the Senate, 'added to their share above mentioned in the Executive department must give them a decided superiority over the House of Representatives'.

[41] *Annals of the Congress of the United States, First Congress* (House of Representatives), 19 May 1789, compiled by J. Gales, Washington, D.C., 1834, vol. 1, p. 380.

[42] The Federal Farmer, Letter XIV, *Storing*, II, 8, 175.

[43] See, An Officer of the Late Continental Army, Letter to the Independent Gazetteer (6 November 1787), *Storing*, III, 8, 3; R. H. Lee, Letter to the Virginia Gazette (22 December 1787), *Storing*, V, 6, 1; The Impartial Examiner, Essay IV, *Storing*, V, 14, 37–40; Brutus (of Virginia), Reply to Cassius by Brutus, *Storing*, V, 15, 1; G. Clinton, Notes of speeches given by George Clinton before the New York State ratifying Convention, *Storing*, VI, 13, 32.

The first and most natural division of the powers of government are into the legislative and executive branches. These two should never be suffered to have *the least share of each other's jurisdiction*, or to intermeddle with it in any manner ... It is therefore a political error of the greatest magnitude, to allow the executive power a negative, or in fact any control over the proceedings of the legislature.[44]

Various Anti-Federalists argued in like manner that the powers and mode of appointment of the judiciary, particularly those of the Supreme Court, violated the maxim of the separation of powers. The Pennsylvania Minority proposed for example that the 'judges would be made completely independent' to the end 'that the legislative, executive and judicial powers be kept separate', thereby implying that the appointment of judges by the executive in concurrence with the Senate transgressed the principle of the separation of powers.[45] Brutus developed an extensive and detailed critique of the proposed judiciary system.[46] The constitution stated: 'The judicial Power shall extend to all Cases, in Law and Equity, arising under this Constitution, the Laws of the United States, and treaties made ... ' (Art. III, sec. 2, cl. 1). Brutus first pointed out that this provision gave to the courts an immense power: by empowering them to judge 'in equity' it gave them the latitude to interpret the meaning of the constitution without being bound to its letter.[47] He then showed that, vested with such a power, the courts, and particularly the Supreme Court, would become superior to the legislature. Brutus wrote:

The supreme court then have a right, independent of the legislature, to give a construction to the constitution and every part of it, and there is no power provided in this system to correct their construction or do it away. If, therefore, the legislature pass any laws, inconsistent with the sense the judges put upon the constitution, they will declare it void; and therefore in this respect their power is superior to that of legislature.[48]

Brutus considered this outcome objectionable on two grounds. First, the Supreme Court would become an uncontrollable power. Second, and more relevant to our question, he also emphasised that the court would thus be constitutionally entitled to trespass the proper boundaries of the judicial power and to exercise legislative functions. 'The *proper province* of the judicial power', he wrote, 'in any government, is as I conceive it, to declare what is the law of the land. To explain and enforce those laws, which the supreme power or legislature may pass, but not to declare what

---

[44] William Penn, Essay II, *Storing*, III, 12, 13–15 (my emphasis).
[45] The Address and Reasons of Dissent of the Minority of the Conventions of Pennsylvania, *Storing*, II, 7, 13, §12.
[46] Brutus, Essays XI–XV, *Storing*, II, 9, 130–96.
[47] Brutus, Essay XI, *Storing*, II, 9, 136–8.
[48] Brutus, Essay XV, *Storing*, II, 9, 193.

the powers of the legislature are.'[49] Brutus concluded his examination of the proposed judiciary by the following remarks:

> To have a government well administered in all its parts, it is requisite that the different departments of it should be separated and lodged as much as may be in different hands. The legislative power should be in one body, the executive in another and the judicial in one different from either. But still each of these bodies should be accountable for their conduct.[50]

Not only is it certain, then, that the Anti-Federalists emphatically advocated the general principle of the separation of powers, it is also possible to discern the principal meaning that the elliptic maxim assumed for them. When they invoked Montesquieu's axiom, they had in mind the principle that *no branch should exercise more than one of the three functions of government*. It was on the basis of this principle that they opposed some provisions which constitutional theory usually regards as checks and balances: the powers of appointment and of treaty-making granted to the Senate, the presidential veto, and the prospect of judicial review. All these provisions indeed vested one department with more than one function. Their reading of the maxim, however, also explains why they did not oppose another feature of the constitution commonly categorised as one of the checks and balances: bicameralism. That interpretation was indeed logically compatible with the division of one function between two branches, provided both branches exercised *only* the function that they shared. Thus the Anti-Federalists could at the same time approve one of the checks and balances and reject the others, while remaining perfectly coherent. They were not hovering between the checks and balances provided by the constitution and the pure separation of powers, without any clear alternative in mind. They did not propose a pure functional separation at all: the pure doctrine would have prescribed to assign each function to one branch only, whereas their guiding constitutional principle was simply: 'one branch, one function'.

This interpretation of the theory of the separation of powers helps explain how the constitutional outlook of the Anti-Federalists combined a certain democratic majoritarianism and a concern for limiting the power of majorities. Their principle, if applied, would have resulted in a limited supremacy of the legislature. For the very characterisation of the governmental functions as legislative, executive and judicial entailed an inherent hierarchy. The executive and judicial functions were necessarily subordinate: the former because it was supposed to put the laws into effect, the latter because it was regarded as the application of laws to particular

---

[49] Brutus, Essay XIII, *Storing*, II, 9, 159. My emphasis.
[50] Brutus, Essay XVI, *Storing*, II, 9, 197.

cases. The nature of the executive and judicial functions poses in fact a complex problem which has given rise to multiple theoretical elaborations in the course of the nineteenth and twentieth centuries. There is no doubt, however, that by the second half of the eighteenth century, following the impact made by *The Spirit of the Laws*, most political actors and theorists conceived these two functions as subordinate to legislation. Once the notion of prerogative power was abandoned, no possibility of legitimately acting beside or against the law was left.[51] Now, because of the hierarchy among the three functions, the constitutional scheme suggested by the Anti-Federalists would have placed the body vested with the superior function (the Congress) in a position of supremacy. In the absence of executive veto and judicial review, the other two branches could have done nothing but carry out and apply the decisions of the legislature. This legislative supremacy, however, would have been limited in two ways. First, the division of the legislature in two branches was intended to prevent the enactment of arbitrary laws: the two chambers would have actively checked each other. Second, the Congress itself would have been restricted to the enactment of laws, that is, of general measures, and therefore prevented from making individual decisions. Thus, the legislature, which the Anti-Federalists regarded as more representative of the people in their diversity than the President, and more accountable to them than the judges, would have wielded a supreme and yet limited power.

The principle: 'one branch, one function', however, revealed another capital dimension of the Anti-Federalist constitutional views. The Anti-Federalists unremittingly advocated precision and certainty in constitutional matters. They complained over and over again that the constitution was 'incomprehensible and indefinite', 'vague and inexplicit'.[52] Looking back at the debate in which she had participated herself, Mercy Warren noted in 1805: 'These judicious men [the Anti-Federalists] were

---

[51] Locke's *Second Treatise* contained the last major theorisation of prerogative power. Locke justified and defined prerogative power in the following terms:

> Many things there are, which the Law can by no means provide for, and those must necessarily be left to the discretion of him, that has the Executive Power in his hands, to be ordered by him, as the publick good and advantage shall require ... This power to act according to discretion, for the publick good, without the prescription of the Law, and sometimes even against it, is that which is called Prerogative. (*Second Treatise of government*, ed. by P. Laslett, Cambridge, 1989, ch. 14, §§ 159–60, pp. 374–5)

Thus in the *Second Treatise*, the three functions of government are legislation, execution and prerogative. Prerogative encompasses the whole 'federative power', but it applies in certain cases to domestic affairs as well. One of Montesquieu's most important innovations was precisely to do away with any notion of a discretionary power in his definition of the three governmental functions.

[52] Denatus, Address to the Virginia Federal Convention, *Storing*, V, 18, 5; Cato, Letter V, *Storing*, II, 6, 33. See also A Columbian Patriot, *Storing*, IV, 28, 4.

solicitous that every thing should be clearly defined; they were jealous of each ambiguity in law or government ... They were of opinion, that every article that admitted of doubtful construction, should be amended, before it became the supreme law of the land.'[53] The Anti-Federalists did not attack the provisions which granted more than one function to one department on the sole ground that the combination of any two functions paved the way for tyranny. They also protested that such an intermixture was a source of ambiguity, confusion and potential conflict.[54] Certainty, they argued, constituted 'a *wall of safety* to the community'.[55] They insisted that the constitution should set in the clearest and most intelligible fashion the bounds circumscribing the jurisdictions of the various governmental bodies. In her observations concerning the proposed judiciary, for example, Mercy Warren complained:

There are no well defined limits of the Judiciary Powers, they seem to be left as a boundless ocean, that has broken over the chart of the Supreme Lawgiver '*thus far shalt thou go and no further*', and as they cannot be *comprehended* by the clearest capacity, or the most sagacious mind, it would be an Herculean labour to attempt to describe the dangers with which they are replete.[56]

The Anti-Federalists' preference for clear limits appeared in their observations on two other constitutional issues: the relations between state and federal governments and the question of a bill of rights. Though these two questions were different from the separation of executive, legislative and judicial powers at the federal level, they had objectively something in common with it. Each case raised, indeed, the problem of

[53] Mercy Warren, *History of the rise, progress and termination of the American revolution, interspersed with biographical, political and moral observations*, Boston, 1805, chap. 31, reprinted in *Storing*, VI, 14, 44.

[54] Mercy Warren, for example, wrote: 'The Executive and the Legislative are so dangerously blended as to give just cause of alarm, and every thing relative thereto, is couched in such ambiguous terms – in such vague and indefinite expressions – as is a sufficient ground without any other objection, for the reprobation of the system, that the authors dare not hazard to a clear investigation.' (Cited in a Columbian Patriot, *Storing*, IV, 28, 4, § 4. The anonymous author of this pamphlet has been identified as Mercy Warren.) Cincinnatus, for his part, denounced as an 'egregious error in constitutional principles' the division of executive powers between the Senate and the President. 'This absurd division', he claimed, 'must be productive of constant contentions for the lead, must clog the execution of government to a mischievous, and sometimes to a disgraceful degree' (Cincinnatus, Essay IV, *Storing*, VI, 1, 33).

[55] Cato, Letter V, *Storing*, II, 6, 34. My emphasis.

[56] A Columbian Patriot, *Storing*, IV, 28, 4, § 3 (my emphasis). Presidential powers were also criticised in similar terms. Cato protested that these powers were 'vague and inexplicit' (Cato, Letters IV–V, *Storing*, II, 6, 31–4). An Old Whig complained that they had no 'bounds' (An Old Whig, Essay V, *Storing*, III, 3, 31). Commenting on the clause that the President 'shall take care that the laws be faithfully executed', William Symmes exclaimed: 'But was ever a commission so *brief*, so *general* as this of our president?' (William Symmes, Letter to Capt. Peter Osgood, Jr., *Storing*, IV, 5, 2, § 11; original emphasis).

the proper method for limiting the legitimate sphere of action of public authorities: the government in general, its various levels, or its various branches. Now it is striking to note that in their arguments over these three constitutional issues, the Anti-Federalists used the same vocabulary: that of precise and fixed lines of demarcation. It was in that language that they expressed their concern for protecting the states against possible encroachments by the federal government. Melancton Smith, for example, declared in one of his speeches at the ratifying convention of the state of New York:

It is necessary that the powers vested in government should be precisely defined, that the people may be able to know whether it moves in the *circle* of the constitution. It is the more necessary in governments like the one under examination; because Congress here is to be considered as only a part of a complex system. The state governments are necessary for certain local purposes; the general government for national purposes ... It is therefore of the highest importance, that *the line* of jurisdiction should be accurately drawn. It is necessary, sir, in order to maintain harmony between the governments, and to prevent the constant interference which must either be the cause of perpetual differences, or oblige one to yield, perhaps unjustly, to the other.[57]

Edmund Randolph, a participant in the Philadelphia Convention who refused to sign the constitution, enumerated in one letter the directions in which the constitution ought to be corrected. '*In drawing a line*', he mentioned among other points, 'between the powers of Congress and individual states; and in defining the former; so as to leave no clashing of jurisdictions nor dangerous disputes: and to prevent the one from being swallowed up by the other, under the cover of general words, and implication'.[58] It is remarkable also that the Anti-Federalists often

---

[57] Melancton Smith, Speech of 27 June 1788, *Storing*, VI, 12, 36, (my emphasis). In his speech of 25 June, Melancton Smith had declared: 'One or the other of the parties [the federal and state governments] must finally be destroyed in the conflict. The constitutional *line* between the authority of each should be so obvious, as to leave no room for jealous apprehensions or violent contests' (*Storing*, VI, 12, 31; my emphasis). A Pennsylvania Anti-Federalist expressed his fear that given the 'undefined, unbounded and immense power' granted to Congress, the only recourse left if the federal representatives abused their power would be sheer force (An Old Whig, *Storing*, III, 3, 12).

[58] Edmund Randolph, Letter of 10 October 1787, *Storing*, II, 5, 41; my emphasis. George Mason, another Anti-Federalist who had attended the federal convention, declared in his speech to the Virginia ratifying convention: 'I hope that a government may be framed which may suit us, by *drawing the line* between the general and State governments, and prevent that dangerous clashing of interest and power; which must, as it now stands, terminate in the destruction of one or the other' (George Mason, Speech in the Virginia State Ratifying Convention, *Storing*, V, 17, 1). The Pennsylvania Minority employed the same vocabulary. 'That therefore', they wrote, 'as there is no line of distinction drawn between the general and state governments; as the sphere of their jurisdiction is undefined, it would be contrary to the nature of things, that both should exist together, one or the other would necessarily triumph in the fullness of dominion' (The Address and

couched their arguments for a bill of rights in a similar language. Brutus remarked that the people in all countries 'where any sense of freedom remained' had found necessary 'to fix *barriers* against the encroachments of their rulers', in the form of bills of rights.[59] Denatus criticised in the same breath the lack of clear lines of demarcation between state and federal governments and the absence of a bill of rights. 'There would be no need of a bill of rights', Denatus wrote, 'were the states properly confederated. The *land-mark* clearly drawn between the powers that give, and the power given ... Had this distinction been clearly fixed, so as to prevent any future controversy, the constitution in question, would have been a glorious, and immortal example of human wisdom.'[60] The remarkable recurrence of the same type of metaphors in these pamphlets suggests that these images expressed a deep and powerful intuition belonging to the core of Anti-Federalist beliefs.

It seems that the Anti-Federalist demand for clear and fixed constitutional barriers and boundaries had three main motivations. First, the opponents of the constitution believed that the limits placed upon the actions of public authorities had to be precise in order to be strong and effective. Their Whiggism took the form of an attachment to constitutional accuracy. They thought that indeterminacy and vagueness in the fundamental law would provide an excuse for endlessly increasing power at the expense of liberty. The notion of flexible yet resistant limits was alien to their constitutional outlook. Second, they regarded precision as a guarantee against disputes and conflicts. In their eyes, the proposed system of checks and balances opened the way to antagonisms between governmental bodies. Indeed, it called for disputes insofar as it relied on the operation of countervailing forces for preventing abuses of power. The Anti-Federalists did not view the possibility of conflict as a source of moderation and compromise, but as a road to either deadlock or the victory of the stronger. Finally, their preference for clear and fixed boundaries reflected the value they attached to the intelligibility of the constitution. One of the essential qualities they expected from a good structure of government was that it could be easily comprehended by the ordinary citizen. They criticised the system devised by the Federal Con-

Reasons of Dissent of the Minority of the Convention of Pennsylvania, *Storing*, III, 11, 23). Centinel deplored the absence of a 'barrier' protecting the state governments (Letter V, *Storing*, II, 7, 99).

[59] Brutus, Essay II, *Storing*, II, 9, 25; my emphasis. 'What excuse can we then make', asked Centinel in his argument in favour of a bill of rights, 'for the omission of this grand palladium, this *barrier* between liberty and oppression?' (Centinel, Letter II, *Storing*, II, 7, 54; my emphasis).

[60] Denatus, Address to the Virginia Federal Convention, *Storing*, V, 18, 7; my emphasis. See also The Impartial Examiner, Essay I, *Storing*, V, 14, 4.

vention, not so much because it limited the power of the people, as because it was *opaque* to the people.

This last point deserves a special emphasis, because it helps clarify a central Anti-Federalist notion, that of 'simple government'. When the Anti-Federalists advocated 'simple government' they were not asking for unlimited popular government, but for a government whose operation, indeed whose very limitation, were easily comprehensible. To be sure, their idea of simplicity was relative. The type of divided and limited government that they had in mind was necessarily more complex than an undifferentiated and absolute popular government. Still, there were, in their opinion, varying degrees of simplicity and complexity. The Anti-Federalists contended that a system of fixed boundaries delineating precisely the jurisdictions of the government in general, and of the various public authorities, was less impenetrable than a structure in which the limitation of each authority resulted from the possible resistance and counteraction of others.

The attachment of the Anti-Federalists to the conceptualisation of governmental functions proposed by Montesquieu must be seen in this context. It is certainly true that by 1787 the distinction between the executive, legislative and judicial functions had become the conventional language of the day. This, however, did not imply that its adoption by the Anti-Federalists was merely superficial. Quite the contrary, in light of their emphasis on constitutional intelligibility, the fact that this conceptualisation had gained such a wide acceptance took on a political import: precisely because the difference between the three functions was so widely recognised and accepted, the operation of the government strictly organised along those lines would have been easily understood by virtually everyone. The Anti-Federalists criticised the constitution because it parcelled out power in an unconventional, and therefore less widely understood, manner.

Furthermore, even though they did not explain exactly why, the opponents of the constitution felt that delineating exactly in the constitution the functions of the several levels and branches of the government would have fostered democratic accountability. As noted above, they held simple government and responsible government as synonymous. Accountability does not necessitate an omnicompetent elected assembly. It can be attained in a differentiated government, if the people know who is responsible for what. This in turn is facilitated if the constitution unambiguously allots different tasks to different authorities and if this division of labour remains stable over time. One can indeed argue, to consider only the case of the legislative, executive and judicial powers, that if the constitution assigns only one function to each branch, the people can relatively easily lay the blame for a particular decision (or for the absence of a decision) of which they disapprove. They have only to determine to what function or type of task that decision belongs. On that basis, they can infer with certainty that the branch to which the constitution assigns that function was involved in the making of the incriminated decision. Voters do not need to inquire into the particular process that led to the decision, because a given function is *always* performed by the same department or combination of departments (in the case of a bicameral legislature). The situation of the electorate is significantly different if, as under the system criticised by the Anti-Federalists, each branch is authorised, but not required, to exercise a part of the function primarily assigned to another. The latter system entails indeed various effects. First, the exercise by one branch of its right to participate in another's function is discretionary and optional. The President may or may not use his right of vetoing legislation. The Supreme Court may or may not decide to hear a case questioning the constitutionality of a law. Thus, a given department is sometimes responsible for one category of decisions, sometimes for another (in combination with another department). This tends to blur the popular perceptions of the various authorities as the people cannot systematically associate each with a certain type of task. Before laying the blame, then, the people must trace *case by case* the particular process which resulted in the decision that they condemn. Depending on the case, a certain type of measure (say, a law) may have involved one, two or even three branches. The combination of branches, moreover, is not identical in all cases: a law may have implicated either the legislature and the executive, or the legislature and the courts. Lastly, when the populace has eventually identified the culprits (in case there was more than one), the accused authorities will most probably attempt to shift the blame onto each other. If, in spite of their protestations, the electorate decides that they are jointly responsible, it must still apportion the blame among them. Since each branch is authorised to exercise only *a part* of the function primarily assigned to another, their respective influences over a given decision are not equal. The faculty of blocking laws, for example, does not exactly coincide with that of making laws, nor does it carry an equal weight. The people presumably know this, at least vaguely. They must, then, try to assess the degree of responsibility of each implicated authority and they cannot resort to the *simple* rule of equally distributing the blame among the various culprits. The intuition of the Anti-Federalists that the system they were rejecting would hinder democratic accountability was no mere fantasy.

However, the Anti-Federalists' advocacy of a system of clear and stable boundaries left a crucial question unanswered: how would these bound-

aries be enforced? The last essay by Brutus hinted that the people themselves, to whom the carefully separated branches of the government
should all be accountable, might be the ultimate guardians of the boundaries. But, as Storing remarks, it was perhaps significant that Brutus
broke off before elaborating the point any further.[61]

III.   The Federalist response

The views of the Federalists on the separation of powers are much better
known than those of their opponents. One can gain, however, a more
precise understanding of the Federalist statements on the subject by
replacing them in the context of the ratification debate. The Federalists
were indeed led to spell out their conception by the need to answer the
objections of their adversaries: the section of the *Federalist Papers* usually
regarded as the most authoritative formulation of the Federalist doctrine
on the separation of powers (*Federalist 47–51*) began as a response.[62]
'One of the principal objections', Madison wrote, 'inculcated by the more
respectable adversaries to the Constitution is its supposed violation of the
political maxim that the legislative, executive, and judiciary departments
ought to be separate and distinct'.[63] Thus, the opening paragraphs of the
Federalist 47 confirmed that it was the Anti-Federalists who raised the
question of the separation of powers in the ratification debate. Moreover,
Madison explicitly framed his argument as a contrast. He did not contend
that there were no alternatives, nor that those alternatives were just
inconsistent and confused. Rather, he scrutinised other proposals (*Federalist 48–50*), and carefully attempted to demonstrate their inadequacy.

Let us recall the first steps of Publius's argument. Madison acknowledged the principle that the accumulation of the three functions in the
same hands 'whether of one, a few or many, self appointed or elective' was
the very definition of tyranny.[64] He argued, however, that what Montesquieu meant was not that the three departments should be kept totally
independent:

His meaning, as his own words import, and still more conclusively as illustrated
by the example in his eye [the British example], can amount to no more than this,
that where the *whole* power [i.e. function] of one department is exercised by the

---

[61] Storing, 'What the Anti-Federalists were for' in *Storing*, I, p. 96, note 38.

[62] The four papers (*48–51*) formed a sequence in Madison's own eyes, as the opening
sentence of *Federalist 52* testifies. 'From the more general inquiries pursued in *the four
last papers*', he wrote, 'I pass on to a more particular examination of the several parts of
the government' (Madison, *Federalist 52*, p. 325; my emphasis).

[63] Madison, *Federalist 47*, p. 301.

[64] *Ibid.*

same hands which possess the *whole* power of another department, the fundamental principles of a free constitution are subverted.[65]

In other words, Montesquieu's doctrine did not prohibit a *partial* participation of each branch in the function primarily assigned to another. Thus, on Madison's reading, what came to be known as the checks and balances among the three branches of the government was authorised by the 'oracle' himself.[66] Next, Madison argued that such a limited mixture of functions was not only permissible, but indeed necessary. He began by emphasising the problem of effectiveness. It was not sufficient, he claimed in the *Federalist 48*, to discriminate 'in theory' the several classes of power; the 'great problem' was to provide 'some practical security for each, against the invasion of the others'.[67] Madison was thus turning the argument of the Anti-Federalists against themselves: the arrangement they criticised (the partial participation of each department in the function primarily assigned to another) was in reality a method better than their own for achieving the result they wanted.

In the *Federalist 48*, Madison asserted first that the precise constitutional boundaries advocated by the Anti-Federalists would be mere 'parchment barriers'.[68] Although the phrase was to become extremely famous, it was quite enigmatic. One could indeed have retorted – and Madison could not possibly ignore – that any written constitution was necessarily a piece of parchment. Was this image, then, more than a powerful rhetorical weapon? To substantiate his assertion, Madison pointed out that the constitutions of Virginia and Pennsylvania which established clear lines of demarcation between the three branches of government had proved incapable of protecting the executive and the judiciary against invasions by the legislature. He proposed, moreover, an explanation of this failure. His account rested in the first place on a general axiom: 'the encroaching spirit of power'.[69] Those who exercised power essentially desired to extend it. Moreover, Madison argued, the legislative branch was 'more powerful' than the other two.[70] He imputed that superiority to a variety of factors. First, the legislative branch was politically more powerful as it was closer to the people, who constituted the ultimate source of legitimacy in a republican government. Although the *Federalist 48* suggested merely indirectly the superior political weight carried by the legislature in a republican regime, there is no doubt that the

[65] *Ibid.*, pp. 302–3; my emphasis.
[66] One could demonstrate that Madison was interpreting Montesquieu correctly (see above, note 3), but the point is rather immaterial here.
[67] Madison, *Federalist 48*, p. 308.
[68] *Ibid.*
[69] *Ibid.*
[70] *Ibid.*, p. 309.

notion played a central role in Madison's doctrine.[71] He laconically made the point in the *Federalist 51*: 'In republican government, the legislative authority necessarily predominates.'[72] The superiority of the legislature had also, for Madison, a purely legal or technical cause: the legislative function was inherently 'more extensive' than the executive and judicial functions.[73] This argument was a direct consequence of the prevailing conception of the three governmental functions: being bound by the laws, the executive and judicial functions were necessarily more restricted than legislation. Thirdly, Madison pointed out, the legislative branch controlled more resources as it alone had access to 'the pockets of the people'.[74]

Madison, however, made another and more surprising claim. 'It is not unfrequently', he wrote, 'a question of real nicety in legislative bodies whether the operation of a particular measure will, or will not, extend beyond the legislative sphere.'[75] The notion that it was in many cases difficult to determine whether a particular measure was of a legislative nature or not reflected a broader conviction. Madison stressed at various points, in the *Federalist* and elsewhere, that the definition of the three functions, simple as it might at first appear, was in reality characterised by a certain objective indeterminacy. 'Experience has instructed us', he wrote for example in the *Federalist 37*, 'that no skill in the science of government has yet been able to discriminate and define, with sufficient certainty, its three great provinces – the legislative, executive, and judiciary; or even the privileges and powers of the different legislative branches.' Even in Great Britain, he insisted, 'where accuracy in such subjects has been more industriously pursued than in any other part of the world ... the jurisdiction of her several courts, general and local, of law, of equity, of admiralty, etc., is not less a source of frequent and intricate discussions, sufficiently denoting the indeterminate limits by which they are respectively circumscribed'.[76] It is worth noting that this passage began with the following remark: 'Not less arduous [than the task of reconciling liberty and energetic government] must have been the task of marking the proper line of partition between the authority of the general and that of the State governments.'[77] It was indeed to support that initial observation

---

[71] In the *Federalist 48*, Madison just noted that the legislature was 'inspired by a supposed influence over the people with an intrepid confidence in its own strength' (*Federalist 48*, p. 309).
[72] Madison, *Federalist 51*, p. 322.
[73] Madison, *Federalist 48*, p. 310.
[74] *Ibid.*
[75] *Ibid.*
[76] Madison, *Federalist 37*, p. 228.
[77] *Ibid.*, p. 227.

that Madison mentioned the example of the three governmental functions: just as it was impossible to draw precise lines of demarcation
between the three functions of the government, so too was it impossible to
trace clear and rigid boundaries between local and national measures.
Thus, there was a symmetry between Madison's views and those of the Anti-
Federalist: both sides established a close connection between the separation of powers and the issue of federalism. Madison's belief in the
ultimate indeterminacy affecting the definition of public functions was
apparently profound: he expressed it also in his private correspondence.
In a letter to Jefferson he wrote,

> The line of distinction between the power of regulating trade and that of drawing
> revenue from it, which was once considered as the barrier of our liberties, was
> found on fair discussion absolutely undefinable. No distinction seems to be more
> obvious than that between spiritual and temporal matters. Yet wherever they have
> been made objects of legislation, they have clashed and contended with each
> other, till one or the other has gained the supremacy. Even the boundaries
> between the Executive, Legislative and Judiciary powers, though in general so
> strongly marked in themselves, consist in many instances of mere shades of
> difference.[78]

The contrast with the views of the Anti-Federalists could hardly be
greater. The assignment of different functions to different authorities was
predicated on an assumption that the Anti-Federalists never questioned:
the possibility of clearly discriminating in theory between various public
functions. The Anti-Federalists did not even formulate that assumption,
so self-evident it was in their eyes.

To return to the *Federalist 48*, the relative indeterminacy affecting the
theoretical definition of the three governmental functions entailed in
particular that the legislative branch was in a position to extend its power
surreptitiously. Thus, in a system of functional boundaries, the legislature
had simultaneously the motivation (the encroaching spirit of power), the
capacity (superior political, legal and financial resources), and even the
pretext for unduly expanding its power. Moreover, the other two
branches could not punish violations of the boundaries by the legislature.
If, in the face of legislative infractions, the executive and judicial departments did not transgress their own functional limits, they had no means of
influencing legislation, because legislation did not depend on execution
and adjudication. Therefore, the initial power base of the legislature
remained beyond their reach. If, on the other hand, the executive and the
judiciary decided to go beyond their constitutional function, they would
be hampered by their inferior resources (in terms of finances and political

---

[78] Madison, Letter to Jefferson, 24 October 1787, in Kurland and Lerner, eds., *The
Founders' Constitution*, vol. 1, p. 646.

legitimacy). Thus, from the standpoint of the legislature, the costs of a violation of the boundaries could never outweigh its benefits. It was inevitably in the interest of the legislative branch to try to modify in its favour the initial distribution of power. The only factor that could prevent this outcome was, then, a sort of moral commitment to comply with the constitutional rules for their own sake. In other words, a system of functional boundaries required that the legislature restrain itself for the sole purpose of obeying the constitutional document. It was the futility of this reliance on pure self-restraint – as opposed to interest and the fear of punishment – that Madison ridiculed through the metaphor of the 'parchment barriers', not the fact that constitutional boundaries existed only on paper. The difficulty highlighted by the metaphor concerned the *particular scheme* that was laid down on paper. Madison was arguing in effect that the constitutional distribution of power suggested by the Anti-Federalists could not constitute what contemporary social sciences call an equilibrium: one of the relevant agents would inevitably want, all things considered, to deviate from it.

Contemporary social scientists, however, also show that when an outcome is such that one actor would be better off deviating from it, that outcome may nonetheless hold if it is exogenously enforced. As a matter of fact, Madison turned to the solution of exogenously enforced boundaries in the *Federalist 49–50*. In these two papers, he examined indeed the proposal to hold periodical constitutional conventions.[79] It is just barely anachronistic to employ the term of exogenous enforcement to characterise the system of constitutional conventions. Madison himself came very close to using that vocabulary. Referring to the system of constitutional conventions he had just criticised, he wrote in the *Federalist 51*: 'To what expedient, then, shall we finally resort for maintaining in practice the necessary partition of power among the several departments as laid down in the Constitution? The only answer that can be given is that as all these *exterior* provisions are found to be inadequate ... '[80] The constitutional conventions were 'exterior' or exogenous in the sense that they were constitutionally placed above the three branches of the government. Although a part of the constitution, they were not on the same constitutional (or logical) level as the authorities they were designed to control.[81] By turning somewhat unexpectedly to the question of

---

[79] Madison, *Federalist 49–50*, pp. 313–20.

[80] Madison, *Federalist 51*, p. 320; my emphasis.

[81] Some French revolutionaries favoured such an exogenous system of limitation of power, both at the time of the Constituent Assembly and in Thermidor. See, in this volume, P. Pasquino, 'The constitutional republicanism of Emmanuel Sieyès'; see also, B. Manin, 'Montesquieu', in F. Furet and M. Ozouf, eds., *Critical dictionary of the French Revolution*, transl. by A. Goldhammer, Cambridge, Mass., pp. 728–41.

constitutional conventions, Madison was not breaking off his argument against the idea of precise functional boundaries. If an authority capable of punishing the transgressions of the limits was set up, a purely functional distribution of power could become an equilibrium: no branch would want to deviate from it, because of the costs attached to such deviations. It seemed that with the addition of a guardian of the constitution, functional lines of demarcation became a much more credible option. Madison had to dispose of that alternative to demonstrate that his own solution was the only viable one.

The principle of recurrent constitutional conventions had been put forward by Jefferson in the context of the debate over the reform of the Virginia constitution. Jefferson's proposal, as cited by Madison, was the following: 'Whenever any two of the three branches of government shall concur in opinion, each by the voices of two thirds of their whole number, that a convention is necessary for altering the Constitution, or *correcting breaches of it*, a convention shall be called for the purpose.'[82] Madison considered the possible adoption of this solution at the federal level and discussed successively the system of occasional conventions (a convention would be called, whenever the qualified authorities claimed that a violation had been committed) and another system, close to the first, of periodical conventions (conventions would be held at fixed intervals to prevent and correct infractions of the constitution).[83] However, Madison insisted that he was exclusively considering Jefferson's proposal as a means of keeping each department within its proper boundaries, and not – which was certainly of equal importance in Jefferson's mind – as a procedure for revising the constitution. Not only did Madison underline, in his citation of the *Notes on Virginia*, the purpose of 'correcting the breaches' of the constitution, he also stated explicitly that he was discussing the propriety of constitutional conventions 'as a provision in all cases for keeping the several departments of power within their constitutional limits'.[84] He reiterated the point in the *Federalist 50*: 'I confine myself to their aptitude [i.e., of the constitutional conventions] for *enforcing* the constitution, by keeping the several departments of power within their due bounds without particularly considering them as provisions for *altering* the constitution itself.'[85] Madison was manifestly eager to stress that he was discussing the role of constitutional conventions only as *guardians* of the constitution.

[82] Jefferson, *Notes on the State of Virginia*, cited in Madison, *Federalist 49*, p. 313; Madison's emphasis.
[83] The system of periodical conventions was discussed by Madison in *Federalist 50*.
[84] Madison, *Federalist 49*, p. 314.
[85] Madison, *Federalist 50*, p. 317; original emphasis.

Madison's arguments against both systems of occasional and periodical constitutional conventions were essentially identical. He assumed that, in accordance with republican principles, the constitutional conventions would be elected by the people. He then developed three main objections. He argued first that reiterated appeals to the people would undermine respect for 'the government'.

Frequent appeals would, in great measure, deprive the government of that veneration which time bestows on everything, and without which perhaps the wisest and freest governments would not possess the requisite stability. If it be true that all governments rest on opinion, it is no less true that the strength of opinion in each individual, and its practical influence on his conduct, depend much on the number which he supposes to have entertained the same opinion ... When the examples which fortify opinion are *ancient* as well as *numerous*, they are known to have a double effect. In a nation of philosophers, this consideration ought to be disregarded. A reverence for the laws would be sufficiently inculcated by the voice of an enlightened reason. But a nation of philosophers is as little to be expected as the philosophical race of kings wished for by Plato.[86]

In this passage, the term 'government' could obviously not mean the persons who happened to hold office at a particular point in time. In a republican government, whose very definition entailed that the governors were periodically subject to re-election and could be dismissed at each election – as Madison recalled several times – the only thing that could earn the 'veneration which time bestows on everything' was, of course, the structure of the government or, in other words, the constitution. When Madison claimed in the same passage that: 'every appeal to the people would carry an implication of some defect in the government',[87] he meant that convening a constitutional convention each time that a governmental branch had trespassed its boundaries would imply in the eyes of the people that the constitution itself was defective, in the sense that it had been unable to effectively restrain public authorities.

Why, however, would conventions entrusted with the exclusive power of maintaining the constitution jeopardise its stability? Madison, it must be remembered, had carefully stressed that he was considering these conventions *only* as a method for enforcing the constitution. The conventions he envisioned, therefore, had only the right to enforce the constitution; they were not authorised to alter it. Thus, they were themselves bound by the constitution: they had to perform a specific and limited task. But who could have guaranteed that a convention, once convened, would confine itself to its assigned task, and not decide to *revise* the existing constitution, rather than *enforce* it? The institution of a guardian of the

---

[86] Madison, *Federalist 49*, p. 314; original emphasis.
[87] *Ibid.*

constitution, whatever its form (either a constitutional convention or a constitutional court), inevitably raises the classical problem: who will guard the guardians? A guardian of the constitution being necessarily the supreme constitutional body cannot be controlled and punished by another constitutional authority. It must therefore *spontaneously* limit itself to the performance of its task. The Jeffersonian system, then, could have been accepted if it had been reasonable to expect the conventions to be animated by a pure 'reverence for the laws' (i.e., the constitutional laws) 'inculcated by the voice of an enlightened reason'. Once again, as in the case of the 'parchment barriers' evoked earlier, one had to suppose the existence of an agent or a body morally committed to comply with the rules for their own sake. In this case, however, the body that ought to be motivated by this pure respect for the rules was not, at least it seemed, a party to the constitutional conflicts. If one branch of the government encroached upon the jurisdiction of another, constitutional conventions could apparently play the role of disinterested umpires. Their own power was not at stake in the adjudication between contending governmental branches. It was therefore apparently less unrealistic to assume a pure willingness to comply with the constitution on their part than on the part of the legislature, whose power and interests were at stake in constitutional disputes. Madison refused nonetheless to make that assumption. Even a disinterested umpire, he thought, had to be motivated by something other than the pure sense of constitutional duty. He envisioned only one alternative motivation: reverence for ancient institutions. Now, this second motive would of necessity be absent when, shortly after the establishment of the constitution, the first infractions by governmental branches would occur. At this stage, Madison implicitly assumed, the conventions would probably transgress their limited task of enforcing the constitution, because they would lack the only realistic motive which could have restrained them. They would most probably alter the constitution. Furthermore, the realisation that the existing constitution had failed to achieve its purpose would give them an additional motive or pretext for doing so. As a result, however, at the next constitutional dispute, another convention would have to enforce a constitutional rule of recent origin. Respect for antiquity would therefore be lacking again with the same result as in the first case, and the process would indefinitely repeat itself. No constitutional rule would ever be sufficiently ancient to command the willing respect of the assemblies. The conventions would never enforce the existing constitution, they would always revise it.

Madison also raised another objection against the system of recurrent constitutional conventions. These conventions, he claimed, would arouse the 'public passions', leading thereby to disorder and strife. The revolution of 1776 did not bring about that result, because the universal hostility to the ancient government helped maintain the cohesiveness and 'concord' of the people. But such experiments, Madison argued, 'are of too ticklish a nature to be unnecessarily multiplied'.[88]

Finally Madison raised 'the greatest objection of all'. Called upon to adjudicate the conflicting claims of the different branches of government, constitutional conventions elected by the people would not in reality be neutral and impartial between the parties: they would inevitably be biased in favour of the legislative branch, because the legislature was the closest to the people, and because the people had the strongest attachment to it. Moreover, the leaders of the legislature would most probably be in a position to secure a seat in the constitutional convention.[89] Each constitutional case, Madison wrote, would not be tried on its own merits, but 'it would inevitably be connected with the spirit of preexisting parties or of parties springing out of the question itself ... It would be pronounced by the very men who had been agents in or opponents of the measures to which the decisions would relate.'[90] By this crucial observation, Madison was denying that in the final analysis constitutional conventions could be a true system of *exogenous* enforcement. The conventions would legally be exterior to the conflicts they had to adjudicate, but they would *de facto* and politically be enmeshed in those conflicts. Not only, then, would the constitution be changed rather than enforced, but the direction of the changes was all too predictable: constitutional disputes would usually result in legislative aggrandisement, at the expense of the other two branches.

Having demonstrated that conventions would not maintain the constitutional separation of powers, Madison could affirm in the *Federalist 51* that the plan submitted to ratification was the only option, thereby bringing to a conclusion the argument started in the *Federalist 47*. In the last paper of the sequence, Madison explained how the proposed arrangement would operate and why it would effectively keep the functions separate. In the course of his explanation, he laid out what he saw as the main properties – and merits – of the system of checks and balances.

The difficulties raised by the other two alternatives could 'only' be overcome, Madison wrote: 'by so contriving the interior structure of the government as that its several constituent parts may, by their mutual relations, be the means of keeping each other in their proper places'.[91] Each department should have the means of exercising some influence and

[88] *Ibid.*, p. 315.
[89] *Ibid.*, p. 316.
[90] *Ibid.*, p. 317; original emphasis.
[91] Madison, *Federalist 51*, p. 320.

control over another. All the branches of the government had to be connected by a network of reciprocal means of influence. Thus, Madison was not presenting the influence of one department on another as a necessary exception to an otherwise valid general rule (the separation of functions), as did the few Anti-Federalists who accepted the presidential veto.[92] For Madison, there was a way of combining Montesquieu's axiom and the need for reciprocal influences: each branch should partially participate in the function primarily exercised by another. The remarkable point was that this partial participation of each department in the function primarily assigned to another was presented as *the* general principle that had to be applied systematically throughout the constitution. Thus, the system of checks and balances was organised by a fundamental principle. That principle was incompatible with the Anti-Federalist demand for precise functional boundaries between the various public authorities.

Madison emphasised first one remarkable feature of the proposed arrangement: it was an endogenous system of limitation of power. The '*interior* structure of the government' was such that each branch could be held in check by another branch, that is, by an authority placed on the same constitutional level. There was no need of an external enforcing agency, such as a guardian of the constitution. In the plan submitted to ratification, no constitutional organ was placed above all the others. Quite remarkably, the Supreme Court itself was not placed in a position where it could be completely immune from any influence by another governmental branch. Not only did the President and the Senate appoint the judges, but the constitution also stipulated that 'the supreme Court shall have appellate Jurisdiction, both as to Law and Fact, with such Exceptions, and under such Regulations as the Congress shall make' (Art. III, sec. 2, cl. 2). Thus, the Congress was authorised to impose limits on what constituted the major power of the Supreme Court (its appellate jurisdiction). This provision was to fall into virtually complete disuse. Nevertheless, its presence in the constitution as it stood in 1787 helps illuminate the fundamental principle of the Federalist plan.

Secondly, Madison pointed out that his scheme made use of a motivation invariably prevalent among those who exercised power.

But the great security against a gradual concentration of the several powers [i.e. functions] in the same department consists in giving to those who administer each department the necessary constitutional means and personal motives to resist encroachments of the others. The provision for defense must in this, as in all other cases, be made commensurate to the danger of attack. Ambition must be made to counteract ambition.[93]

[92] The Federal Farmer, for example. See above, p. 36.
[93] Madison, *Federalist 51*, pp. 321–2.

The last sentence, which was to figure in every history textbook, must be understood in contrast to the type of motivation required by the alternatives examined earlier. Madison's plan did not demand that any actor – neither the legislature, nor the guardian of the constitution – be animated by a pure willingness to comply with the constitutional law for its own sake. In Madison's argument the notion of 'ambition' had its implicit but precise opposite. The system of checks and balances postulated only that the members of the various branches desired to retain and expand their own power. Each department, being authorised to exercise a part of the function primarily assigned to another, could inflict a partial loss of power to another if the latter did not remain in its proper place. Assuming, then, that all the branches were motivated by a desire to retain and expand their power, each would be discouraged from encroaching upon the jurisdiction of another by the fear of retaliation and the prospective costs of such an encroachment.

If each department did what was best for itself (given the foregoing assumption about the motivations of the actors), the initial distribution of power would hold: no relevant actor would want to deviate from it. The language of contemporary social science, which characterises distributions of this kind as self-enforcing equilibria, brings out a central feature of Madison's plan. If the distribution of power he suggested could be established *once*, it would perpetuate itself. In light of Madison's concern for constitutional stability as it appeared in his critique of the Jeffersonian conventions, it seems likely that he had at least an intuition of this remarkable property, even though he did not mention it explicitly.

Paradoxically, the contemporary concept of a stable equilibrium describes more accurately the distribution of power advocated by Madison than the notion of equilibrium as it was used in eighteenth-century political theory. Indeed, one of the most striking features of the Madisonian plan was that it did not intend to give each department equal weight. 'But it is not possible', Madison remarked, 'to give to each department an equal power of self-defense. In republican government, the legislative authority necessarily predominates.'[94] In the *Federalist 51*, this observation served to justify the division of the legislature into two branches. However, even within a legislative department thus divided into two chambers, Madison did not expect a strict equality of weights. In the *Federalist 63*, while defending the powers granted to the Senate, he pointed out that the more popular branch of the legislature would in fact have a superior power. Drawing on the examples of Great Britain, Sparta, Rome and Carthage, which all had a senate (the House of Lords in Great

[94] *Ibid.*, p. 322.

Britain) and some representatives of the people (the Ephori in Sparta, the Tribunes in Rome), he emphasised 'the irresistible force possessed by that branch of a free government, which has the people on its side', and carefully noted that in all three cases the more popular representatives had prevailed over the senate.[95] He regarded this imbalance as an inevitable characteristic of republican governments, even though he expected the American Senate to offer a greater resistance than its ancient counterparts. Moreover, Madison hinted at various points that the people would in most cases side with the House of Representatives because they elected it directly and for short terms, whereas the Senate was elected indirectly and for longer terms. If there was, then, an imbalance within the legislative department, which was itself more powerful than the other two branches, the distribution of power suggested by the Federalists could not be described as an equilibrium in the sense given to the term by most eighteenth-century political theorists. In reality, the central property of the arrangement was its stability: whenever the constitutional partition of power was modified, the system set in motion reactive forces *that brought it back to its initial state*, however unequally power was distributed in that initial state. Now, this is the contemporary concept of a stable equilibrium.

The stability of the system understood in this fashion had one important implication. Suppose that one branch took the initiative of extending its jurisdiction to better confront an exogenous disturbance (say, a war or an economic crisis). If the other branches agreed that the situation did require such a departure from the initial distribution of power, they could hold off their normal reactive strikes. The limits separating the jurisdictions of the different branches could then shift, as long as there was general agreement on the necessity of the modification. That would have been impossible under a system of boundaries. The Anti-Federalist principle was to write the limits prescribed to each branch into the constitution: the lines of demarcation were thus necessarily fixed once and for all. One could argue, then, that a system of checks and balances was more capable of coping with contingencies and emergencies than a system of boundaries. Although Madison did not mention this characteristic, Hamilton stressed several times that a good constitution ought to give the government the means of confronting unforeseen circumstances and exigencies.[96] There is little doubt that the greater flexibility and resilience of a system of checks and balances played a role in the constitutional choice of the Federalists.

The fact that Madison expected an imbalance between the various

[95] Madison, *Federalist 63*, p. 389.
[96] See in particular Hamilton, *Federalist 23, 26, 28, 31*, pp. 153, 170, 178, 194–5.

branches of the government was important in another respect: it under-lined a major contrast between the Federalist plan and the traditional notion of the mixed constitution. As noted at the beginning of this study, historians have long remarked that in the proposed constitution the various branches of government did not embody distinct social forces. This, however, was not the only difference between the mixed constitution and the plan submitted to ratification. Nor was this difference completely decisive in itself as the Polybian version of the mixed regime did not emphasise the representation of social forces, but insisted almost exclus-ively on the notion of equilibrium among institutions.[97] The crucial element, common to all interpretations of the mixed constitution, yet absent from the Federalist scheme, was rather the notion of equilibrium understood as an equality of weights. It was particularly significant that Madison had recourse to the examples of Great Britain, Sparta and Rome to demonstrate the superior weight carried by the popular branch of the legislature. For, these regimes were generally regarded as the paradigma-tic cases of mixed constitutions. Madison even referred explicitly to Polybius.[98] His conclusions, however, were far different from those of Polybius. Madison pointed out that in Sparta, the Ephori, the annual representatives of the people, 'finally drew all power into their own hands', and that 'the Tribunes of Rome who were the representatives of the people prevailed, it is well known, in almost every contest with the senate for life, and in the end gained the most complete triumph over it'.[99] In Madison's eyes, the governments that were widely considered as the embodiments of the ideal mixed regime ended in reality as popular regimes. Not only, then, did Madison believe that the constitutional plan he was defending would not create the equality of weights praised by the partisans of the mixed constitution, he even denied that a republican regime equilibrated in this sense was ever able to maintain itself. The ideal of the mixed constitution was thus dismissed as unsustainable and in the end illusory.

The Federalists believed that under the constitution they were propos-ing, the will of the people would ultimately prevail. They regarded the system of checks and balances as a protection against the risks entailed by

---

[97] On the difference between the Aristotelian and the Polybian versions of the mixed constitution, see in this volume the study by W. Nippel, 'Ancient and modern republi-canism: "mixed constitution" and "ephors"'. See also W. Nippel, 'Bürgerideal und Oligarchie. "Klassischer Republikanismus" aus althistorischer Sicht', in H. G. Königsber-ger, ed., *Republiken und Republikanismus in Europa der frühen Neuzeit*, Munich, 1988, pp. 11–12.

[98] 'To these examples', he wrote, 'might be added that of Carthage, whose senate, according to the testimony of Polybius . . . ' (Madison, *Federalist 63*, p. 389).

[99] *Ibid.*

that prevalence, which they judged both inevitable and legitimate. In the ratification debate, in order to answer the objections of the Anti-Federalists and to assuage their fears, they emphasised that checks and balances would effectively maintain the separation between three functions of government. There is no doubt, however, that in the minds of Madison or Hamilton the partition of power among authorities capable of holding each other in check also served a purpose broader than the functional separation of powers: it aimed to place restraints on what the Federalists expected to be the predominant power, the power of the people. How could checks and balances limit the power of the people, and yet not contradict the principle of popular government?

Two passages of the *Federalist Papers* clarify what the Federalists had in mind. To demonstrate the necessity of a senate capable of holding the more popular branch in check, Madison put forward the following argument:

As the *cool* and *deliberate* sense of the community ought in all governments and actually will, in all free governments, ultimately prevail over the views of its rulers; so there are particular moments in public affairs when the people, stimulated by some irregular passion or some illicit advantage, or misled by the artful misrepresentations of interested men may call for measures which they themselves will *afterwards* be the most ready to lament and condemn ... In these critical moments, how salutary will be the interference of some temperate and respectable body of citizens in order to check the misguided career and to *suspend* the blow meditated by the people against themselves *until* reason, justice and truth can regain their authority over the public mind.[100]

In the *Federalist 78*, Hamilton defended another check on the popular will which the Anti-Federalists strongly criticised: the Supreme Court was authorised to strike down a law passed by the legislature on grounds of its unconstitutionality. Hamilton argued first, as is well known, that judicial review derived from the superiority of the popular will expressed in the constitution over the popular will reflected by the legislature at any particular moment. He also put forward, however, another argument which is worth quoting at some length. Judicial review, he claimed, was necessary

to guard the constitution and the rights of individuals from the effects of those ill humors which the arts of designing men, or the influence of particular conjunctures, sometimes disseminate among the people themselves, and which, though they *speedily* give place to better information, and *more deliberate* reflection, have a tendency in the meantime, to occasion dangerous innovations in the government, and serious oppressions of the minor party in the community.[101]

---

[100] *Ibid.*, p. 382; my emphasis.
[101] Hamilton, *Federalist 78*, p. 469; my emphasis.

It was, he continued, 'a fundamental principle of republican government' that the people had the right

to alter or abolish the established Constitution whenever they find it inconsistent with their happiness; yet it is not to be inferred from this principle that the representatives of the people, whenever a *momentary inclination* happens to lay hold of their constituents incompatible with the provisions in the existing constitution would, on that account, be justifiable in a violation of those provisions ... Until the people have, by some solemn and authoritative act, annulled or changed the established form, it is binding upon themselves collectively, as well as individually.[102]

There was a striking parallel between Madison's defence of the Senate and Hamilton's argument in favour of judicial review: their common emphasis on momentary inclinations as opposed to deliberate wills. Madison and Hamilton did not expect either the Senate or the Supreme Court to block the popular will forever. The primary purpose of these two prominent checks and balances was thus only to *slow down* the will of the people and to *delay* its action. These checks were not supposed to operate as bulwarks that stopped definitively the popular will, but only as obstacles which could be overcome, but after a while. One could observe that this was yet another difference with boundaries. In a system of boundaries, no constitutional actor was supposed ever to be in a position to surmount the barriers set to its will. Under a system of checks and balances, if the people persistently willed something (including a change in or the abolition of the constitution), they would in the end prevail. Since the people had thus the final say, they were sovereign in the precise sense that political theory gives to that term. The modern concept of sovereignty was constructed in explitic opposition to the ideal of the mixed regime (by theorists such as Bodin and Hobbes). There was a strict incompatibility between the notion of sovereignty and the model of the mixed constitution. On the contrary, checks understood as delaying devices were compatible with the existence of a sovereign.

However, in the Federalist conception, it was not *any* popular will that ought to prevail, but only the 'cool and deliberate' sense of the people. The system of checks was designed to secure that effect. For if all the wills of the people had to pass through a delaying process before they were implemented, some popular wills would never be translated into governmental decisions, because the people, though sovereign, would have changed their minds when the time had finally come to carry out their will. The system of delaying checks aimed to filter out the transient wills of the people. Both Madison and Hamilton assumed that persistent wills

---

[102] *Ibid.*, my emphasis.

were more likely to be reasonable than ephemeral ones. Their psychological postulate was that passions cooled with the passing of time. Since, however, irrational wills or whims had the formal characteristic that they did not stand the test of time, purely procedural restraints in the form of delaying devices would secure substantive effects: non-reasonable wills would be automatically screened out, even in the absence of a gatekeeper eliminating them on the basis of a substantive judgement.

Aside from this broader result, the checks and balances proposed by the Federalists undoubtedly provided a coherent answer to the problem of the separation of powers. The issue of the debate, however, was not a proof that there was no alternative to the Federalist plan. There was also a logic governing the objections of the Anti-Federalists and their suggestions. The argument over the separation of powers did indeed oppose two alternative methods for limiting power. The Anti-Federalists proposed to write into the constitution the precise boundaries circumscribing the legitimate spheres of action of the various public authorities. To limit power, the Federalists designed an arrangement in which each actor was confronted with the resistance and counteraction of other actors. The former method could be described as a system of lines, the latter as a system of forces. Not only did the Anti-Federalists have a coherent conception, they also put forward some arguments and objections which the other party was apparently unable to refute. The Federalists did not respond to the powerful accusations that their system was opaque to the people and hindered democratic accountability or that it might clog the government.

Thus, the debate over the separation of powers offered a real choice. After the discussion had brought to light some properties and probable effects of the two alternatives, one side simply won.

3   From utopia to republicanism: the case of Diderot

Gerolamo Imbruglia

'On retrouve partout la base et les détails de son *Contrat social*:[1] in 1782 Diderot seemed to subscribe to this judgement, which offers an interesting indication of the spread of republican ideas in the middle of the eighteenth century, but denies Rousseau's masterwork any greatness. Of course, Diderot's view reflects the lively conflict between the two *frères ennemis* – a conflict that was still stirring Diderot's mind. Already in 1774, Diderot regarded the republican tradition as not very useful, because it was inescapably linked to small societies: these, in the age of great national states, could have only a precarious existence.[2] It seems therefore that we are at the end of the *longue durée* of the republican theme, so well illustrated by Quentin Skinner. Mine, therefore, is a research about a silence. But in the history of French political thought this silence has perhaps been of no less importance than the inflamed discourse of Rousseau. This silence nurtured inside it the word of truth: 'il faut qu'elle reste, cette vérité, ou que tout périsse avec elle'.[3] This is the truth of the ideal political society, where happiness, liberty, and virtue reign:[4] it is the truth of the republic. 'Les vérités enterrées dans les ouvrages des Gordon, des Sydney, des Machiavel, elles en sortent de tous côtés.'[5] Consequently, it was no longer enough just to meditate upon this truth; it was necessary to think of it within history, even if it was just this difficulty which had wrecked the earlier theories, in particular that of Rousseau.[6]

[1] *Essai sur les règnes de Claude et de Néron, et sur les mœurs et les écrits de Sénèque, pour servir d'introduction à la lecture de ce philosophe*, in *Œuvres complètes*, ed. by J. Assézat and M. Tourneux (henceforth AT), 20 vols., Paris, 1875–7, vol. 3, p. 95.
[2] Diderot, *Réfutation suivie de l'ouvrage d'Helvétius intitulé l'Homme*, in AT, vol. 2, p. 390.
[3] *Ibid.*, p. 446.
[4] Diderot, *Pages contre un tyran*, in *Œuvres politiques*, ed. by P. Vernière (henceforth *OP*), Paris, 1963, p. 138: 'la société ne peut donc subsister sans la vertu? et la vertu, qui n'est que le vrai dans les mœurs, peut-elle être sans la vérité? la société ne peut donc être sans la vérité'.
[5] Diderot, *Réfutation*, p. 446.
[6] See the letter of A. Deleyre to J.-J. Rousseau of 18 February 1765, in J.-J. Rousseau, *Correspondance générale*, ed. by Théophile Dufour and P. P. Plan, 20 vols., Paris, 1924–34, vol. 13, p. 22; but see esp. Rousseau, *Lettres écrites de la montagne*, in *Œuvres complètes*, Paris, 1964, vol. 3, p. 895.

Thus Diderot wondered: 'Pourquoi décourager les nations, pourquoi désoler les philosophes en restraignant le nombre des causes de bonheur? ... Il paraîtra, il paraîtra un jour parce que le temps amène tout ce qui est possible, et il est possible, l'homme juste, éclairé et puissant que vous attendez.' This man would not have sacrificed to his *volonté de pouvoir* and his desire of glory 'l'impulsion de la bonté, de la justice, de l'humanité'.[7]

Something totally different from renunciation is at the heart of Diderot's silence about republicanism. As is always the case with him, there is the need to understand how an idea could become a cultural and political ethos. The problem of the republic was becoming in Diderot that of history and revolution; and we could say that it was just through these two problems, that the republican themes re-emerged in his thought.

This perspective had already started to assert itself on Diderot during his involvement with the *Encyclopédie*,[8] and strengthened itself in the years between 1768 and 1776. This periodisation has recently been discussed with great insight by Franco Venturi, who speaks in this sense of the 'first crisis of the *ancien régime*'.[9] These were the years of the American revolution, of Wilkes and liberty, of Pugacév in Russia – and Diderot was there; the years of the great crisis in France, with the defeat of the reformers, the 'coup d'état' of Maupeau, the great financial crisis, the 'guerre des farines' in 1775. Diderot chose to be silent: after 1765 his main works were either circulated in manuscript, or appeared anonymously, or were known only within a very narrow group of friends. In those years of despair, Diderot addressed Seneca: 'Quoi faire donc alors? S'abstenir de penser? Non, mais de parler et d'écrire.'[10]

The *Encyclopédie*: between Montesquieu and Rousseau

According to the Diderot of the *Encyclopédie* France is a society in turmoil, where power has not assumed despotic features: this is demonstrated by the reassuring image, at the end of the article 'Autorité politique', of Henry IV listening to the wise men of his kingdom.[11] Diderot seems almost to place himself among those men in the reasonable hope of being able to guide the movements which he sees in the society of

---

[7] Diderot, *Réfutation*, p. 446.

[8] See G. Imbruglia, 'Dopo l'Encyclopédie. Diderot e la saggezza dell'immaginazione', *Studi Settecenteschi*, vol. 11–12 (1988–9), pp. 178ff.

[9] F. Venturi, *Il settecento riformatore*, vol. 3, *La prima crisi dell'Antico Regime (1768–1776)*, Turin, 1979; transl. as *The end of the Old Regime in Europe, 1768–1776*, Princeton, N.J., 1989.

[10] Diderot, *Essai sur les règnes*, p. 25.

[11] 'Autorité politique', in *Encyclopédie*, Paris, 1751, vol. 1, p. 889.

his times. If the role of the *philosophe* is to know the spirit of his nation, to guess its direction, and to be ahead of it,[12] this ideal was not incompatible with the Bourbon monarchy. The *gens de lettres* had to stay aloof and be indifferent to the lure of the *grands*,[13] but could at the same time rely on the structures of the monarchy. In an interesting letter written to Helvétius in 1761, Diderot describes this task in greater detail.[14] The work of the first generation of the Enlightenment had been that – he says – of discussing what 'religion et gouvernement' were, but the answers which had been given to these questions were no longer sufficient. It was necessary to move from a sceptical critique to a positive vision of society and man, otherwise French youth, which was for Diderot the very heart of public opinion, would think not only that old laws were iniquitous, but that laws as such were unjust. The risk of 'anarchie' was coming closer and closer, and this was a risk that not only the *police*, but also the *philosophe* must confront. His commitment was thus the elaboration of a 'plan de philosophie politique', which would sketch the ideal order according to which the new political life should be constructed; a new plan, but also a realistic one. As Marmontel's article 'Critique' said, there were two kinds of criticism: one able only to describe, and the other capable instead of thinking of 'modèles transcendants', that is gifted at the same time with realism and ideal strength.[15] Montesquieu had been an example of the latter type, and it was from him that came the ideal model, monarchy.

The definition of this model is set out very well in Holbach's article 'Représentants', where sovereignty is centred around the concept of *mandat impératif*, with which citizens, divided into six orders, invest their representatives, in whom therefore national sovereignty is embodied. In this way a clear and rigorous difference between monarchy and despotic monarchy is stated:[16] in contrast with the second, the first is the only perfectly legal political form, as the articles 'Autorité politique' and 'Puissance' maintain, against Rousseau. Diderot's attention does not focus upon the problems of the *pactum associationis*, but rather upon the constitution of the government. It is the relationship between *police* and sovereignty which interests him from the beginning.[17] For him, as for

[12] *Encyclopédie*, vol. 5, p. 637.
[13] See d'Alembert, *Essai sur la société des gens de lettres et des grands, sur la réputation, sur les Mécènes, et sur les récompenses littéraires*, Paris, 1753.
[14] In Helvétius, *Correspondance générale*, Oxford and Toronto, 1981, vol. 1, p. 351. See F. Venturi, *L'antichità svelata e l'idea del progresso in N. A. Boulanger*, Bari, 1947, p. 66.
[15] 'Critique', in *Encyclopédie*, vol. 4, p. 492.
[16] See e.g. also the articles 'Obéissance', 'Puissance', 'Tyran'.
[17] 'Vingtième', *Encyclopédie*, vol. 17, p. 856. Compare S. Goyard-Fabre, 'Les Idées politiques de Diderot au temps de *l'Encyclopédie*', *Revue Internationale de Philosophie*, vol. 38, (1984), nos. 148–9, pp. 91–119, and J. Lough, 'Les Idées politiques de Diderot dans

Boulainvilliers, even the state born out of the conquest can be legitimate. The monarchy which is here both idealised and proposed is the English monarchy, considered by Diderot a model of liberty.[18] Modern monarchy, often presented in terms which do not coincide with those of the *Esprit des lois*, in particular on the question of the division of the power, allows the division of legislative power between crown and parliament:[19] an interpretation *pro domo sua*, which emphasises the constitutional ambiguity of the French parliamentarians with the purpose of continuing to trust the Bourbon monarchy.

If we compare this monarchy with that of the *Esprit des lois*, we see an important difference between the two. In the *Encyclopédie*, monarchy was contrasted with despotism but not with republic, while for Montesquieu the second contrast was as clear as the first. Between monarchy and republic there was in fact neither contiguity, nor continuity; instead in the *Encyclopédie*, monarchy was idealised precisely because of its ambivalent capacity for absorbing elements which came from the republican tradition. In this way, the project of monarchy came to contest the superiority of the republican model, gathering exclusively unto itself the quality of being an ideal. Thus in the *Encyclopédie* monarchy was always the positive side of the republican ideal; its model was the one outlined by Montesquieu, who managed to give it its extraordinary theoretical strength.

Montesquieu and the republic

In the *Esprit des lois* each of the three political forms corresponds to a specific cultural, economic and moral system, the elements of which cannot be transferred from one form to the other. The leading characteristic of the republic is the fact that among those areas of individual and social life a 'virtuous' circle is created, which brings forth a peculiar form of liberty and sovereignty. While in a monarchy men cannot be but *sujets* and therefore, as such, they are 'comme des poissons dans un grand filet: ils se croient libres et pourtant ils sont pris',[20] in a republic on the contrary 'la liberté de chaque citoyen est une partie de la liberté publique. Cette qualité dans l'Etat populaire est même une partie de la souveraineté' (*Esprit des lois*, Book XV, Chapter 2). There, people have 'droit d'y

l'Encyclopédie', in Raymond Trousson, ed., *Thèmes et figures du siècle des lumières. Mélanges offerts à R. Mortier*, Geneva, 1980, pp. 137–46.

[18] See the letter of Diderot to S. Volland of 12 October 1760, in Diderot, *Correspondance générale*, ed. by G. Roth, 16 vols., Paris, 1955–70 (henceforth: *Corr.*), vol. 3, p. 129.

[19] See the articles 'Pouvoir', 'Souverains'.

[20] Montesquieu, *Mes pensées*, in *Œuvres complètes*, ed. by R. Caillois, Paris, 1951, vol. 1, p. 1431.

prendre des résolutions actives' (XI,6; XIX,27), because in the republic political liberty and philosophical liberty (XII,2) coincide, while in a monarchy they are completely separated. Liberty is the soul of the republican institution, and the individual is not its subject, but rather its 'citizen'. He alone knows the passion for virtue, which is precisely love for the republic, for its liberty and for its conditions, which are democracy, equality and frugality. He is a figure unknown to other states, where only subjects exist: that is, individuals who live with honour but without virtue, under monarchy, and with fear, without even honour, under despotism. Furthermore, because virtue is 'un sentiment et non une suite des con-naissances' (V,2), it allows man to attain happiness, a feeling which grows from the unification of the political and moral dimensions. The love for democracy is nothing but 'le seul désir, le seul bonheur de rendre à sa patrie de plus grands services que les autres citoyens' (V,3). Thus, it is not a world without passions. As we find in monarchy, there is a combination of natural and 'factices' passions: but here it is the 'passions générales' which prevail over the 'passions particulières' (V,2). The republic is for this reason the only political form which is at the same time 'composée de gens heureux' and itself 'très heureuse' (V,3).

To describe republican life, Montesquieu resorted to a brilliant formula, where the anthropology of politics is very clear: in the republic one finds 'nos arts sans notre luxe, et nos besoins sans nos désirs' (IV,6). Why is the republican citizen happier than the monarchical subject, who nonetheless has more 'passions particulières'? An interpretation of the *Esprit des lois* which emphasises only the novelty of its political classifi-cation would be seriously distorted. The novelty of its theory lies precisely in the new foundations of politics, which broke with the structures of tradition, including the sensationalist tradition of Locke. For Montes-quieu man was not just a purely passive animal machine, sensitive only to external stimuli. He was motivated not only by fear, but also by wonder, which is the capacity for understanding events which seem mysterious and for giving them order and sense. Man followed not only the law of need, but also that of desire. Man was by his nature gifted with an internal energy, which saved him from a rigid subjection to mechanical laws and permitted him to disobey them. Liberty was thus a structure of necessity. For Montesquieu the inescapable artificiality of politics must not betray this complexity. The republic was an ideal form of society, because in it there was activity, but desires were lacking; *industrie* offered an answer to need, while virtue and happiness were combined. Monarchical man was instead the one described in Mandeville's *Fable*, which denounced as a symptom of modernity the split between public and private life, between ethics and politics: such a man could not be happy.

Montesquieu was well aware that the modern condition was the fruit of the new society and of its economy: the fruit of luxury. Luxury was incompatible with the equality of the republic, which had to be limited to a small size, so as to make frugality and equality possible. It was therefore a political form inadequate for modern societies and nations, which are large and stratified. According to Montesquieu, in the eighteenth century the republics were all in decay, with a single exception, which I invoke for its relevance. In the Jesuit state of Paraguay Montesquieu saw a republic which, though similar to the ancient republics, was still healthy. In this way Montesquieu gave the republic the character not of myth, but of true utopia, possible in history, even in modern history.

With Montesquieu one could finally say what was needed to make a republic possible.[21] Before him, examples of republican life had been discussed: now those examples had become the very object of the theory itself. It was a critical theory, which approached the republican utopia in a new and yet realistic way.

It was not the utopia that the *Encyclopédie* had chosen. In order to take apart this republican ideal and to assert the monarchical model, two strategies were adopted. In his article 'République' de Jaucourt argued from a line of reasoning which was above all sociological and historical. The republic was a legitimate form of politics, but it was outmoded historically.[22] Montesquieu would never have used this kind of argument, since he did not reason in terms of progressive historical evolution. But just as the ways of procuring one's *subsistence* analysed by Montesquieu were then organised, in the first instance by Turgot, into the pattern of a succession of stages, similarly the political forms were also arranged in an historical sequence. De Jaucourt borrowed the categories of the *Esprit des lois*, but he organised them differently. In his reconstruction, Europe had a new form of political life, which was no longer the direct participation of the Greek *polis*, but the representation born of feudalism. Along with this new politics, there was also an economic change. The modern states had to be large and to produce luxury. The difference between the systems which Montesquieu had described was no longer only a theoretical one. The republic had become impossible.

For his part, Saint Lambert tried to deny the difference between the two models bridging the gap that Montesquieu had postulated between monarchy and republic by adopting a psychological perspective. In his

---

[21] From this point of view, cf. the not completely satisfactory J. N. Shklar, 'Montesquieu and the new republicanism', in G. Bock, Q. Skinner and M. Viroli, eds., *Machiavelli and republicanism*, Cambridge, 1990.

[22] In *Encyclopédie*, vol. 14, pp. 150–1.

article 'Législateur' he demonstrated that in all rational political forms (that is excluding despotism), 'l'esprit de propriété' was transformed into 'esprit de communauté'. In the republic the transformation was easier thanks to 'constitutives' laws, while under monarchy it was possible only thanks to the *police*.[23] In any case the two systems were not incompatible. In another article of his, 'Honneur', he argued that virtue and honour were the same thing, since the correct definition of the former is 'amour de l'ordre politique', and thus the acceptance of any state. Here Saint Lambert saw clearly enough that behind Montesquieu there was Mandeville and that the new *maître à penser* was Hume and his 'principe de l'utilité'.[24] This utilitarian Hume undoubtedly reached Saint Lambert through the mediation of Helvétius, who in *De l'esprit* (1758) had solved the problem of relativism with the principle of public utility. From Helvétius Saint Lambert also borrowed the argument of the possibility of a republic of large dimensions.[25] For him in a large state, 'both a republic and a monarchy', the same laws apply: in these superficial but illuminating pages one can see the gradual disappearance of the concept of sovereignty in favour of the notion of *administration*: this move would be a point of fundamental importance from approximately 1765 onward for those political theorists who wanted to defend monarchy against republic.

If Saint Lambert brought monarchy and republic together in order to promote a monarchical ideal, there were those who tried instead to assimilate republic and despotism. This was incidentally the position of Voltaire, in his tireless struggle against Rousseau, but also against Montesquieu, to whom he dedicated his last work, *Commentaire à l'Esprit des lois*. The political solution which Voltaire sustained was absolute monarchy, represented by Frederick of Prussia, and this point of view was not far from that of the other editor of the *Encyclopédie*, d'Alembert.

Another interesting contribution to the issue of republicanism in the *Encyclopédie* came from Nicolas Antoine Boulanger, an engineer, who died in 1759, and whose writings fascinated Diderot. According to him, there had been an age in the history of mankind, when men had been happy, which he called the patriarchal age. 'Plus de tien, plus de mien: tout appartenoit à la société, qui n'avoit qu'un cœur et qu'un esprit'.[26] The patriarchal age was in fact the state of nature: it represented a world of families or tribes. It is likely that his conception here re-echoed that of

---

[23] *Ibid.*, vol. 9, p. 358.
[24] *Ibid.*, vol. 8, p. 288.
[25] *Ibid.*, pp. 289 and 290.
[26] *Ibid.*, vol. 1, p. 368. Also Diderot thought that this patriarchal age had been 'l'âge d'or' in the history of mankind. See 'Agriculture', *ibid.*, vol. 1, p. 183.

Hobbes: 'Americani, excepto quod per familias parvas legibus paternis subditi sunt, quarum familiarum concordia similitudine sola cupiditatum sustinetur, ita vivunt.'[27] For Boulanger the nature of this savage community was different from the despotic one of the Roman *familia* or *genus*. The difference had already been stressed by Lafiteau, a widely read Jesuit missionary, when he wrote: 'les familles sont ce qu'étaient autrefois les tribus'.[28] The savage community was one in which men entered spontaneously, and the unity of which was not due to political law: in other words, the theory of Chapters 5 and 8 of Locke's *Treatise* and of Montesquieu's argument in his Book XVIII.

But Boulanger gave a different explanation of how men had emerged from this condition. He did not accept the theory of the change of the military chieftainship into the political one. In his view, the change was within men: men were deeply affected by inner as well as external experiences, which generated new passions. Facing great natural events, such as earthquakes, floods, etc., men discovered fear. They discovered that their lives were no longer dominated by the law of nature, but by the need to fight against nature, which Boulanger perceived as deeply ambivalent. Moved by fear, men lost their natural reason and independence: they discovered gods and religion, they accepted the new political power, which was theocracy. From this first government, people passed to Oriental despotism. But there could also be another primitive passion: enthusiasm, and its form was the republic. What the republic wanted was 'ramener toujours au règne et à l'état des habitants du Ciel le gouvernement et l'état des hommes sur la terre'. Its means were violent because its principle was supernatural: 'quand on veut être sur la terre plus qu'un homme, l'humanité est bientôt perdue'. In practice, in order to erect such republics, recourse was made to 'moyens forcés, violents et surnaturels', which were consistent with the enthusiastic millenarism of these men: 'le partage des terres, l'abolition des dettes, la communauté des biens, le nombre et la valeur des voix législatives, une multitude des lois sur le luxe, sur la frugalité, sur le commerce'. In these republics men 'se firent égaux, ils furent tous Rois, ils furent tous législateurs'; they wanted to believe that 'cette égalité était de l'essence de la liberté'.[29] The republic which Boulanger had in mind here was precisely the one theorised by Montesquieu, no longer considered however as a harmonious encounter between passions and reason, but rather as the bleak product of enthusiasm and

---

[27] Hobbes, *Leviathan*, ch. 13, in *Opera Latina*, London, 1839, vol. 3, p. 101.

[28] J.-F. Lafiteau, *Mœurs des sauvages américains comparées aux mœurs des premiers temps*, Paris, 1983, vol. 1, p. 76.

[29] N. A. Boulanger, *Recherches sur l'origine du despotisme oriental*, place of publication unknown, 1761, pp. 233–4, 409, 410, 411.

irrationalism. Virtue was not natural to man, because it was the other side of fear; in the cases both of religion and republican politics true human nature was violated, and in both the same result was reached: 'Le système républicain cherchait de même une contrée fabuleuse; il fuyoit le despotisme, et partout de despotisme fut sa fin.'[30] Monarchy was different, exactly because it was the only political form which had reason as its principle. Seen from this anthropological perspective, the republic was not only an impossible political form for modern times, it was something we could say as being *contra rerum naturam*: it was what man creates against man, and against himself.

Both these trends of criticism can be found in an article written as late as 1764. The article is 'Vingtième', and it discussed this tax; its history is still partly mysterious, since we know that it was written by Damilaville, considerably enlarged by Diderot, but, strangely enough, signed by Boulanger, who by 1764 had been dead for five years. In Sparta, we are told, 'où le peuple, et non pas les officiers, étoit le peuple, il ne falloit point d'impôts'.[31] The article explores the many questions that this simple fact raises: what the state is and how it was born; whether taxes are right and whether there is a common good that legitimates them, and why government is necessary. What is the origin of the state? There are two hypotheses: either 'a sudden and extraordinary transition' from the state of nature: this is Rousseau's theory; or 'through imperceptible and gradual changes men have all along uncovered a better way of life'. Either the *Contrat social* or evolution. One could of course mention Hume, but the article itself quotes Robertson's *History of Scotland* (which had been translated in 1764). The state Diderot analysed here is the one unknown to the ancients, born during feudalism: feudalism which, as Montesquieu said, was an event which happened 'only once in the world', and was the cause of the modern world. In assuming this perspective, Diderot had to accept the consequence, largely adopted by the Scottish thinkers, but still new for France, and rejected by Montesquieu, which consisted in abandoning the idea of a *législateur*.

Diderot's reading of Montesquieu was therefore different from that which dominated the culture in France in those years, precisely because of his closer proximity to themes which could be called philosophical history. The model for his interpretation was Hume's *Natural history of religion*, which he had read with admiration as soon as it was published. To Saint Lambert's very long article 'Législateur' Diderot added the very short item 'Législation', of only eight lines and of a completely different inspiration. In it he recognised that public interest had to be one of the

30 *Ibid.*, p. 412.
31 'Vingtième', *Encyclopédie*, vol. 17, p. 855.

terms of reference for political and moral life. However, in contrast with Saint Lambert's and Helvetius's utilitarianism, he emphasised that individual interest was different and not necessarily coincident with public interest. In order to follow the human natural code, legislation therefore must not go against human passions, or use them for its own ends, as Helvétius had thought: 'la meilleure législation est celle qu'est la plus simple et la plus conforme à la nature'.[32] In this idea of a code of nature, we recognise Diderot's desire to keep a distance from utilitarianism, for which the only foundation of politics was the conventional system of laws. He wanted instead to re-assert that the natural rights of men, which must always be respected, were at the origins of laws. At the same time, however, he wanted to restore the doctrine of natural right in a way different from that chosen by Rousseau.

This theme had already been touched upon in 'Citoyen', an article in which Diderot considered closely Hobbes's position. Diderot seems struck by Hobbes's imposing analysis, in which *citoyen* and *sujet*, republic and monarchy are, from the point of view of power, the same thing. But for him the *citoyen*, who has a 'moral' relationship with the sovereign analogous to the 'physical' relationship between the *sujet* and the tyrant, has also 'des droits qu'il se réserve' and which he must not give up. Here Diderot hides from Hobbes in the shadow of Montesquieu. But then he moves on to consider the question also from a different perspective. In Hobbes, the legitimacy of the state derives from the rights of the individual: and it is to this Hobbes that Diderot is drawn back. In the same article Diderot refuted Locke's theory of the necessity of divinity as a guarantee of political order, and he consequently refuted the interpretation, also Lockean, of natural law as obligation. The code of nature must grant not only the principle of universality, but also, against Locke, that of equality. In this sense the context of the discussion is very significant. This question originates 'dans les tems de troubles', when factions are created in the state and political points of reference for the citizen no longer exist. The citizen can only choose the 'parti ... qui sera pour l'égalité des membres et la liberté de tous'. Equality and liberty: here, in a revolutionary situation, as an incontrovertible moral answer, the republican model of Montesquieu suddenly re-emerges. 'Plus les citoyens approcheront de l'égalité des prétentions et de fortune, plus l'état sera tranquille: cet avantage paroit être de la démocratie pure, exclusivement à tout autre gouvernement.'[33] And yet this 'pure' democracy could stand only with the help of the violence of ostracism, a useless remedy, because it is impossible to stop the movement of life towards death, which affects

[32] *Ibid.*, vol. 9, p. 363.
[33] *Ibid.*, vol. 3, p. 489.

the state as it does 'la vie animale'. The claim that the republic was immortal was indeed the fruit of enthusiasm; 'le meilleur gouvernement est celui qui dure le plus longtemps et le plus tranquillement'. Diderot seems to shut himself into a cul de sac. On the one hand the republic finds its roots in natural right, which makes itself heard just when the positive laws are no longer useful; on the other hand, just as Boulanger had argued, the republic itself produces violence, and alters the natural laws of historical life. In order to escape from this impasse and assess the republican theory, and since political theory itself seemed no longer sufficient, Diderot turned to the history of mankind.

The rejection of utopia

In 'Vingtième' Diderot attacked the abstractness typical of Hobbes, by making appeal to Hobbes's own theory. Hobbes had been right to anchor political life in the natural rights of individuals, but he had been wrong to reduce these to survival alone. The society thus conceived was a 'chimère', because it led men to 'une existence misérable [qui] ressembleroit à celle d'un être dont on déchargeroit des membres pour les faire vivre'.[34] The society of *Leviathan* was a sort of negative utopia, where men lost their own reality in the name of an original nature which had instead become extraneous to them. It was a principle which must be refuted because it produced despotism.

Men had undergone so many transformations in the course of their history, that they had ended if not with assuming another nature, at least with changing their primitive nature radically. As Rousseau had argued in his *Discours sur l'inégalité*,[35] the statue of Glaucus was no longer recognizable. But then Rousseau's own utopia was a mistake, since both the primitivist and the republican models were fictional reconstructions unknown to history. By now, Rousseau and Diderot are divided on this point. In *Emile*, Rousseau had attacked Montesquieu, because in his opinion he had deprived history of all ideals, confining himself to a simple descriptive science: for him, on the contrary, in order to understand 'ce qui est', one must first know 'ce qui doit être'.[36] Diderot believed also that a descriptive science was not sufficient, but he did not agree with the position of Rousseau, who tended to ignore a realistic consideration of facts. For Diderot, who in this respect followed Buffon, Hume[37] and

---

[34] 'Vingtième', *ibid.*, vol. 17, p. 861.
[35] Rousseau, *Discours sur l'origine et les fondemens de l'inégalité parmi les hommes*, in *Œuvres complètes*, vol. 3, p. 122.
[36] Rousseau, *Emile*, in *Œuvres complètes*, vol. 4, pp. 836–7.
[37] See G. Goggi, 'L'ultimo Diderot e la prima rivoluzione inglese', *Studi Settecenteschi*, vol. 7–8 (1985–6), pp. 349ff.

Robertson, an ideal model had to be born out of history. His discussion of the Spartan utopia, a utopia completely unacceptable in the modern epoch, is a clear example of this. His polemical target was clearly Rousseau's *Contrat social*: a society could not longer continue to look only to itself; men no longer wanted to spend their entire lives in assemblies; they had elaborated new psychological structures, and their new needs imposed a new ideal of liberty and of security. A desire for happiness had been created, which required a new relationship between politics and morality. To repropose in this case the ancient republic meant to create 'un état sans peuple, un souverain sans sujets, une cité sans citoyens':[38] a world without men.

The reproposition of this way of thinking at the end of the 1760s must have seemed unreal to Diderot. What in 1760 was considered a danger averted,[39] now seemed to threaten France again. Despotism was spreading; one could no longer speak of 'gouvernement, religion et mœurs'.[40] This condition of crisis greatly upset the philosopher. 'Je ne sais que devenir', he sighed.[41] He had lost the faith of his youth. 'Je sais que je ne réformerai rien', he concluded in his article 'Vingtième'.[42] Projects and utopia sounded false to him, even if they were, in another sense, his only remaining anchor. 'Je m'accommode encore des rêves en poésie; mais je ne peux plus les souffrir en politique ni en philosophie, à moins que ne soient les miens.'[43]

Diderot's impatience thus embraced the entire production of the *Lumières*, utopians and reformists alike. He felt that nothing was talked of except *chimères*, and surprising though it may seem, he extended his judgement to the physiocrats. Initially Diderot had been very enthusiastic about physiocracy, in particular about the book by Mercier de la Rivière, in which the physiocratic doctrine and especially its political implications were explained with great clarity. In a letter addressed to Damilaville, the editor of 'Vingtième', Diderot, in all probability referring to this article, listed no fewer than seventeen reasons to be enthusiastic. He seemed to agree with its principles of natural right: defence of property, the principle of the 'évidence' and the fact that it was 'essentiellement' nature which controlled 'l'ordre des sociétés'. The physiocratic proposal was the only one that 'put donner de bonnes mœurs nationales constantes', while Rome and Greece had only had 'bonnes mœurs passagères'. He even introduced the author of this book – 'celui qui la consolera de la perte de

---

[38] 'Vingtième', *Encyclopédie*, vol. 17, p. 861.
[39] See the letter of Diderot to S. Volland of 14 October 1760, in *Corr.*, vol. 3, pp. 135ff.
[40] *Ibid.*, vol. 7, p. 56, letter of Diderot to Falconet of 15 May 1767.
[41] *Ibid.*, vol. 5, p. 193, letter of Diderot to S. Volland of 30 November 1765.
[42] 'Vingtième', *Encyclopédie*, vol. 17, p. 866.
[43] Diderot, *Mélanges*, in AT, vol. 4, p. 84. The text is there dated to the years 1764–5.

Montesquieu'[44] – to Catherine the Great. But it was a short-lived enthusi-asm. Soon Diderot considered that the physiocratic conception of natural rights was too narrowly sensationalist and 'Lockean', because it turned the idea of right into that of obligation, in contrast with his own views. Physiocracy had excessively reduced the scope of political life, erecting instead that of *administration* as the principal element of public life, thus in fact mutilating it.[45] Finally its anthropology was too poor, because it reduced the desires of men to the mere attempt to satisfy primary needs. In his *Salon de 1767* Diderot introduced a digression on luxury, aimed at revealing to the physiocrats that the *bonheur* which they predicted for society was in reality sacrifice and loss of happiness.

The abbé Galiani played a major role in causing Diderot to change his mind.[46] In his *Dialogues* he had demonstrated the 'absurdity' of the physiocratic doctrine, the principles of which were approximate and lacking in scientific rigour. 'C'est leur cœur et non leur expérience qui a tracé les idées de leur imagination.'[47] The physiocrats had approached the question with enthusiasm, but enthusiasts are always dangerous, especially if they have good intentions, because they lack realism and they deceive themselves. For Galiani, the true politician must love virtue, but he must also have the lucid calm of a criminal, if he wants to 'faire du bien aux hommes'.[48] *L'économie politique*, the 'grande science de l'admi-nistration' which is 'la science de la conduite des hommes', thus requires that one proceed case by case. We can see that for Galiani *administration* is the same as *police*, while for the physiocrats it is the expression of the laws of nature, and regulates property. For Galiani, as long as men live according to nature, *police* will be useless; but as soon as the initial con-ditions are altered, it becomes necessary: if 'il y a foule, if faut une police'.[49] When nature begins to relate to *art* (as in the case of every advanced civilisation), one can no longer invoke the 'natural' course of laws, because another dynamic has taken over. In fact, if we consider human history, we discover that men have done nothing but fight against nature. 'Il faut ... faire un équilibre qui soit celui de l'art, contraire à la

[44] Letters of June 1767, in *Corr.*, vol. 7, p. 78, and *ibid.*, p. 95, of July 1767, to Falconet.
[45] On these theories see K. Baker, 'The idea of representation at the end of Old Regime', in F. Furet and C. Lucas, eds., *The political culture of the Old Regime*, Oxford and New York, 1987, pp. 1–44.
[46] See F. Venturi, 'Galiani entre les encyclopédistes et les physiocrates', in his *Europe des lumières. Recherches sur le XVIIIe siècle*, Paris and The Hague, 1971, pp. 172–92, and M. Minerbi, 'Diderot, Galiani e la polemica sulla fisiocrazia', *Studi Storici*, vol. 14 (1973), pp. 147ff.
[47] F. Galiani, *Dialogues sur le commerce des bleds*, in *Opere*, ed. by L. Guerci and F. Diaz (Illuministi Italiani, vol. 6), Milan and Naples, 1975, p. 519.
[48] *Ibid.*, pp. 548 and 546.
[49] *Ibid.*, pp. 546, 440, 550 and 611.

nature'.[50] The *économistes* defended in the name of nature 'cet esprit triste d'économie et d'épargne',[51] ignoring the fact that the principal value that every man, albeit unknowingly, follows, is that of happiness. Inevitably, their social politics was blind and inane, unable to understand and to avoid popular revolts.

This line of attack was at once accepted by Diderot. In the debate between the Neapolitan abbé and the physiocratic Morellet, he did not hesitate: Morellet 'est un raisonneur abstrait, utopique', who 'ne connaît rien'; Galiani 'connaît les hommes et les choses'. In answer to the physiocratic method of 's'occuper d'abord de la recherche d'un principe général sauf à spécifier les exceptions', Diderot commented: 'Je n'entends rien à cette logique.' In fact 'la folle philosophie ... veut s'assujettir les lois de la Nature et le train du monde', and on the contrary 'la bonne philosophie est celle qui reconnaît ces lois et qui s'assujettit à ce train nécessaire'.[52] His criticism is thus clear: 'Vous utopisez à perte de vue.'[53] Consequently the physiocrats' project for reform was also absurd. Not having taken into account men and their passions, the physiocrats thought of a 'machine' without considering frictions and oppositions. Thus Diderot found himself between on the one hand those who denounced evils but did not know how to indicate the remedies, and on the other those utopists who had imagined 'la machine saine et toute neuve'.[54] 'D'un côté, point de remède, de l'autre, nul moyen de l'appliquer.'[55] This was the case that 'malheureusement' had made 'rentrer le livre de la Rivière dans la classe des Utopies'.[56] The result of their utopia is similar to the Hobbesian chimaera: a culturally and emotionally poor society. 'C'est une belle chose que la science économique, mais elle nous abrutira.'[57]

Nor had the problem been approached in a better way by those utopian writers who were not economists, as, for example, the Benedictine dom Deschamps, the author of the most extreme utopia of those decades.

Diderot was very familiar with the theory of dom Deschamps, with whom he had various encounters, and whose original personality fasci-

---

[50] *Ibid.*, p. 579.

[51] *Ibid.*, p. 421.

[52] Diderot, *Apologie de l'abbé Galiani*, in *OP*, pp. 97, 87, 90.

[53] *Ibid.*, p. 51. See S. Baudiffier, 'La notion d'évidence: La Mercier de la Rivière, Diderot, Mably', *Studies on Voltaire ...*, vol. 216 (1983), pp. 278–80.

[54] Diderot, *Apologie de l'abbé Galiani*, p. 108: 'C'est qu'il y a un point que l'abbé Galiani et l'abbé Morellet ont méconnu tous les deux; ils ont à l'envi sauté par-dessus en sens contraire; et le saut fait, ils se sont trouvés l'un et l'autre également loin de la vérité.'

[55] Diderot, *Observations sur l'Instruction de l'impératrice de Russie aux députés pour la confection des lois*, in *OP*, p. 366.

[56] *Ibid.*, p. 365.

[57] Diderot, *Salon de 1769*, in *Salons*, ed by J. Seznec, Oxford, 1967, vol. 4, pp. 111 and 112.

nated him, but did not convince him. Dom Deschamps's *Vrai système* tried on the one hand to reveal the reasons that had given birth to the social and political institutions to which men owed their unhappiness, on the other hand to introduce through 'le despotisme de son évidence' the new social ideal, which would triumph as soon as it spread and was understood, without shedding blood, but in peace and concord.[58] Dom Dechamps outlined a world without property, where everything was in common; where there were no laws, because they would be useless, in which life flowed along quietly and uniformly, to the point that individuality was completely swallowed up. 'Le bonheur particulier ne peut exister que par le bonheur général':[59] the most individual of all passions – the fear of death and the feeling of wonder – were cancelled and even language tended to disappear. 'Natural, too natural', Diderot seems to have commented on this vision, which for him was a chimaera, in the sense we have already seen of something that does not exist. *Vrai système* was therefore in reality a falsehood.

Diderot was well aware that the major risk that the entire *philosophie* was taking was precisely that of falling into an abstract utopism, which would lead it straight to the positions of its enemies. Diderot in fact passionately defended, against Frederick of Prussia, Holbach, who had avoided that danger: 'il n'a donc pas fait un monde idéal'.[60] By confronting physiocracy and naturalistic utopism, Diderot was able to emphasise the two elements which he regarded as central to the 'plan de philosophie politique'. The first of these was the recognition of the importance of politics, as distinct from *administration*, which must in fact be subordinated to it.[61] The second is the need for a realist observation of men, 'tels que nous sommes', in order to construct a true science.[62] Because they had not considered these questions, the utopists' proposals for change were also absurd, and had no connection with history.[63]

Diderot did not want to give up completely on utopia, on that truth

---

[58] Dom Deschamps, *Le vrai système ou le mot de l'énigme métaphysique et morale*, ed. by J. Thomas and F. Venturi, Paris, 1939, pp. 85, 205, 140.

[59] *Ibid.*, p. 155.

[60] Diderot, *Pages contre un tyran*, p. 135. We find the same observation against Helvétius: see *Réfutation*, p. 393, about his platonism.

[61] Diderot, *Pensées détachées. Contributions à l'Histoire des deux Indes*, ed. by G. Goggi, Siena, 1976, p. 103, where we find a clear distinction between 'administration' and 'gouvernement', which is the condition of liberty.

[62] This perspective, which is of course at variance with that of Rousseau and of any other utopist in the eighteenth century, is very near to that of Buffon. See Diderot's article in *Correspondance littéraire*, vol. 3 (1756), pp. 256–9.

[63] Diderot, *Pages contre un tyran*, in *OP*, p. 146. Among the philosophes who imagine 'un édit qui ordonne le renversement des églises, dans la même journée', there is probably also dom Deschamps. See for instance dom Deschamps, *Le vrai système*, pp. 158 and 204–5.

which 'l'homme cherche sans cesse',[64] but he tried to turn it into a different theory, founded upon a new anthropology and a new vision of history.

Utopia: anthropology and politics

'Dans cette recherche, quel est le premier objet à connaître? ... Moi ... Que suis-je? Q'est-ce qu'un homme? Un animal? sans doute; mais le chien est un animal aussi; le loup est un animal aussi. Mais l'homme n'est ni un loup ni un chien ... Quelle notion précise peut on avoir du bien ... et du faux, sans une notion préliminaire de l'homme?'[65] Rousseau had been wrong to speak of an isolated man of nature: in the beginning there was the group, in which fear and reflection, the fundamental passions of men, are formed. Diderot remained faithful to Shaftesbury's thesis of the innate sociability of men, though he articulated it in different ways. For Diderot, as for the *Esprit des lois*, man did not follow natural laws in a mechanical way, because he had the gift of reflection. The dialectic between nature and culture had its origin in this being, which was both inside and outside of nature.[66] Reflection pushed man to discover the fear of death, which became the dominating passion in his life, and which condemned him to unhappiness. But on the other hand, imagination tried to hide this reality, generating an omnipotent feeling of attachment to life. The relationship between reason and imagination is thus thought of by Diderot in a new way, different from that of sensationalism, by attributing to the latter an equally active role. The ideal for human life was neither the serene and strict control of reason nor the unconscious and uncontrolled behaviour of the enthusiast. If these two attitudes were separated, one would lead to folly, and the other to the dry misery of intellect: either to *le neveu de Rameau* or to *le moi*. The recognition of facts 'tels qu'ils sont' led Diderot to accept life as a contrast of movements which were sometimes converging and sometimes conflicting: man was neither only spontaneity, nor only self-control. Morality could not be separated from the science of man, from the recognition of his complex nature.

Not only in ethics, but in politics as well such a 'préliminaire' theory was needed. In human history three codes could be seen to operate, dissociated one from another, 'le code de la nature, le code civil et le code religieux'.[67] Because of the contrasts among them, it had always been

[64] Diderot, *Pages contre un tyran*, p. 135.
[65] Diderot, *Salon de 1767*, in *Salons*, vol. 3, p. 148.
[66] See Diderot's letter to Mlle de la Chaux, of May 1751, in Diderot, *Corr.*, vol. 2, p. 121.
[67] Diderot, *Pensées détachées*, p. 50.

impossible to be 'ni homme ni citoyen, ni religieux'.[68] In order to rediscover their unity, one had to 'suivre la marche constante de la nature'.[69]
To do this, it was necessary to recover primitive energy, and to return to
the primitive times (the Homeric or Ossian ages) in which the fundamental codes had been elaborated. As in the moral world, rediscovering
this energy meant to trace a natural history of man and of politics, to
discover the profound forces of history and follow their successive transformations. To observe nature was thus not sufficient. At the origin of the
bonds that sprang forth from *sociabilité* was precisely the struggle against
nature.[70] Along with nature, there were society and culture. Ideal society,
the natural community, could not be an alternative to this historical
world. The life of the savages – the only condition really close to nature –
was shorter, thus more miserable than that of Western men; it might
perhaps be less corrupted, but it was certainly less happy:[71] 'oui, M.
Rousseau, j'aime mieux le vice raffiné sous un habit de soie, que la
stupidité sous une peau de bête'.[72] But were happiness and virtue irremediably separated? Was this the truth in the modern world, or was it the
calculated *mensonge* of the power which had civilised and was still
civilising men badly, as the final pages of the *supplément* denounced? And
in order to join happiness and virtue together once again what model
should be followed? A hint, interesting also for its possible further
developments which it allows us to guess at, was found by Diderot in
Chastellux's work.[73]

Chastellux had asked himself if 'en devenant grand on devient plus
heureux?'. His objective had thus not been to teach *how* to make a society
happier, but only to observe whether in the modern world there was more
happiness than in the ancient one.[74] A happy people was not for Chastellux that which lived in a condition of continual tension, but rather that
which, having given up the passion of glory (a violent and self-sacrificing
passion), knew how to enjoy 'l'aisance et ... la liberté', without any
desire for a change of conditions. It was no doubt true that in the origins
of civilisation, the tranquil rural world had been overwhelmed by the

---

[68] Diderot, *Supplément au voyage de Bougainville*, in *Œuvres philosophiques*, ed. by P. Vernière, Paris, 1964 (henceforth *OPH*), p. 505.
[69] Diderot, *Fragments politiques échappés du portefeuille d'un philosophe* (1772), in *Mélanges
et morceaux divers. Contributions à l'Histoire des deux Indes*, ed. by G. Goggi, Siena, 1977
(henceforth *MEL*), p. 354.
[70] *Ibid.*, p. 307.
[71] Diderot, *Réfutation*, p. 287: 'Il ne suffit pas de m'avoir démontré qu'il y a plus de crimes,
il faudrait encore me démontrer qu'il y a moins de bonheur'.
[72] *Ibid.*, p. 411.
[73] Quoted and very well judged in *Réfutation*, p. 431.
[74] F. J. Chastellux, *De le félicité publique*, Paris, 1822, vol. 1, pp. 111 and 33.

violence of hunters and robbers.[75] Civilisation had thus been born from *police*, 'irréconciliable ennemi de la propriété'. Slowly, alongside this, which was also called 'gouvernement des hommes' in Galiani's terminology, another sense of *administration* was also developing. *Administration* was called 'gouvernement des propriétés' and its advent was a clear signal of the turning point in the history of civilisation.[76] Liberty, tranquillity and the law of nature gradually took over from violence and convention. Chastellux defended the ideal of a society in which *bonheur* and *éclat* were both present. 'Un peuple heureux n'est pas celui qui vit de peu.'[77] The comparison between the ancient world and the modern one, if posed in terms of the question 'Ce peuple était-il heureux?', left no room for doubt. Only modern social conditions allowed for the increase in liberty, in wealth, in population, which were the 'natural' sources of happiness. Even Chastellux realised that his optimism was in some way 'magique',[78] and Diderot's approval was accompanied by doubts.

Diderot returned to the idea of *administration* but, instead of contrasting it with *police*, as Chastellux had done, he opposed it to the 'société civile ou politique'.[79] The liberty of each individual must be found not in *administration*, which is bound to have 'la forme et la rigidité monastique', but in the political sphere. This defence of unrestrained individual liberty to the point of *ius abutendi* was not in Diderot a return to the positions of the physiocrats, but rather a correction of those of Galiani. It was above all a polemic against those, like dom Deschamps or Helvétius,[80] who defended the right of the state to limit or to direct the action of individuals; that is, to make individual *bonheur* a function of public *bonheur*. The polemic against this utopianism and utilitarianism significantly widened the horizon of Diderot's discussions and also revealed their critical potential. The utopianism he fought against was not only a false theory, but was also, one would say today, a calculated ideology of power.[81] Against these utopians, against Helvétius, Diderot chose Rousseau.

The ideal society which Diderot aimed at was made up of the 'heureuse médiocrité', between the enormous luxury of Western man and 'l'indigence étroite de l'homme brut', between richness and misery: its characteristic was *l'aisance*.[82]

---

[75] *Ibid.*, pp. 37–8.
[76] *Ibid.*, p. 120. It is apparent here that Chastellux uses the language of physiocracy and not that of Galiani.
[77] *Ibid.*, p. 177.
[78] *Ibid.*, vol. 2, p. 244 (added in 1776; the first edition was published in 1772).
[79] Diderot, *Fragments*, p. 314.
[80] See Diderot, *Réfutation*, p. 419.
[81] Diderot, *Fragments*, pp. 315–16.
[82] Diderot, *Fragments*, p. 308.

'Si Rousseau, au lieu de nous prêcher le retour dans la forêt, s'était occupé à imaginer une espèce de société *moitié policée et moitié sauvage*, on aurait eu, je crois, bien de la peine à lui répondre.'[83] Thus Diderot's model was that of a primitive people 'assez sage pour s'être arrêté de lui-même à la médiocrité',[84] but it was also woven into the history of *civilisation*. The starting points[85] were the mechanical arts, agriculture, and not the disappearance of *industrie*, as dom Deschamps had preached; moderate inequalities, which reflect differences in talents and merits, must be accepted. Thus even a modern society could control its development, without falling into stagnation; that is, it could rediscover the virtue of happiness.[86] Here, the opposition between Diderot and Helvétius is clear. The latter tried also to imagine a new state, where republican institutions would fit into the interests of a large modern society, in which the republic could have the form of an empire. Diderot's ideal republic was instead a small state, the institutions of which must be reconciled with the passions of its citizens. Echoing Montesquieu, this republic had to be 'heureuse' because men were happy, and not because of their sacrifice to 'l'intérêt public'. For Diderot, in other words, liberty was one of the forms of the relationship between virtue and happiness.

The project thus conceived was not 'utopistic' in the derogatory sense that we have seen, because it respected the true nature of man. The comparison between the ancient world and the modern one made Chastellux appear to be right not only in the answer he gave, but also in his question. In the course of history the conditions of life had changed, men had created new structures of thought and of desire, so that the superiority of the modern world was unquestionable. Happiness, as Saint-Just would later say, was a new idea born together with the new world. But Diderot then shifted this comparison, expanding it to that between the natural and the civilised worlds. His answer was fainter here, but clearer. 'Vous préférez donc l'état sauvage à l'état policé? Non.'[87] The savage world kept intact its potential for criticism of institutions, but it did not offer a practical model. The natural place for men was society. No natural state existed which was not social.[88] Human life took place within this horizon: the evolution away from *sauvagerie*, the development of its own conditions, and finally decadence. In the commentary to *De la félicité* one

---

[83] Diderot, *Réfutation*, p. 431 (italics are mine).
[84] Diderot, *Supplément*, p. 503.
[85] See Diderot, *Fragments*, p. 350. These *Fragments* have been intelligently discussed by G. Goggi, 'Les fragments politiques de 1772', in 'Editer Diderot', *Studies on Voltaire . . .*, vol. 254 (1988), pp. 449–60.
[86] Diderot, *Réfutation*, p. 418.
[87] *Ibid.*, p. 411.
[88] Diderot *Supplément*, p. 508.

can hear the echo of another work, precisely the effort of thinking about the relationship between virtue and happiness in the modern epoch, which had set aside the previous categories of history and of nature, in order to present a new one, that of society. Ferguson's *Essay on the history of civil society*, cited by Chastellux, and widely read at that time (a fact about which little is yet known), seems here to be present in Diderot's mind, in a singular *mélange* of memories of Rousseau. Once again, as in the debate between Galiani and physiocracy, it was between Rousseau and Ferguson, between *art* and nature, that Diderot searched for a solution. He ended up far from both because his idea of *civilisation* was different. It was not a question of recognising the naturalness of it, as in Ferguson, nor was it a question of succeeding in imagining one which, radically conventional, was able to recreate the paths of nature, as in Rousseau. The singular interpretation which Diderot had given of *natural history* allowed him to unite those terms that others separated.[89]

In order to avoid the risks and the emptiness of utopianism and to elaborate his plan of political philosophy considering civilisation in a way that would be both critical and realistic, Diderot made use of a notion in which he re-elaborated his anthropological theory of society and of man. The notion of *mélange* could in fact make nature and culture converge in a configuration that was completely original. This allowed not a superficial synthesis of various ideas, but deep insights into the natural history of men. It was precisely the use of this category to describe the birth of civilisation that permitted Diderot to open a new breach in human history, in its rhythms, and in its destiny.

History and revolution

It is possible to argue that, since about 1765, Diderot had come closer to a theoretical perspective of 'natural history'. So that the wonderful *salons* from 1765 to 1769 seem in effect to trace a 'natural history' of art and morality *à la Diderot*. It was a way of thinking of philosophy different from the one he had sketched in the *Encyclopédie*, a way in which imagination now had a predominant role. But the very conditions of the role of the *philosophe* had also changed. If his faith in the power of the state failed him, the *philosophe* went back to be *l'honnête homme* of the years between 1740 and 1750, isolated in his uprightness. But could he still

---

[89] See Diderot, *Pensées détachées*, p. 163: 'Mais depuis qu'on a vu que les institutions sociales ne derivaient ni des besoins de la nature ni des dogmes de la religion, puisque des peuples innombrables vivaient indépendants et sans culte, on a découvert les vices de la morale et de la législation dans l'établissement des sociétés.'

'garder le silence' in the face of unjust laws? Hardly.[90] Through he might be isolated, the *philosophe* must not abandon his critical function: here Diderot introduced the beautiful and disquieting image of the 'invisible church',[91] made up from the group of intellectuals who were far from the 'gros de la nation', and divided from within. The group of the *gens de lettres* had fallen apart and it was now a constellation united more by needs and epochal ideas than by ties and projects in common, as it had been before. The *philosophe* was no longer a political guide, but an external observer, at the same time close and far away, of society.[92] On this image of the *église invisible* one point should be emphasised: what now united the intellectuals was a passion common to them: love of glory, their way of thinking about the future and for the future. Like every poet, like every man whose destiny had the imprint of genius, the *philosophes* were also made of passions and reason. But they knew how to feel, using their voices, the unique sense of life. Like the poet, the *philosophe* was a prophet, relating both to the past and to the future.[93] He lived on the threshold between these two worlds, he permitted them to communicate with each other. The problem was no longer that of the law-giver nor was it that of the plan of legislation; the problem was to understand the movement of history.

Unlike Condorcet, Diderot was not interested in foreseeing a state, but rather in describing a process. This process was that of *tâtonnement*,[94] *mélange* of imagination, reason and experience, in which ideas, sentiments and the forms of civilisation were worked out, sometimes even unintentionally. The *philosophe* must know human and social energy very well. As Diderot said with respect to Galiani's thought, in order to be realistic, the philosopher must think of politics 'en moraliste'.[95] This was not the defence of an abstract dimension, either utopistic or moralistic, but of the

[90] Diderot, *Pages contre un tyran*, p. 144.
[91] 'Il est un certain nombre d'hommes sensés et justes; ils n'élèvent point leur voix; ils se donnent le temps d'écouter; ils ont beaucoup vu, beaucoup plus médité; ils se respectent, cependant ils ont leur voix, leur prétention, leur passion, leur esprit de religion; mais ils se tempèrent les uns par les autres; et ce sont eux qui forment à la longue le sentiment de la Nation, de cette nation dont l'historien écrit le jugement. (Diderot, *Inventaire du fonds Vandeul*, ed. by H. Dieckmann, Geneva and Lille, 1951, p. 233)
See also *Eléments de physiologie*, ed. by J. Meyer, Paris, 1964, p. 338 and the letter to Falconet of September 1766, in *Corr.*, vol. 6, p. 306.
[92] See Diderot's letter to S. Volland of 25 July 1762, in *Corr.*, vol. 4, p. 71.
[93] 'C'est peut-être que les poëtes et les prophètes commercent par état avec les temps passés et les temps à venir; c'est qu'ils interpellent si souvent les morts, ils s'adressent si souvent aux races futures, que le moment de leur pensée est toujours en deçà ou en delà de leur existence': letter of Diderot to Falconet of 15 February 1766 in *Corr.*, vol. 6, p. 71.
[94] About this concept, see esp. the Introduction to the *Salon de 1767*, and also *Pensées détachées*, pp. 104–5.
[95] This observation is reported by Mme d'Epinay to Galiani in her letter of 28 September 1770, in *Corr.*, vol. 10, p. 77.

capacity to find the elements of crisis, to listen to the profound, anthropological dimension of social life. This new *philosophe* had discovered in this way, through his *tâtonnement*, not only a new reality but also a new subject he could relate to. If he had lost the present, he had conquered the future. Just as philosophical history had allowed a look into the remote past and reconstruction of those long undocumented periods, so, it seemed to Diderot, it could also look towards the future. Posterity was the notion, which, elaborated by his theory of imagination and of passion for glory, sustained Diderot's new vision of history.

The new *philosophe* must be a preacher of liberty and of truth. In a society in decadence he had the task of bringing ancient moral enthusiasm back to life. When a society was corrupt, when despotism reached its tragic zenith, the *philosophe* knew that a revolution was imminent. The *philosophe* became a spectator of revolutions.[96] If a nation was 'déchue, il n'appartient pas à un homme de la relever. Il semble que ce soit l'ouvrage d'une longue suite de révolutions.'[97] Their cause was not, as dom Deschamps had ingenuously said, philosophy, but rather 'l'impossibilité de souffrir davantage'. The *philosophe* could in fact prepare 'aux révolutions',[98] but he was not essential. His role was that of blocking the violence of despotism,[99] and of allowing the expression of the voices of rebellion.[100] 'Dans les émeutes populaires on dirait que chacun est souverain, et s'arroge le droit de vie et de mort.'[101] For this reason, revolt was always lawful when the people felt they had lost their sovereignty. Never must they allow the 'prétendus maîtres de faire même le bien contre [sa] volonté'. In the moments of revolt, it was the *philosophe* who must speak: that revolution which he had not caused, could be saved by him. The 'peuple indigné de sa longue souffrance' never missed the opportunity 'pour rentrer dans ses droits'. But then this rebellion would become 'anarchie', because the people 'n'a ni vue ni projet'. The *philosophe* was necessary, because knowing how to free himself from the present, he knew how to link up the primordial past – the energy of nature – and the future. In the midst of the riots nothing is heard 'qu'un cri: Liberté'. Only the *philosophe* knew how to save liberty,[102] because he alone knew how to

---

[96] Letter of Diderot to Wilkes of 19 October 1771, in *Corr.*, vol. 11, p. 210.

[97] *Pensées détachées*, p. 71.

[98] Diderot, *Mémoires pour Cathérine II*, ed. by P. Vernière, Paris, 1966, p. 235.

[99] 'L'intérêt général de la multitude suppléerait peut-être à la pénétration du génie, si on le laissait agir en liberté: mais il est sans cesse contrarié par l'autorité dont les dépositaires ne s'entendent en rien, et prétendent ordonner de tout': Diderot, *Observations sur le Nakaz*, in *OP*, p. 367.

[100] 'La nature parle plus haut que la philosophie et que l'intérêt': Diderot, *MEL*, p. 243.

[101] Diderot, *Principes de politique des souverains*, in *OP*, p. 177.

[102] Diderot, *Fragments*, p. 313 and p. 337.

think about it, although like him and with him all men felt the need to do so.

These were not empty words. The famous appeal for the 'rugissements'[103] of the people, this extreme choice on the part of the revolution was connected with the dramatic situation of the France of Maupeau. 'Nous touchons à une crise qui aboutira à l'esclavage ou à la liberté.'[104] This revolution, as Diderot knew, would not be painless: it could only be 'un bain de sang', the only way to achieve the regeneration of the social body, just as Medea had done with Aeson.[105] But, were these transformations still imaginable? History seemed to teach both how terrible ancient revolutions had been, like natural cataclysms, and that they were now impossible.[106] Enthusiasm and spirit of conquest had disappeared; mild sentiments and sleepy utilitarian passions had replaced them.

And yet history could still teach something: 'En vérité je crois que le fruit de l'histoire bien lue est d'inspirer la haine, le mépris et la méfiance avec la cruauté.'[107] History was food for the imagination and could make room for those sentiments which the bleak present and the reigning despotism seemed to prohibit. 'Le livre que j'aime et que les rois et leurs courtisans détestent, c'est le livre qui fait naître des Brutus.'[108] There were no more republics, and their memory had been cancelled; one could only hope for the birth of new republicans.

Perhaps even these ideas were part of the ongoing dialogue between Diderot and Rousseau. The problem in the face of which Rousseau had deposed his arms seemed to find a solution: perhaps it was possible to avoid corruption and to think of a new project for the regeneration of a declining nation. The dilemma of *Emile* and the *Contrat social*[109] seemed to have been reappropriated and resolved in this passionate defence of virtuous posterity. In the heart of the republicans the truth of the ancient world, of Machiavelli, of the English republican tradition would be born again. The English republican tradition had undergone an important transformation: through the reflection of Montesquieu, Rousseau and Diderot it had found a new fertility, which within a few years would bear its fruits.

103 Diderot, *Pensées détachées*, p. 311.
104 Diderot, *Corr.*, vol. 11, p. 20.
105 Diderot, *Pensées détachées*, p. 71. On this image see G. Goggi, 'Diderot et Médée dépeçant le vieil Eson', in *Diderot: Colloque international (Paris 4–11 July 1984)*, Paris, 1985, pp. 173–83.
106 Diderot, *Fragments*, pp. 218–19.
107 Letter of Diderot to S. Volland of 28 September 1761, in *Corr.*, vol. 3, p. 320.
108 Diderot, *Lettre apologétique de l'abbé Raynal à M. Grimm*, of 25 March 1781, in *OPH*, p. 640.
109 Rousseau, *Contrat social*, II,7, in *Œuvres complètes*, vol. 3, p. 383; *Emile*, p. 859.

4   Cordeliers and Girondins: the prehistory of the republic?

Patrice Gueniffey

At the beginning of the revolution, no one, or almost no one, seriously believed that France could one day cease to be a monarchy. The proclamation of the sovereignty of the nation did not prevent the majority of revolutionaries from holding as sacred the person of the king, and even the institution of the monarchy. The idea of transforming France into a republic did not unite more than a handful of sectarians, at least until Varennes. Divided in their definition of republican government, condemned to political impotence by their isolation, republicans never formed a 'party', only 'one of those conspiracies of ideas, in which the members occasionally meet but more often act singly, according to individual initiative'.[1]

They remained unnoticed for a long time. The existence of a republican faction began to be discussed toward the spring of 1790, after the king had been stripped of all prerogatives of sovereignty. The *Révolutions de Paris* at the time remarked on the prudent silence maintained by numerous deputies in regard to the king, 'for fear of leaving an opening for the accusation, so often repeated, that they ... want to make France a republic'.[2]

The first writings to call openly for an abolition of the royalty were also published during this period.[3] The ex-poet Lavicomterie began in September 1790 with *Du peuple et des rois*, which was followed in November by a more substantial article by François Robert[4] which was echoed in different articles published by journals close to the radical circles of the capital. Militant republicanism, at this time, was the business of a tiny sect

[1] F.-R. de Chateaubriand, *Mémoires d'outre-tombe*, 3 vols., Paris, 1973, vol. 2, p. 467.
[2] *Les Révolutions de Paris*, issue of 12–19 June 1790.
[3] From the beginning of July 1789, Camille Desmoulins declared himself in favour of the republic, in *La France libre* (Paris, 1789, pp. 52–75). But this denunciation of the monarchy, a 'detestable form of government', took aim above all at the king of the Old Regime whose royal *séance* of 23 June seemed to indicate that he intended to take vigorous control of the situation.
[4] P.-F.-J. Robert, *Le Républicanisme adapté à la France*, Paris, 1790. This work was republished after Varennes, with a few modifications, under the title *Avantages de la fuite de Louis XVI, et nécessité d'un nouveau gouvernement* (Paris and Lyon, 1791).

gathered around François Robert and his wife, Louise de Keralio[5], which was alone, not only in proclaiming the incompatibility of liberty and the monarchy, but in affirming the possibility of establishing the republic immediately.

Such abrupt professions of faith did not fail to excite a certain degree of mistrust in the other republican circle of the period, which included most notably Brissot, Condorcet, and the entourage of Madame Roland. Certainly Brissot had proposed a toast, in July 1790, 'to those who had the good sense to pronounce the executive power elective and not hereditary', but he was hardly bound by that, and when he took up his pen once more, it was to reproach Robert and Lavicomterie for underestimating the obstacles that stood in the way of an immediate installation of the republic and, above all, to define the latter in terms of the archaic form of direct democracy.[6] This disagreement permits us to delineate two relatively distinct currents of republicanism. The division was an old one that dated to the first weeks of the revolution, when all was mingled in the struggle that would continue until the spring of 1790: it opposed the militants of the Paris districts, eager to preserve the sovereignty won in 1789, to members of the general council of the Commune, on which sat notably Brissot, Bancal des Issarts, and Bonneville, who wanted to endow the capital with a representative regime. The latter finally carried the day with the law of 21 May 1790 which ended the districts' claims, but their victory was brief: they were not re-elected to the general council. Henceforth deprived of all public responsibility, they participated in the creation of the Confederation of the Friends of Truth, while the republican partisans of direct democracy joined the club that succeeded the radical district of the Cordeliers.[7]

This episode, in provoking the separation of the first republicans into two branches, reveals the existence of two conceptions of republicanism: the one democratic, drawing upon the models of antiquity as well as upon those of the national history; the other representative, inspired in particular by the American experience. The more marginal was not the most archaic. The first group, formed by the 'Cordeliers', was born of the struggle against a double usurpation of the rights of the people: representation and the attack that was launched against national sovereignty when the Constitution accorded the suspensive veto to the king. This group expressed the most radical currents, but it was situated well within

---

[5] On this group, see A. Aulard, *Histoire politique de la révolution française. Origines et développement de la démocratie et de la république (1789–1804)*, Paris, 1901.

[6] Cf. *Le Patriote françois, Journal libre et impartial* (hereafter *Pf*), no. 498, 19 December 1790).

[7] On this episode, see G. Kates, *The Cercle Social, the Girondins, and the French revolution*, Princeton, N.J., 1985.

the arena of the revolution. Matters were quite different for the second group, all of whose members would come together in 1792 in the Girondin 'party'. This group was not born with the struggles of 1789; rather it pre-existed them. If the revolution brought together Fauchet, Bonneville or Buzot, and estranged a few others, the majority of members had already known one another for quite some time. Toward the middle of the 1780s, the partnership formed by Brissot and Clavière had become, through agreements, polemics and meetings, the centre of a network[8] of friendships and intellectual affinities whose essential coherence was based on the inherited values of the Enlightenment and upon an unbounded admiration for the American republic. This double heritage would prove to be burdensome, at the very least, and it would place this group not simply at the margins of the arena of revolutionary politics, but outside of it.

On 21 June 1791, the king's flight threw the 'republicophiles' into turmoil. For the first and last time, they formed a coalition. 'The sword is now drawn', cried Brissot in supporting Robert's petition calling for the abolition of the royalty, 'it is necessary to throw the scabbard far away, and not to profit from this lesson by halves.'[9] The illusion did not last three days. The arrest of Louis XVI at Varennes and his return to the capital sounded the death-knell of republican hopes, whose chances depended on the success of the royal project. With the king departed, and the country delivered from its burden, everything became possible, including a republic. With the king returned, his flight transformed into a 'kidnapping', the establishment of a republican government was condemned.[10]

The Cordeliers persisted in pleading with the French to deliver the final blow to the monarchy, reminding them that 'the opportunities for recovering liberty are ... rare for nations'.[11] Brissot's friends, joined by Achille du Châtelet and Thomas Paine, who was living in Paris at the time, sought more modestly to offer public opinion a 'complete course in republicanism', by rallying in the short term to a project that was supported by a faction of the Jacobins, and which called for a decree of deposition followed by a regency. These men showed great indecision and weakness during these crucial days, philosophising when action was needed and

---

[8] R. Halévi, 'Les Girondins avant la Gironde: esquisse d'une éducation politique', and P. Gueniffey, 'Brissot', in F. Furet and M. Ozouf, eds., *La Gironde et les Girondins*, Paris, 1991, pp. 137–68, 437–64.

[9] *Pf*, no. 683, 22 June 1791.

[10] Cf. *Mémoires de Madame Roland*, ed. by C. Perroud, 2 vols., Paris, 1905, vol. 1, p. 205.

[11] J.-N. Billaud-Varenne, *L'Acéphocratie, ou le Gouvernement fédératif, démontré le meilleur de tous, pour un grand Empire, par les principes de la politique et les faits de l'histoire*, Paris, 1791, p. 55.

pushing the most audacious to compromise themselves while they prudently kept in the background.

The defeat of this movement, on 17 July at the Champ de Mars, marked the end of the history of this first republicanism. The debate on the form of government was provisionally closed. Pursued by justice, the Cordeliers went into hiding; curiously spared, Brissot and Condorcet turned all their attention to the convocation of the next Legislative Assembly, whose decree of non-reeligibility opened the doors to them. The Cordeliers, amnestied after the proclamation of the Constituent Assembly, reintegrated themselves into the sectional movement from which they had issued, while the 'brissotins', henceforth in command, would find themselves, once the throne had collapsed for good, tested by the impasses and contradictions of the impossible project in which their politics of reason enclosed them.

Republicans do not like kings. There is no reason to doubt the sincerity of the sentiments expressed repeatedly by a Robert or a Lavicomterie, and this at a time when the French had not yet been called upon to hate royalty. These men had only one aim: to topple the old idol, and it was against 'ALL HELL of the monarchy'[12] that they went to war, launching a first (literary) attack in the autumn of 1790, after Necker's resignation, and then a second in the spring of 1791, as the Constituent Assembly prepared to debate the organisation of the executive power.

Their language remained the same from one attack to the other, freed of useless subtleties. 'I cannot forbid myself a remark', wrote Desmoulins in his journal at the beginning of April 1791.

In all truth, the national assembly is indebted to me. Because while Cazalès and this d'Eprémesnil, three years ago, interrogated the king on the stand ... crying out that the national assembly degraded the monarchy ... not only did I shout, but I proved by proper syllogism that the national assembly is capable of cowardice, of flabby condescension toward the Capets, that out of its superstition for the royalty it sacrifices daily ... its own decrees ... to the extent that, in the criminal process to which the monarchists submitted the assembly, my journal may be considered a continual petition for mitigation, and a collection of justificatory acts.[13]

---

12 The phrase from a later date, is that of Thomas Paine, in his letter to Sieyès, published in *Le Républicain ou le Défenseur du Gouvernement représentatif* ..., no. 3, 16 July 1791, p. 54.

13 *Révolutions de France et de Brabant*, 1st ser., issue of 4 April 1791. I would like to thank Henry Aureille who very kindly shared with me several articles published in the Paris press, from the journals of Desmoulins and Carra to the *Révolutions de Paris* and *La Bouche de fer*.

The essentials of the Cordeliers' indictment are contained in these few lines. They accused the Constituent Assembly of having renounced its principles, betrayed the revolution and exposed the nation to falling once more, in the near future, under the yoke of despotism. Not only had the members of the Constituent Assembly consecrated the right of an individual to command by hereditary succession or in perpetuity, without the consent of the nation, but they had also given him the political means to protect that right and even, by placing him above the law, to recover one day the ancient power of which several symbolic attributes – such as the right to pardon or reference to divine will in the choice of the reigning dynasty – reminded him. Republican on the day after the popular insurrection of 14 July, when Louis XVI was constrained to bow before the majesty of the sovereign people, France became monarchic once more when the Assembly alienated a part of the national sovereignty with the veto.

This interpretation of the Constitution was singular, at the very least, because it consisted in defining royal prerogatives within the context of the new principles as so many concessions in favour of the former sovereign. The principal targets of republican attack were the veto and the political inviolability of the constitutional monarchy. In taking for themselves Sieyès's arguments of 7 September 1789 against the absolute veto, and turning them against the suspensive sanction, the Cordeliers accused the Constituent Assembly of having ceded all legislative power to the king whose will, effectively capable of blocking the national will, became 'the soul and principle' of legislation.[14] Certainly, the affirmation of the all-powerful nature of the popular will accorded ill with the veto, even a suspensive one, which *de facto* limited the power to apply that will, but the Cordeliers' line of argument was based on a confusion between absolute and suspensive vetoes. In 1789, the Constituent Assembly had adopted the suspensive veto as a means to respond to demands for the separation of powers which would not, however, make the monarch's will an integral element in the constitution of the general will, as would the absolute veto. The sanction, intervening after the legislative's vote on a law, neither added anything to, nor detracted anything from it. It could only suspend execution for a specified length of time after which, as Barnave recalled, the law would be applied to its full effect.[15] The suspensive veto had been adopted as a prerogative of the head of the executive power, who was

---

[14] Cf. Robert, *Le Républicanisme adapté à la France*, pp. 39–50. This interpretation is currently that of certain jurists, like M. Troper, *La Séparation des pouvoirs et l'histoire constitutionnelle française*, Paris, 1980, pp. 23–35.

[15] *Moniteur universel*, 24 March, 1791, in *Réimpression du Moniteur universel ...*, 32 vols., Paris, 1863–70, vol. 7, p. 716.

charged with guarding against usurpations by the Assembly. Even sup-posing that the king were designated as a co-legislator, as Barnave suggested after the events of June 1791, it would have been under the auspices of representation and not of sovereignty. Similarly, inviolability was not, as the editor of *Révolutions de Paris* pretended, the 'corollary of the heritability of the throne'.[16] In placing the monarch beyond reach, this measure was intended, on the one hand, to maintain the distinction between the two powers and, on the other, to guarantee the subordination of the executive to the legislative by making the ministers – i.e. the agents of executive power – responsible to the legislative, without exposing the state's stability to the shocks provoked by a direct confrontation between the two powers.[17] The absence of responsibility of a monarch who did not act, but was simply 'charged to elect and revoke [ministers] in the name of the people', was, as Sieyès would underscore in his debate with Paine,[18] the pre-condition of the responsibility of the agents charged with direct execution.

The Orleanist Laclos, who was close to the republicans but who certainly would have preferred that their attacks spare the throne to concentrate on its current occupant, reminded the republicans with a felicitous phrase that 'the constitution [was no longer] in the monarchy, but the monarchy in the constitution'.[19] The republicans were manifestly mistaken about the period. Their adversaries did not fail to accuse them of quarrelling over nothing, of wanting to engage in a useless 'battle of words' (Sieyès) by confusing the current regime, in which a law made by all was enforced by a king who was himself subject to the national will in the exercise of his functions, with the former monarchy, in which an individual will was invested with all sovereignty. The Cordeliers, but also Brissot's entourage, were setting out to battle with the monarchy as France became a republic in which the general will animated all, including the monarch. Robespierre, himself suspected of yearning for the abolition of the monarchy after Varennes, returned to the Rousseauist definition of

---

16 *Les Révolutions de Paris*, issue of 9–16 April 1791.
17 Cf. speech on ministerial responsibility delivered by Barnave on 17 August (*Moniteur*, vol. 5, p. 417) and 23 December 1790 (*ibid.*, vol. 6, p. 714).
18 Text published in the *Moniteur*, 16 July 1791 (vol. 9, pp. 137–9). On 6 July, Sieyès undertook to prove the superiority of monarchic government in order to defend himself from the suspicions of republicanism that weighed on him (*ibid.*, vol. 9, pp. 46–7). Thomas Paine took up the challenge (letter published in issue 3 of the *Républicain*, pp. 52–4), and Sieyès replied with an exposé of his principles on 16 July. At this time, Paine had already left Paris for England, but he replied in turn in the second part of the *Rights of Man*, published at the beginning of 1792 (T. Paine, *Les Droits de l'homme*, ed. by C. Mouchard, Paris, 1987, pp. 199–213). On this controversy and its subsequent interpre-tations, cf. the synthesis of J.-D. Bredin, *Sieyès. La clé de la révolution française*, Paris, 1988, pp. 202–3.
19 *Journal des Amis de la Constitution*, issue of 1 March 1791, vol. 2, p. 36.

the republic – representation included – to affirm that 'the current French constitution' was nothing other than a 'republic with a monarch' placed at the head of the government.[20] A few months earlier, Dubois-Crancé had made the same assertion in responding to Brissot who maintained, in an open letter, that a good republican should have 'the ultimate conviction that *kings are man-eaters'* and the royalty 'a political scourge'.[21] 'In adopting this definition', wrote Dubois-Crancé, 'I affirm that I understand by the word *royalty*, indefinite power, and not the monarchy, whose head reigns legally, and which I respect infinitely more than do those who call themselves royalists.'[22]

The issue was so decisive that even the most virulent republicans, like François Robert, found themselves forced to admit that the monarch of 1789 had nothing in common with the old 'absolute despot'.[23] But they added immediately that the Constituent Assembly, after overturning the Old Regime, had instituted a sort of 'mixed government', half-way between slavery and liberty, whose fragile equilibrium was, moreover, abandoned to the hazards of heredity. If this latter condition frequently resulted, according to Thomas Paine, in 'a mule in lion's clothing', it might also place a resolute and intelligent king on the throne whose constitutional prerogatives would become so many means of usurpation placed at his disposal. Brissot was inclined to compromise. He wrote in September 1790 that France was no longer 'a monarchy, in the sense understood by royalists and [ministerials]', but 'a free government, popular in its representation and hereditary in its executive power'.[24] In defining the Constitution as quasi-republican ('à un élément près'), non-elective and irremovable, he minimised the importance of his disagreement with the members of the Constituent Assembly. Hostile to heredity in the choice of the magistrate charged with applying laws, he did not accuse the Assembly of having established a reputedly 'mixed' constitution.

The republican arguments that opposed the revolutionaries in 1790 and 1791, even within the camp of the partisans of a representative system, may seem surprising, because the installation of the republic does not date from 10 August 1792, and the preceding period does not constitute its 'prehistory'. The French revolution was at once republican. The proclamation of equal rights, the collective appropriation of sovereignty, the

[20] 13 July 1791, to the Jacobins, in A. Aulard, ed., *Recueil de documents pour l'histoire du Club des Jacobins de Paris*, 6 vols. Paris, 1889–97, vol. 3, p. 12.
[21] J.-P. Brissot, *Lettre ... à M. Barnave*, Paris, 20 November 1790, pp. 70–3.
[22] *Archives parlementaires de 1787 à 1860. Première série, de 1787 à 1799*, 91 vols. to date, Paris, 1862– , vol. 20, p. 607.
[23] Robert, *Le Républicanisme adapté à la France*, p. 28.
[24] *Pf*, no. 412, 24 September 1790.

institution of representative powers and the circumscription of royal authority within a domain – the executive – that was already understood to be subordinate, marked the institution of a republican regime in 1789, but without the name. In 1792, the form of the executive power changed; there was a revolution *within* the republic, in a history which is that of the revolution itself. If there is a 'prehistory', it must be sought earlier on, in the movement of ideas which, through the progress of notions of contract and above all the practice of treating the institution of the monarchy as an 'executive power', helped to strip the monarchy of the mystical principle of its sovereignty. The first republican partisans' obsessional hatred of kings undoubtedly prevented them from recognising the scope of the revolutionary break. In fact, republican discourse contains an element of irrationality that defies analysis. Brissot's remarks about 'kings, man-eaters', Madame Roland's anguish in the face of the spectacle of 'the abasement of a humiliated man before his fellow man, who protects him', or again the injustice which, according to Robert, placed the king's son above his own,[25] did not constitute a theory, but fed a passion. However, if France was republican, if it possessed the thing, most revolutionaries refused to give it the title.

'Republic' and 'republican' did not do well after 1789, sounding to most French ears, according to Brissot, like a 'blasphemy'. This negative inversion, after a long period of positive evolution,[26] is one of the singularities of the period. To declare oneself a republican, of the 'utmost good taste' in the 1780s, became almost an indictment with the revolution. Certainly the republic – that of the ancients – had never constituted a practicable model. One admired the virtues of its citizens without really believing it possible. Its establishment and, above all, its maintenance rested on such a fragile equilibrium of geographic, social and moral conditions that the slightest change had always brought about ruin. Founded upon the reign of virtue, incompatible with the progress of the 'spirit of commerce', as the aristocratic character of republican regimes surviving in several modern European states demonstrated, the republic belonged to the past. The American revolution had rescued the idea from its pure democratic wrapping, but it had uprooted it from the past to transpose it to the new world which was, above all, another world. Did not M. Broglie, many years later, speak of his daughter, dead at the age of thirteen, by saying: 'It seems as though my daughter is in America'?[27]

---

[25] *Mémoires de Madame Roland*, vol. 1, p. 192; *Républicanisme adapté à la France*, 34–5.
[26] Cf. J. Deprun, 'Deux images du républicain dans quelques dictionnaires français, de 1691 à 1788', in J. Viard, ed., *L'Esprit républicain*, Paris, 1972, pp. 130–1.
[27] Stendhal, *Vie de Henry Brulard*, ed. by B. Didier, Paris, 1973, p. 73.

America was a miracle for Europeans, a 'new birth of nature', the fruit of an encounter between prodigious nature and new men, without history and without prejudice, ignorant of honorific distinctions and great inequality. If Europe admired this people who made the right to happiness the foundation of their institutions, it was especially taken with the virtues and mores whose rebirth became possible in the exceptional case that was America. But in 1789, the republic no longer evoked mores but institutions: it became a problem of politics. The republican was no longer an idealist, as had been Lafayette, or the more common Cincinnatus of the salon dreaming of pitching his tent under the acacias and handling a plough; he was now an enthusiast of direct democracy, now an enemy of the king, of this monarch inherited from the Old Regime that the revolution had undertaken to nationalise.

The republican controversy was not based on a simple misunderstanding. If the pronounced republicans and the constitutionals shared the same, purely republican political arena, there remained between them the king, not as an idea, but as *this* king. The existence of a monarchy that was instituted and empowered by the general will was founded on a precondition: the forgetting of history. Before comparing the respective advantages of monarchy and republic, Sieyès wrote in a letter to Paine that it was necessary to 'isolate all the examples. In regard to the social order', he continued, 'M. Paine cannot be any happier than I with the models that history offers us: thus the matter between us can be treated only theoretically.'[28] This was the whole difficulty. The automaton that Barnave still dreamed of in July 1791[29] was *this* king, issued from *this* dynasty, which the Constituent Assembly had been constrained to accommodate, thus finding itself confronted with the delicate problem of the source of this legitimacy. The right to reign had been given to the king by the law, but the Assembly had not chosen him, it had inherited him. He occupied the throne by virtue of an altogether different 'election', that was rooted in national history. France became a republic, but with the king of the Old Regime who, in a present reconstituted on principles of reason, incarnated a history that the revolution wanted to tear apart. The republicans seem to have understood this. Even as the prevailing discourse treated all in terms of principles alone, the republicans made themselves historians, tirelessly covering the 'fourteen centuries of insults, barbarism and infamy' that, according to them, constituted the history of

[28] *Moniteur*, vol. 9, p. 137.
[29] Cf. his speech of 15 July 1791 on royal inviolability, in F. Furet and R. Halévi, eds., *Orateurs de la Révolution française, I. Les Constituants*, Paris, 1989, pp. 28–42.

the monarchy, to prove that before he was 'king of the French', Louis XVI was still heir to a long and negative history.'[30]

No obstacle *a priori* stood in the way of transforming the king into the head of the executive power, with the exception that it was necessary to make the heir of the 'first throne of the world' into a living automaton. Even taking into account the pale figure of the heir in question, he was not easily brought down from his throne to be placed in the seat of this new power. Unlike Sieyès or Barnave, the republicans did not consider an abstract, hypothetical monarchy, but the French monarchy. When they put heredity on trial, it was to denounce not so much its intrinsic absurdity[31] as the inevitable effects of this precise historical context: the impossibility of the functional monarch that the Constituent Assembly desired, described as 'a negative being, abstract, an absence',[32] effacing himself behind the function. The symbolic power associated with the monarchy remained too strong for there to be any hope of abolishing the patrimonial character of the royal function, theoretically delegated by the nation but concretely possessed by historical election, or of blocking the identification of the function with the person who held it.

The conjuncture created by Varennes led the supporters of the Constitution to believe that the hour of the new royalty had at last arrived. The Assembly was paralysed by fear of the void, the opposition was divided, the king above all vanquished and forced to abandon all hope of a return to the past ... At the same time, Barnave devoted all of his efforts to saving this monarchy distinct in the person of the king, a fixed point incarnating the unity of the state and serving as a bulwark against usurpation wherein neither the 'qualities' of the man placed there by birth nor his 'personal actions' had any bearing on the maintenance of liberty. Nonetheless, Barnave himself gave evidence of the vanity of this project, preaching ceaselessly in his secret correspondence with the court of the reinforcement of ties between king and people that had been too lax since 1789.[33] The need to find the support of popular opinion for an authority that sought, at the same time, to inscribe itself in the one and only constitution

---

[30] Cf. above all L. Lavicomterie, *Du peuple et des rois*, Paris, 1790, and *Les Crimes des rois de France, depuis Clovis jusqu'à Louis XVI*, Paris and Lyon, 1791. This work having achieved a certain commercial success, Lavicomterie specialised in the denunciation of the falsehoods and baseness of the powerful. He attacked the popes (1792), then the German emperors (1793), and finally Turkish despots (1795).

[31] On this critique, cf. T. Paine, *Le sens commun/Common Sense* ed. by B. Vincent, Paris, 1983, pp. 73–91, the essentials of which inspired the French republicans.

[32] The phrase is that of L. Lavicomterie, *Les Droits du peuple sur l'Assemblée nationale*, Paris and Lyon, 1791, p. 88.

[33] Cf. M. Ozouf, 'Barnave et la reine', in F. Furet and M. Ozouf, eds., *Terminer la révolution. Mounier et Barnave dans la révolution française*, Grenoble, 1990, pp. 115–30.

illustrates the whole difficulty of preserving an ancient monarchy in a political universe that had been entirely rebuilt on reason.

On 5 July 1791, Brissot published a lengthy exposé of his principles. 'I understand by republic', he wrote, 'a government in which all powers are, firstly, delegated or representative; secondly, elective by and for the people; thirdly, temporary or removable'.[34]

At the time, it was a common strategy to affirm the impossibility of a large nation becoming a republic by invoking the example of the antique city-states, whose enlargement of territory and even prosperity had, by multiplying interests and weakening civic ties, always led to 'political death', anarchy and tyranny. In defining modern republicanism as a wholly representative system, in which no power escaped popular election, Brissot distinguished himself at one and the same time from the constitutionals, by excluding heredity, and from the Cordeliers, as partisans of direct democracy. In this way, he intended to dismantle the assimilation between republic and pure democracy that led his contemporaries to reject the former. Representation, as he stressed from the time of his first writings on the United States, published in 1786–7,[35] placed liberty within reach of the Moderns, and this in spite of the fact that in modern communities citizens would not be available for full-time political activity, and despite the inequality of abilities. On the one hand, *limiting* public intervention by citizens permitted them the true exercise of their political rights, because participation that was too broad would *de facto* cancel itself to the benefit of small 'ceaselessly active oligarchies';[36] on the other hand, *delegating* the exercise of sovereignty, by selecting leaders to meet in assemblies sufficiently restricted to ensure the proper conduct of deliberation, increased the likelihood of reaching decisions in conformity with the interests of the collectivity.

Brissot never compromised on the need for representation, even in the exercise of constituent power: after having declared himself in favour of direct ratification of the constitution by the *bailliages* (the administrative districts under the Old Regime) in 1789,[37] he recommended, from the beginning of 1790, the calling of a convention charged with conducting this vote in place of the nation, 'a means [that] is perhaps better suited to the circumstances, character, and number of the French'.[38] Above all, this

---

[34] *Pf*, no. 696–7, 5–6 July 1791.
[35] Cf. in particular J.-P. Brissot and E. Clavière, *De la France et des Etats-Unis, ou de l'Importance de la Révolution d'Amérique pour le bonheur de la France*, London, 1787.
[36] Cf. for example *Pf*, no. 106, 22 November 1789.
[37] *Pf*, no. 38, 9 September 1789.
[38] *Pf*, no. 186, 10 February 1790, and the following year, J.-P. Brissot, *Discours sur les conventions, prononcé à la Société des amis de la Constitution ... le 8 août 1791*, Paris, n.d.

system had the advantage of permitting a proper examination of each article, while the referendum envisaged by Condorcet, in calling the citizenry to pronounce with a 'yes' or a 'no', did not in reality deliver the decision to the electors, but to those who had the ability to 'present the question in terms most favourable to their interests'.[39]

Brissot's unflagging defence of representation, most notably during the struggle that he led in 1789–90 within the Paris municipality against the districts' pretensions to the immediate exercise of sovereignty,[40] does not, however, place him in the camp of the partisans of the representative system that was installed in 1789.

The Constituent Assembly, treating the nation as a collection of equal individuals and representation as a deliberative organ charged with expressing the common will, had broken with the traditional doctrine of representation by annulling imperative mandates. Representation was no longer taken to mean the plurality of interests that existed in practice, but the common quality of citizenship; it no longer sought to mediate between opposed interests, but to define the necessarily single interest of the united nation. The radical exclusion of interests from the public sphere led in concrete terms to the institution of representation as a substitute for the 'Rousseauist' people which in reality did not exist:[41] the assembly did not 'represent' anything, but it gave existence to the nation in whose name it was called to speak. The installation of such an absolutist system was undoubtedly the price to be paid for putting an end to the division of corporate interests, by opposing to them the will of all; but the postulation of an identity of will and interest between the nation and its representation blocked the development of a more democratic system – in the modern sense of the term – in which the exercise of citizenship would not be limited to the right to relinquish one's right. The purpose of election within this uncompromising plan of representation was less to delegate – hence to control the use of this proxy – than to effect an identification between the nation and the assembly of its elected. In other words, the problem of legitimacy exhausted the guarantee of liberty, because the assembly's reunion of the conditions of legitimacy endowed it with, in the deputy Frochot's words, the 'efficacious gift' of the general will.[42]

39 J.-P. Brissot, *Plan de conduite pour les députés du peuple aux Etats-Généraux de 1789*, n.p., 1789, p. 30; *Discours sur les conventions*, p. 16.
40 Cf. *Motifs des commissaires pour adopter le plan de municipalité qu'ils ont présenté à l'Assemblée générale des représentans de la Commune, par J.-P. Brissot de Warville ... Suivis du projet du plan de la municipalité*, Paris, (12) août 1789.
41 Cf. M. Gauchet, *La Révolution des droits de l'homme*, Paris, 1989, pp. xii–xv.
42 31 August 1791: 'You admit', he said to his colleagues, 'that the Legislative speaks in conformity with the general will in the creation of laws! because your whole system of

When, in light of their principles, Barnave made the Jacobins adopt an address recognising the National Assembly's right to '*invariably* fix the charter [of the] constitutional laws', Brissot replied that no power, no matter how legitimate, could arrogate a right that belonged to the nation, or forbid it in advance the right to change the form of its institutions when judged necessary.[43] 'A well-governed state', he said in August 1791, 'should have a body to make laws, one or several persons to represent the nation in the execution of those laws, and a power subsisting in itself [through the periodic meetings of conventions], to resist the usurpations of any of the members of government, and to keep all within the bounds of duty.'[44] In 1786, Condorcet had defined republicanism by the existence of legal recourse against the decisions of the political power,[45] a definition that Bergasse, who was closely tied to these sorts of republicans before 1789, would take up in a letter that he addressed to the president of the Assembly on 6 February 1790, to protest against the decree requiring oaths of fidelity to the constitution.[46] The Constituent Assembly had recognised the superiority of the constituent power over constituted authorities, but without really accepting all of the consequences. It had thus prudently adjourned, hence buried, the inclusion in the declaration of the right of revision that was demanded by LaFayette and Mont-morency, fearing the anarchy which might result but, above all, loath to admit the responsibility of a contradiction between law and rights by adopting an appeal against the general will.

Brissot was convinced of the opposite. He believed neither in the necessary soundness of the representative will, nor that the deputies, as Rabaut-Saint-Etienne had argued in September 1789, 'represent all and act as substitutes for nothing'.[47]

The refusal to identify the nation with its representation, and to confuse the legitimacy of authority with the beneficence of its acts, such as the affirmation of the right − belonging to 'all classes of men and to every citizen' − to denounce laws contrary to fundamental rights, are at the heart of Girondin republicanism. These principles reveal the magnitude of the Girondins' debt, on the one hand, to a political rationalism inherited from the physiocrats, whose democratic potentials Condorcet

---

government is founded on that ... You prohibit the use of *cahiers* and mandates because you admit that the representatives have the efficacious gift of the general will.'
[43] *Pf*, no. 586, 17 March 1791.
[44] J.-P. Brissot, *Discours sur les conventions*, p. 5.
[45] M.-J.-A.-N. Caritat, marquis de Condorcet, *Vie de M. Turgot* (1786), in *Œuvres*, ed. by A. Condorcet-O'Connor and M.-F. Arago, 12 vols., Paris, 1847–9, vol. 5, pp. 209–10.
[46] Published in Furet and Halévi, eds., *Orateurs de la Révolution française*, pp. 134–9.
[47] *Archives parlementaires*, vol. 8, p. 570.

had – in the wake of Turgot – tried to explain;[48] and, on the other hand, to the American experience, understood and analysed as a new opportunity (after the failure of Turgot's ministry) for the advent of a government of reason.

The rationalist definition of the law, as a 'truth deduced by reason from the principles of natural law' and not as 'the expression of a will' – even the general will – made both Condorcet and Brissot strangers to the 'superstition' of the law that was so characteristic of the French revolution. In suppressing all influence of the will in the formation of laws, and above all in considering laws to be simple deductions from pre-existing rights, this rationalism led to a dissociation of the validity of the law from the legitimacy of legislative authority. Condorcet had thus, at least until 1788, minimised the question of institutions, claiming to prefer an absolutism of reason – in which the prince had abdicated his own will – to a republicanism of the will in which the fate of the citizenry rested on the decisions, even legal ones, of an ignorant multitude.[49] The localisation of sovereignty lost its importance if liberty consisted less in making, than in obeying laws founded on reason. In any case, even in a republic, the problem of legitimacy could not overwhelm that of liberty. If, in a principled government, election was necessary to exercise any portion of collective power, the legitimacy that was conferred by suffrage did not permit any presumptions about results. A legitimate power, regularly elected by the people, could just as easily make mistakes or allow itself to be corrupted, and in no case should its decisions be considered in advance to be the right ones. In a passage published in 1789, Condorcet insisted on the difference between despotism and tyranny: while the former consisted of 'the use [even just use ...] of legitimate power ... which did not issue from the nation', the latter was the result of 'the violation of natural right effected by a legitimate or illegitimate power'.[50] Certainly, popular choice diminished the risk of abuse, but without eliminating it. It offered a partial guarantee that should not prevent citizens from preserving, as Brissot had written in 1784, 'the right and the force ... to censure political misconduct'.[51]

[48] Cf. K. M. Baker, *Condorcet. Raison et politique*, French translation, Paris, 1988, esp. pp. 266–81 and 319–41.

[49] Cf. Condorcet, *De l'Influence de la Révolution d'Amérique, sur l'Europe* (1786), in *Œuvres*, vol. 8, p. 7; and in 1788: *Lettres d'un citoyen des Etats-Unis, à un Français, sur les affaires présentes*, in *Œuvres*, vol. 9, pp. 102–3.

[50] Condorcet, *Idées sur le despotisme, à l'usage de ceux qui prononcent ce mot sans l'entendre* (1789), in *Œuvres*, vol. 9, p. 164. In other words, if an illegitimate power could take action in regard to individual rights, as the 1787 edict on the Protestants demonstrated, a legitimate power could violate these rights, as the Constituent Assembly proved in adopting the decree on the *marc d'argent*.

[51] *Journal du Lycée de Londres*, no. 5, vol. 1, pp. 320–1.

The idea of control over the law, so dear to our republicans, originated in this preconception, largely indifferent to the question of sovereignty, whereby liberty consisted less in instituting a popular power than in containing authority within the limits of its 'législatrices' functions while prohibiting it from usurping the power of the 'législacteur'.[52] This approach led Condorcet, most notably, to take up unusual positions, even after he rallied to the principle of universal suffrage in 1789. In September 1789 again, he proposed placing a council alongside the legislative body, to be charged with 'guiding' the deputies and checking the validity of their acts,[53] a proposal that was, at the very least, incongruous for the time, because it tended to limit sovereignty at the very height of the battle being engaged for its appropriation.

Condorcet had discovered the model for this committee of sages in the constitution of Pennsylvania, the most atypical of American constitutions and yet the most celebrated by French republicans. With its single assembly and its collegiate executive with purely consultative powers, it seemed to them to offer, according to Brissot, the 'blueprint of a democracy as perfect as man could imagine';[54] one in which it became possible to block the despotism of the will by means of the council of censors acting in concert with the recognised right of citizens to demand, 'through addresses, petitions, and remonstrances the rectification of wrongs that they believed had been done against them.

Brissot also borrowed the typology of the three powers cited above from America – perhaps from Madison's speech before Congress on 8 June 1789, in favour of the reinforcement of the judiciary's competence to protect individual rights against usurpations of power,[55] although neither Brissot nor any other republican envisaged making the judicial power guardian of the constitution. As the citizens of Germantown affirmed in their deliberations of 4 July 1791, published by Brissot,[56] the verification of the validity of laws belongs to the citizens themselves, whether through the periodic meeting of national conventions or, more widely, through the

[52] This celebrated distinction of Quesnay's is taken up again by Condorcet and Dupont de Nemours in the annotations to the translation of J. Stevens, *Examen du gouvernement d'Angleterre, comparé aux constitutions des Etats-Unis ... par un cultivateur de New-Jersey ...* London and Paris, 1789, no. XIX: 'On the meaning of legislative authority, and how far it may be delegated', pp. 177–82. (On the authorship of this work, sometimes attributed to W. Livingston, cf. the synthesis of D. Lacorne, *L'Invention de la république. Le modèle américain*, Paris, 1991, pp. 34 and 170.)

[53] Condorcet, second of the *Lettres à M. le Comte Mathieu de Montmorency, député du bailliage de Montfort-l'Amaury* (6 September 1789), in *Œuvres*, vol. 9, pp. 378–83.

[54] J.-P. Brissot, *Examen critique des Voyages dans l'Amérique septentrionale, de M. le marquis de Chastellux*, London, 1786, p. 112.

[55] Quoted by Lacorne, *L'Invention de la république*, p. 195.

[56] Cf. *Pf*, no. 809, 28 October 1791, 'Sur la liberté qu'ont les citoyens d'émettre leur opinion contre une mauvaise loi'.

possibility of denouncing bad laws even while continuing to submit them until they had been legally revoked by parliamentary means.[57]

Brissot – and this is the most interesting dimension of his thought – also defended all that might broaden the arena of debate over the public interest beyond the limits of the representative sphere, so that the social body might become simultaneously the dispenser of all authority, the informer, the interlocutor, and the censor of political power. Here, Brissot's thought contrasted markedly with the revolutionaries' poorly elaborated concept of political democracy, of which Le Chapelier's speeches of 1791 provide eloquent illustration. Against the widely-shared illusion of a democracy that was peaceful because it was confined to the public sphere of representation, Brissot several times recalled[58] 'that there is never an end to debate amongst a free people; that liberty cannot exist but by debate, that silence announces its extinction', and that a free people could not adopt the slogan: 'do you want good laws? Do not bother your legislators, nor agitate.'[59]

He was an intransigent partisan of the right of petition as of the right of association – even to the benefit of his political adversaries[60] – which the Constituent Assembly recognised without any great enthusiasm, instinctively mistrustful of demonstrations of public opinion which were undoubtedly useful in fighting against a despotic regime, but dangerous when a representative assembly was called upon to express the will of the nation.[61] He also advocated – though without much success – legislation of open candidacy for elections,[62] in order to encourage political debate, through the publicity of electoral competition, before the meeting of the legislative, and to strengthen and give political content to the ties between electors and elected. The requirement that candidates declare themselves, state their opinions and their programmes, make commitments that would become indispensable to their gaining a majority of votes, meant

---

[57] Cf. *Pf*, no. 79, 26 October 1789, no. 486, 7 December 1790, etc. Condorcet laid down the same conditions: cf. notably *Aux amis de la liberté, Sur les moyens d'en assurer la durée* (August 1790), in *Œuvres*, vol. 10, pp. 174–87.

[58] Cf. *Pf*, no. 17, 17 March 1791.

[59] J.-P. Brissot, *Mémoires (1754–1793)*, ed. by C. Perroud, 2 vols., Paris, n.d., vol. 2, pp. 115–15.

[60] For this reason he condemned the authoritarian closing of the Society of the Friends of the Monarchic Constitution (*Pf*, no. 619, 19 April 1791).

[61] Cf. M. Ozouf, 'Esprit public', in F. Furet and M. Ozouf, eds., *Dictionnaire critique de la révolution française*, Paris, 1988, pp. 713–14. (Translated as *Critical dictionary of the French revolution*, Cambridge, Mass., 1989.)

[62] Brissot declared himself in favour of the publicity of candidatures from the beginning of 1789 (*Plan de conduite*, p. 91). The critical text on this question is his *Réflexions sur l'état de la Société des électeurs patriotes, sur ses travaux; sur les formes propres à faire de bonnes élections ...*, Paris, 25 December 1790.

giving representation the *representativity* which it had been denied by reason of its own principles.

If Brissot and Condorcet shared identical principles, they diverged in their choice of means. The former never adhered to the procedures, elaborated by the latter, that allowed citizens to exercise their right of censure. He believed such procedures to be too democratic, hence unworkable. In giving the social body the means to express itself, Brissot did not want to condemn the assembly to powerlessness, but to rationalise the functioning of the representative system. The aim of enlarging the arena of debate was not to set representation in opposition to democracy, but to organise a dialogue, to gather advice and useful knowledge from wherever it could be found so that those who governed could order their conduct according to the opinions issuing from society.

This is why Brissot turned all of his attention to the arbiters that might intervene between the populace and its leaders to alleviate direct confrontation and, at the same time, to contribute to making informed decisions. The principal role was to be given to the press, which alone was capable of quickly putting the mass of citizens in communication with one another without exposing them to any of the inconvenience of large assemblies. As a substitute for a direct democracy that was impossible, a free press would become the privileged intermediary between governed and government, transmitting to the former the decisions of the latter, and to the latter the opinion that issued from the social body. If the press permitted the gathering and comparison of all opinions, it offered as well the means to clarify them. Brissot accorded it distinguished status because it gave the power of speech to the people without giving it to the multitude; rather it gave it to an intellectual elite charged with passing popular discourse through a filter of reason.[63]

Brissot's republicanism was largely based on this idea of 'representative democracy', wherein representation was tempered by democracy which, in turn, was tempered by the tutors of the people, so averting the dangers that either the governors or the people harboured for liberty. Less democratic and more influenced by the enlightenment than Condorcet, Brissot sought in the development of arbitration between political power and the social body the same result that Condorcet hoped to obtain by extending the competence of the citizen.[64] Together they denounced the supposed ability of representation alone to discern the general interest, and, by

[63] Cf. the *Prospectus* of the *Pf* of 16 March 1789; J.-P. Brissot, *Mémoire aux Etats-Généraux, sur la nécessité de rendre dès ce moment la presse libre, et surtout pour les journaux libres*, n.p., June 1789; *Pf*, no. 656, 26 March 1791; J.-P. Brissot, *Mémoires*, vol. 2, pp. 80–1.

[64] Cf. J. Jaume, *Le Discours jacobin et la démocratie*, Paris, 1989, pp. 305–18.

different means, they both sought to promote the formation of rational decisions through the broadest possible participation. Brissot's intentions should not be misunderstood. His praise of 'restlessness' and 'movement' was not intended to legitimate divisions within public opinion but rather to restore it to the unity of general opinion through permanent debate. Public opinion, he wrote in reference to the press, 'bursting forth from all sides, from all parties at once, is elaborated and purified by frank and open opposition, and by comparisons which settle the dross to leave nothing on the surface but a limpid liquor':[65] reason. In calling all citizens to participate in the formation of collective decisions according to their capacities, the institution of representative democracy imbued the law with a degree of certitude that was sufficient to reinforce the motives of each to obey it, and to substitute the reign of thoughtful consent for blind obedience to a will backed by force.

In large states, the adoption of republicanism confronted a major obstacle: the need to 'move beyond a very powerful government [executive power]'. From Montesquieu to Rousseau, the century's philosophy had taught that the republic was viable only in small states, in which the proximity of citizens and the limited development of particular interests did not require the imposition of a strong executive to ensure submission to the law. The objection was tailored to those, Cordeliers and Girondins alike, who since 1790 had wanted to replace the monarch by an elective council without independence which was, above all, deprived of political prerogatives, financial means, and the use of public force. The problem was to find an alternative principle that ensured that the cohesion and unity of the social body which the government was no longer in a position to guarantee. The project of rationalising the political order so that power became an *instrument* in the service of reason, which emanated from the social body – a project already sketched in Turgot's and Dupont de Nemours's *Plan de municipalités*[66] – sought to create this alternative. It did not, however, address the real problem, because it took as given that individuals were capable of rational conduct, which was the only means to ensure the regulation of society without recourse to coercion.

The republicanism of reason was at an impasse, and Brissot ceaselessly warned republicans who were in too much of a hurry: 'I love republican government', he wrote in September 1790, 'but I don't believe that the French are yet worthy of this saintly regime. Conquering liberty is nothing; knowing how to preserve it is all: but it cannot be preserved without morals, and we do not have those which can bear the weight of

[65] *Pf*, no. 656, 26 May 1791.
[66] Cf. K. M. Baker, *Condorcet*, pp. 277–81.

republican liberty.'[67] In contradiction to his own analyses of the representative system as a substitute for the absence of virtue,[68] he offered a classical response to a no less classical problem: morals, the principle of the republic – thus he rediscovered at the end of the road, at the moment of placing the last stone in the republican edifice, the most hackneyed discourse on *homo civicus*. The American experience clearly had a powerful influence on this dimension of Brissot's discourse, most notably when, in 1787, the creation of a quasi-monarchic federal executive seemed to confirm his most pessimistic predictions of the inevitable decadence of large republics. Very much current with what took place on the other side of the Atlantic, Brissot had, in a letter to Clavière in 1786,[69] evalued the extent of the serious crisis then sweeping across the confederated America. In his eyes, the responsibility for this crisis was not to be found in ties between the thirteen states that were too lax, as many of the partisans of reinforcement of the union believed, but in important changes in the moral climate of the country. He accused the too rapid progress of the spirit of commerce and the ills of using paper money of having created artificial needs, broadened social inequalities, and embittered relations between citizens. Ignoring all political considerations, he entreated Americans to combat commerce and to remain attached to agriculture: in short, to preserve their morals, if they wanted to remain republicans, and, in all seriousness, embarked on an extravagant eulogy of barter.[70]

Brissot was one of the most zealous propagandists of a mythic America, populated by farmers with simple ways whose virtues were so solidly established that it had long been possible to confine all administration to a 'small number of agents entrusted with legal transactions and the control of criminals'.[71] Moreover, he was not alone in this illusion. It took all the lucidity and pessimism of a Mably to discover that, behind the myth, there were men who had set aside all reason in their passionate pursuit of riches and glory.[72] Brissot had even travelled to the United

---

[67] *Pf*, no. 412, 24 September 1790. Carra used the same language until 1792 (cf. H. Aureille, 'Les annales patriotiques ... Etude d'un quotidien politique pendant la Révolution française, 1789–1797', unpublished, 1992).

[68] Sieyès's ambition was to find the guarantee of liberty in the institutional mechanism, which virtue, absent among the Moderns, could no longer ensure.

[69] J.-P. Brissot and E. Clavière, *De la France et des Etats-Unis*.

[70] *Ibid.*, p. 24.

[71] The phrase is that of the abbé Fauchet, in *La Bouche de fer*, 3rd year, no. 29, 10 March 1791, p. 492.

[72] Abbé de Mably, *Observations sur le gouvernement et les loix des Etats-Unis d'Amérique*, Amsterdam, 1784. 'My friends sometimes, jestingly, call me the prophet of misfortune', he confessed, 'and it is true, Monsieurs, that I know men well enough that I don't easily hope for the best' (p. 177). Cf. also the other great pessimist, J. Adams, *Défense des constitutions américaines, ou De la nécessité d'une balance dans les pouvoirs d'un gouvernement*

States but, unlike Chateaubriand who made the voyage only a few months later,[73] he did not lose his illusions upon discovering Philadelphia. With the faith of the true believer, he marvelled *de visu* at the extraordinary spectacle of a society in which, as Crèvecœur had sworn, men could 'experience the different events of a long life ... without being obliged, during this long period, to have recourse to the Law'.[74]

Certainly, the France of 1789 had nothing in common with the puritanical communities of Pennsylvania that Brissot so admired, where the assimilation of moral principles was so strong as to render useless any visible system of constraint. Brissot did not mean to transform the French into Quakers,[75] but he believed, like Condorcet, that citizenship could become the sufficient principle of social cohesion, the component of a unity constructed at the base through a general alliance of wills, and no longer embodied at the summit through the unifying principle of the royal will or national sovereignty.[76] If Girondin republicanism had any unity, it was in this utopia which made the rational conduct of individuals dependent on the establishment of this 'heavenly government' in which 'the maximum of liberty', in Fauchet's words, accorded 'with the minimum of authority'.[77]

Modern and archaic, accommodating interests but, in the last resort, founded on virtue, Brissot's republicanism, and more generally that of the Girondins, testifies above all to an extraordinary misunderstanding of what was at stake, as its most characteristic traits reveal: the subordination of sovereignty to reason, and the critique of the tyranny of the

libre (1787), French translation, 2 vols, Paris, 1792, notably vol. 1, pp. 185–220 (letters 23 and 24).

73 Cf. *Mémoires d'outre-tombe*, vol. 1, pp. 271–2 (chapter written in 1822) and, more contemporaneously, *L'Essai ... sur les Révolutions* (1796), quoted in F.-R. de Chateaubriand, *De l'Ancien Régime au Nouveau Monde. Ecrits politiques*, ed. by J.-P. Clément, Paris, 1987, pp. 332–4.

74 M.-G.-J. Crèvecœur, *Lettres d'un Cultivateur Américain, écrites à W. S. Ecuyer, depuis l'année 1770, jusqu'en 1781*, 2 vols., Paris, 1784, vol. 2, p. 180.

75 However, he maintained that the Constitution of 1791, in spite of its faults, reinforced 'ties between the society of Quakers and free France': J.-P. Brissot, *Nouveau voyage dans les Etats-Unis de l'Amérique Septentrionale, fait en 1788*, 2 vols., Paris, 1791, vol. 2, pp. 248–9.

76 Cf. L. Cornu, 'Fédéralistes! Et pourquoi?', in Furet and Ozouf, eds., *La Gironde et les Girondins*, pp. 265–89.

77 C. Fauchet, 'Sur le gouvernement en général et le principe qui le constitue', *La Bouche de fer*, 3rd year, no. 29, 10 March 1791, pp. 485–97. Against the Rousseauist thesis of the impossibility of liberty in a large state because of the need for a powerful executive power, Fauchet, on the contrary, affirmed that the government was especially useless in large states. 'In fact', he said, 'motives for obeying the law increase with the expansion of the republic, because the probability of obtaining a "true" decision increases with the number of voters – with the condition, naturally, that they are capable of forming a rational judgement, and still more, capable of adopting the judgement of the majority as their own'.

general will. The idea of the censure of laws took shape in a very different context. As Marcel Gauchet and Philippe Raynaud have recently demonstrated,[78] the problem in America was one of protecting threatened, but already-held, rights and liberties against political power while, in France, it was necessary to institute these rights and liberties by collective authority and to define their content by law. The possibility of protecting pre-existing rights against the general will made no sense, to the extent that a right could not be separated from the law which gave it existence. In the last resort, the guarantee of liberty resided entirely in the legitimacy of the sovereign authority that was charged with creating law.[79]

The two strains of primitive republicanism further distinguished themselves around the principal stake of sovereignty. Contrary to the Girondins, the Cordeliers inscribed themselves within the revolutionary arena. They denounced not an excess of sovereignty, but the Constituent Assembly's attacks upon this principle. If, like the Girondins, they criticised this 'stupid enthusiasm' required of citizens in regard to the law or the 'new *papism of political infallibility*',[80] it was only because the right of expressing the general will had been confiscated from the people by its representatives. They did not mean giving *citizens* the right to *verify* the conformity of laws with their rights, but returning to the *people* the power to *make* the law, in order to establish, thanks to the immediate exercise of sovereignty, the absolute reign of the general will.

Misunderstanding the decisive importance of sovereignty, attached to a politics of reason in a universe governed by will, republicans of the Girondin variety were by no means armed for a confrontation with the new times, as Elisabeth and Robert Badinter have nevertheless claimed of Condorcet.[81] It was exactly the reverse: condemned to advance blindly into a period to which they were strangers, they would pay a high price for this incomprehension once a republic was installed in 1792 which owed them nothing, but which owed everything to the principles of 1789. But perhaps, as Buzot is supposed to have said in the twilight of his life, their mistake was too beautiful to even dream of repenting.[82]

[78] M. Gauchet, *La Révolution des droits de l'homme*, pp. 36–59; P. Raynaud, 'Révolution américaine', in Furet and Ozouf, eds., *Dictionnaire critique de la révolution française*, pp. 860–71.

[79] Cf. the objections, outside of this subject, of the republican Buzot at the time of the revision of the Constitution (*Archives parlementaires*, vol. 29, pp. 271–2).

[80] The phrase is that of R. de Girardin, *Discours sur la nécessité de la ratification de la loi par la volonté générale* ... (7 June 1791), Paris, n.d., p. 20.

[81] E. and R. Badinter, *Condorcet (1743–1794). Un intellectuel en politique*, Paris, 1988, p. 249.

[82] *Mémoires inédits de Pétion, et Mémoires de Buzot et de Barbaroux*, ed. by C.-A. Dauban, Paris, 1866, p. 31.

5 The constitutional republicanism of Emmanuel Sieyès

Pasquale Pasquino

After Thermidor French politics and political theory were dominated by a major challenge: namely, how to save the principle of the republic while obliterating the experience of its practical realisation. The key problem for French republicans, starting with Benjamin Constant and Germaine de Staël, was to establish a disjunction between republicanism and the Terror, or to make people forget the bloodshed associated with the establishment of the republic by appealing to the hopes and principles of 1789.

In considering, as I shall do here,[1] the early years of the revolution, 1789–91, there is an additional difficulty, because the Constituent Assembly gave the French a government which had the form of a constitutional monarchy[2] rather than a republic – at least in the ordinary modern sense of the two terms. Not only was representative sovereignty shared between an elected legislative assembly and an hereditary monarch, but the latter, in his capacity as head of the executive and co-legislator, was entitled to a right of veto – a right to suspend his formal sanction of laws proposed by the Assembly – for a period of four years.[3]

Among historians of the revolution, the Constituent Assembly has never enjoyed much favour. Too moderate, and excessively bourgeois for some, it has been considered by others to have been at the true origin of the Terror. The first view, largely dominant in France until very recently, is undoubtedly closer to historical reality, at least as far as the argument about its moderation is concerned – and this in spite of the strong ideological bias common to the Jacobin and Leninist disqualification of 1789. The second view seems to rest on the other hand upon a dubious metaphysics of potentiality, which confuses a principle of historical causality with the truism *post hoc ergo propter hoc*.

---

[1] See also the contribution of P. Gueniffey in this volume.
[2] Cf. *titre* 3, art. 2 of the French constitution of 1791.
[3] The best analysis of the constitution of 1791 is still the book by M. Troper, *La Séparation des pouvoirs et l'histoire constitutionnelle française*, Paris, 1980; see, in addition, his recent article 'Sur l'usage des concepts juridiques dans l'analyse historique' (forthcoming).

My intention here is not to reopen the debate on the Constituent Assembly, a debate in relation to which I should (if asked) side with liberals like Constant and de Staël.[4] I shall instead consider the political theory of Sieyès before 1792, in order to show the sense in which it is possible to talk of his republicanism.

Before doing so, however, I should like to deal briefly with a text which, to my knowledge, has never been published, and which may throw light on the true nature of the constitution of 1791: a constitution of which, contrary to a common misconception (which has perhaps its origin in Burke), Sieyès was by no means the author. We shall consider subsequently the reasons why he chose not to criticise it publicly. This text is a memoir drafted on 8 Germinal Year II (28 March 1794) and addressed to the Committee of General Security by Jacques-Guillaume Thouret, the man who made the greatest contribution to the provision of the constitution during the summer of 1791. The memoir was written during the trial which resulted in the author himself being sentenced to the guillotine.

> I refer to the Decree approved in 1791 on which I reported to the Assembly, which stated that the king was merely a *fonctionnaire public* [public official][5] ... I supported it warmly because, by *denaturing the ancient royalty*, it established the essence of a *republican constitution* under the guise of monarchy.[6]

Even if we allow for the circumstances in which Thouret drafted the text, while imprisoned in the Luxemburg under threat of impending death, we cannot doubt the historical value of his testimony: for without actually abolishing the monarchy the Constituent Assembly divested it of its sacred character by turning the head of the executive into a mere *fonctionnaire* (official). The Feuillants – in particular Thouret and Barnave – aimed to make the king part of a constitutional machine which would prevent *gouvernement d'assemblée* (government by assembly); exactly the kind of government which was to prevail under the Convention. Long before his trial, on 13 August 1791, Thouret made a very important speech to the Assembly[7] in which we read:

---

[4] Cf. B. Manin, *Un voile sur la liberté. La révolution française du libéralisme à la Terreur*, Paris, 1993.

[5] This refers to the decree concerning the regency of the kingdom presented to the Assembly by Thouret on 22 March 1791 (*Archives parlementaires*, vol. 24, pp. 260–4). Here royalty is defined as the 'supreme magistracy of the nation'; its hereditary character is a simple *délégation* made in the 'public interest'; *Moniteur*, vol. 7, p. 684. (For full bibliographical details of the *Archives parlementaires* and the *Moniteur* see ch. 4, nn. 22 and 15.)

[6] Archives Nationales, Paris, F7 4775²⁹ (cf. in the same folder Thouret's memoir of 14 Frimaire); emphasis added.

[7] This speech is not included in F. Furet and R. Halévi, eds., *Orateurs de la révolution française, I. Les constituants*, Paris, 1989.

We must not include such a clause[8] in the Constitution since a Constitution must not sanction measures which may be acceptable during a revolution and only during a revolution. When, after a long period of despotism, a nation wakes up and gives itself a new constitution, its chief *enemy* in such circumstances is the executive power, since it is the executive which is corrupted and the agent of oppression. It is against it that the revolution has occurred, not to destroy it but to drive it back and contain it in future within its proper *limits* ... But when the revolution is over and it is time to establish a true government, the constitution is not merely a set of written clauses, but the living mechanism of the political organisation. We believe that it is a serious mistake to continue to *treat the executive as the enemy of the commonwealth* and national liberty. Is not the executive power a power of the nation, emanating from it like the legislative one? Is it not vital for the nation that it should be exercised, within the prescribed limits, *with all the vigour of which it is capable* and with all the means that can be put at its disposal? Would it be able to perform its function unless it is thus constituted? And unless it does, and does so with great energy, who will guarantee domestic order, and *who will defend the commonwealth from the undertakings of the legislative body*? Finally, and in a few words, is not the executive power as necessary to liberty as the legislative?

And further on he adds: 'The legislative power on the one hand, and the executive on the other are the *two essential components* of the political system.'[9]

If we take judgements of this kind into account it is difficult to talk, as it is increasingly, of the *législativocentrisme*[10] of the Constituent Assembly, especially because the opinion quoted above, far from being marginal, was that of the head of the Comité de Constitution and its representative at the Assembly. F. Furet and R. Halévi[11] rightly describe Thouret as 'one of the key figures of the great debates and of the great texts which reorganised the kingdom' and as 'one of the most influential architects of the new legislation'. He was in fact not only an independent and moderate voice, but also the best expert on public law in the Assembly.[12]

---

[8] Thouret refers to the article passed by the Assembly on 7 April 1791 and left out – as noted by de Saint-Martin – by the Comité de révision, presided over by Thouret, an article which called for a strict separation of powers: 'No member of the current Assembly, nor of the following Legislatures ... may be promoted to the position of minister, nor may receive any position or gifts ... from the executive power or from its agents, while they are in the Legislature and for four years after the end of their mandate.'

[9] *Archives parlementaires*, vol. 29, pp. 399–400; emphasis added.

[10] This clumsy word makes sense, if we understand by it the absolute supremacy of the legislature *vis-à-vis* the other powers. The word *légicentrisme*, on the other hand, is either a synonym for expressions such as rule of law or *Rechtsstaat*, or it has no clear sense, unless it is the antonym of *décrétocentrisme* specific to a despotic government.

[11] *Orateurs de la révolution française*, p. 1573.

[12] The same views are presented by Duport and also by Barnave in his famous speech on the inviolability of the king given on 15 July 1791. *Ibid.*, pp. 28–42 (esp. p. 31: 'this power accorded to the King to *limit* the legislative power'); and Duport's speech given on 14 July on the same subject, pp. 319–30 (esp. p. 323: 'it is necessary ... to have alongside the

But just as Mounier and Lally-Tollendal had been unable to impress upon the Assembly the difference between a bicameral system and a society of orders during the summer of 1789,[13] so Thouret and Barnave, in spite of their good standing in the Assembly, were unable to persuade French opinion of the need for a strong executive power, largely because of the growing hostility to the person of Louis XVI. I shall return to this point in discussing Sieyès's attitude after the king's flight to Varennes. I shall now turn to the political and constitutional theory of the abbé.

Even the most reliable of recent studies of Sieyès's political theory – the work by Murray Forsyth, *Reason and revolution. The political thought of the abbé Sieyès* – represents the image of Sieyès as a supporter of constitutional monarchy in 1789.[14] Michelet, in a lecture at the Collège de France on 6 May 1847,[15] made the following judgement about the 'priest' Sieyès, for whom he clearly had little sympathy: 'Externally a daring and free spirit, Sieyès nevertheless remained the slave of his clerical garb and his desire for a quiet life: he wanted the clergy, he wanted royalty.'

In contradistinction to this received opinion I would like to show:

1 That Sieyès was a republican. His principles in 1789–91 were not compatible with the monarchical system – meaning by this the presence at the head of the government of an hereditary representative; and that he was to become, after Varennes, a 'monarchist of reason', to echo the German term *Vernunftrepublikaner* used under the Weimar republic to indicate those who, despite their principles, had nevertheless accepted the republic.

2 That he was a *modern* republican and a liberal, since he spoke the language of rights and of the limits of power, and built a theory of

legislative Body a *brake*, a way to stall its action if it be too hasty or arbitrary': 'the monarch ... in order to stop or moderate the action of the legislative power'; and pp. 324–5 on the despotism of the legislative body) (emphasis added). See, also, the anecdote on Thouret, the day when the king came to swear allegiance to the constitution, in Michaud, *Biographie universelle*, Paris, n.d., vol. 41, p. 446:

> Thouret was chosen to present to the King the Constitution; and, named president [of the Assembly] ... for the fourth time, he welcomed the monarch when Louis XVI went to the Assembly to declare his acceptance of the Constitution. Seated in a chair very similar to that of the King, the president kept his legs crossed all the time; and without moving from this position, he praised at length to the King the advantages of a constitution which for the most part he himself had written.

See also *Moniteur*, vol. 9, pp. 662–3, on the session of 14 September: 'At the time that the King will be sworn – said Thouret – the Assembly must be seated.'

13 Cf. P. Pasquino, 'La Théorie de la "balance du législatif" du premier Comité de constitution (1789)', in F. Furet and M. Ozouf (eds.), *Terminer la révolution. Mounier et Barnave dans la révolution française*, Grenoble, 1990, pp. 67–89.

14 Leicester, 1987, p. 179.

15 Unpublished text which François Furet has kindly allowed me to consult.

representative government upon popular 'authorisation', that is to say upon the juridical mechanism of general and periodic elections.

I shall start from this second point, and in particular from the issue of the limitation of power, which will allow me to develop and specify arguments I have already discussed elsewhere.[16] I shall refer to some manuscripts of the abbé which I have since had the opportunity to examine more closely.

One of the most remarkable texts to be found amongst his papers – now in the Archives Nationales in Paris – is what 'seems to be the draft of a newspaper article on his book *What is the Third Estate?* written by Sieyès himself.'[17] It is in fact a review of his book which no doubt Sieyès intended to publish anonymously in order to draw the attention of the public to the importance of his text – yet another sly device of the abbé. The review was never published, a fact which is easily explained if we consider the immediate and extraordinary success of the book. This text deserves to be reproduced. Here I shall simply signal some of the passages most relevant to my purpose. Here is how he begins:[18]

I have just finished reading the work entitled *****. At last, I find an author who has provided me with some principles. I have always thought that political morality was not just a matter of sentiment, but forms a true science and that this science must be either incomplete or ill-known if in all possible circumstances it did not offer us the remedy as well as an analysis of the disease. But I can also see that this science could not be the product of superficial inquiry.

After a series of flattering comments of this kind – 'There are men of a scholarly disposition who have devoted themselves silently to the study of the great social morality for years' – a comment which of course refers to the abbé himself, Sieyès proceeds to summarise the central arguments of his book:

I learn from this work that what we must call a constitution is by no means an attribute of the nation, but belongs to its government alone. It is the government, not the nation, which is constituted.

I see too that the *constituted power* and the *constituent power* cannot be confused. Consequently the body of the ordinary representatives of the people, that is to say those who are entrusted with ordinary legislation, cannot without contradiction and absurdity *interfere with the constitution.*[19]

[16] Cf. P. Pasquino, 'E. Sieyès, B. Constant et le "gouvernement des modernes"', in *Revue française de science politique*, vol. 37, no. 2, (April 1987), pp. 214–29, and 'Le Concept de nation et les fondements du droit public de la révolution: E. Sieyès', in F. Furet, ed., *L'Héritage de la révolution française*, Paris, 1989, pp. 309–33.
[17] This comment in the margin of Sieyès's manuscript is in the hand of H. Fortoul, who had access to the abbé's papers towards the middle of the nineteenth century.
[18] Archives Nationales, 284 AP 4, doss. 8.
[19] Emphasis added.

These statements are clearly of great interest. A work which has been always presented as the manifesto of the revolution, as a *cri de guerre* (Tocqueville's words) and as the very model of political radicalism, is instead presented by its author as a tract of political and constitutional science, in which a central role is attributed to the issue of the *limitation of legislative power*!

All those who have even a superficial knowledge of Sieyès's political writings are aware that he always attached a great importance to the distinction – which he in fact claims to have introduced to political theory – between *pouvoir constituant* and *pouvoir constitué*, as he states in his *Discours de l'an III*. No doubt Sieyès's claim was made in good faith. There is however a much earlier work, published in London in 1660, in which this distinction appears already in a clear form and which I should like to recall briefly. I do not believe that this work could have directly inspired Sieyès, but it helps us to understand the political and theoretical relevance of this distinction, one which has completely escaped the attention of such recent interpreters of Sieyès as K. M. Baker and B. Baczko.[20] The work I am referring to is *Politica sacra et civilis or a modell of civil and ecclesiasticall Government* by George Lawson,[21] who had published, three years before, in 1657, another book, which like *Politica sacra* was a polemical tract against Hobbes – entitled in fact *An examination of the political part of Mr Hobbs his Leviathan*. Together with Philip Hunton, Lawson is certainly the most important of those seventeenth-century English political theorists we no longer read.

In this text, written in a curious mixture of Latin and English, Lawson begins by establishing a distinction between two types of sovereignty or authority (*majestas*) which he calls respectively *real* and *personal*.

On page 34 of *Politica sacra*, we have the schema shown in figure 1.

According to Lawson *real sovereignty* belongs to the community and is superior to *personal sovereignty*, which is the power of constituted commonwealth. *Real majesty* is defined as the power *to model a state* (p. 35) and this *power of constitution* is attributed to the community (in Sieyès's language, the *nation*). This distinction has the explicit function of limiting the power of the Parliament (the legislative power), whose members, being the depositories of a simple personal sovereignty, 'cannot alter or take away the cause whereby they have their being, nor can they meddle with the fundamental Laws of the constitution, which if it once cease, they cease to be a Parliament'.

---

[20] K. M. Baker, *Inventing the French revolution*, Cambridge, 1990; B. Baczko, 'Le Contrat social des français', in K. M. Baker, ed., *The French revolution and the creation of modern political culture*, vol. 1: *The political culture of the Old Regime*, Oxford, 1987, pp. 493–513.

[21] Cf. C. Condren, *George Lawson's Politica and the English Revolution*, Cambridge, 1989.

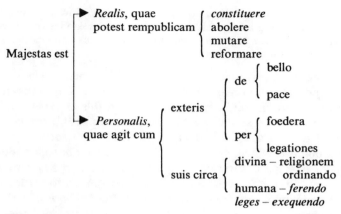

Figure 1

I shall not discuss here the radical criticism of Hobbes's theory of representation implicit in this view. My aim is simply to show how the distinction between constituent and constituted power is introduced against the view (which Lawson attributed to Hobbes) of the absolute sovereignty of the Assembly: 'The personal Soverain [that is to say the] persons who are trusted with the exercise of it [legislative and executive powers] ... hath no power to make fundamental Laws concerning the constitution, but only for the administration' (pp. 36, 39).

It is therefore this same preoccupation of limiting the power of representatives which Sieyès asserts in 1789 through his distinction between *pouvoir constituant* and *pouvoir constitué*; a distinction which the manuscript mentioned above considers as one of the central points of his book on the Third Estate.

It is not necessary to make appeal to Sieyès's manuscripts to realise that 'His thought is essential to understanding the articulation of revolutionary philosophy with what preceded it – Enlightenment rationalism – and what followed it – the liberal line of Constant–Staël'.[22] It is sufficient to read his *Préliminaire de la Constitution* of July 1789:[23]

In a large society individual liberty has three kinds of enemies to fear. The least dangerous are malevolent citizens: in order to repress them, ordinary authority is sufficient ... Individual liberty is far more endangered by [the second enemy: the] undertakings of the *Officers encharged to exercise some part of public power*. Simple isolated public officials, entire bodies, the government itself in its entirety, can cease to respect the rights of the citizen. A long experience proves that *nations*

22 Furet and Halévi, eds., *Orateurs de la révolution française*, p. 1523.
23 Reprinted *ibid.*, pp. 1004–18, which unfortunately does not reproduce the third and last edition of the text which I cite here; emphasis added.

are not sufficiently cautioned against this sort of danger. How disgraceful to see a public official turning against his fellow citizens the weapons or power he has received to defend them and ... turning into instruments of oppression the means entrusted to him for the common protection!

After this diagnosis, the author proposes his remedy: 'The separation, and a good constitution of public powers are the only guarantee that nations and citizens might be preserved from this extreme evil.'[24] (The third enemy of liberty mentioned in the text is a possible foreign enemy.)

When I described Sieyès's doctrine as a liberal theory of the state, I meant a doctrine which, as shown in the text cited above, considers that *too great a power* concentrated in the hands of those who govern or in the institutions of the state represents a danger or a *threat* for order, security and the freedom of individuals. In his essay *Die Diktatur* of 1921,[25] Carl Schmitt wrote that all excessive political power represents, for Montesquieu and his liberal followers, the enemy. We can also say that 'modern constitutionalism' (or more precisely the doctrine of the *Verfassungsstaat*), which rests upon the idea of fundamental rights and the mechanism of the division/balance of powers, is in fact the answer to the threat which comes from inside the *polis*, such as it is conceptualised by the (in this respect exemplary) text by Sieyès.

Having clarified this, I shall now return to my initial point: Sieyès's republicanism. Here too I shall comment on a manuscript and a published text by the abbé, both written shortly after the flight of the king on 20 June 1791. The manuscript[26] is once again of great interest. It contains the text of a speech that Sieyès intended to read before the Assembly during the debates on the revision of the constitution, in any case after 10 August, as is shown by a reference to a speech by Barnave which can be precisely dated.

[Amongst the propositions of the Comité de constitution] there is one so important, so strange and so subversive of our constitution, that I feel obliged to present to you some observations upon which I rest my beliefs ... It is the ultimate answer to this question: France has a representative Constitution, the representatives are the legislative body and the King.

In this text Sieyès explains better than anywhere else one of the most important concepts of his political theory: that of representation. This concept does not only refer to the principle developed by the Scottish political economists of the division of labour; but defines also the specific

---

[24] 3rd edn, Paris, 1789, pp. 29–30. The edition published by Furet and Halévi (pp. 1010–11) begins this paragraph with the words: 'Une bonne constitution de tous les pouvoirs publics ets ... '
[25] Reprinted Berlin, 1964.
[26] Archives Nationales, 284 AP 4, doss. 12.

relation between governors and governed in his republican model of representative government (emphasis added): 'All public officials are representatives of the people in the broadest sense of the term, *because all powers emanate from the people*' (representatives are not, therefore, governors *sui juris*).

On 10 August, on the other hand, Barnave had argued in the Assembly that the representatives of the people were only those who were encharged to *will* for it:[27] an argument which allowed him to attribute the role of sovereign representative to the king as well as to the legislative assembly. This was, moreover, the position sanctioned by the constitution of September 1791. Sieyès, for his part, did not accept the position of the Comité de constitution. To begin with he pointed out that 'we find the exercise of some will in all public functions', in the legislative body as well as in 'the public official with the most limited authority'. Secondly, against the line of thought which connects Rousseau to Condorcet, he stressed that 'the application of the law does always imply the exercise of a will'. Finally, and this is the most crucial point, he came more forcefully than Thouret to demand a republican constitution:

According to the Comité the legislative body is divided in two branches, the Assembly and the King. In this case, the legislative power is formed by two wills, the national will exercised by the temporary system of the elected and the hereditary royal will. At the time of the debates on the royal sanction [in 1789] the nature of this sanction was not discussed. The King has the right of sanction, this is true, but what was not discussed is that the exercise of this sanction implied a legislative will, since if a legislative will can be attributed to an hereditary magistrate, it is evident that this will cannot any longer be mistaken for the will of the people.

And further: 'We must ask whether the possibility of forming the common will which will be the law can be entrusted to anyone other than men elected for a time by the people. *The answer is evidently no.*'[28] Hence follows the conclusion that: 'In this precise sense, the king cannot therefore be a representative.' We can see here quite clearly that Sieyès refuses the role of legislative representative – 'the most essential function of all', he writes – to an hereditary public magistrate. In fact the 'election for a period of time' is considered as a necessary and compulsory condition for prescribing the law and expressing the will of the nation. *No (legislative) representation without election*: with this formula we can summarise the republican argument expressed by Sieyès in the draft of his speech.

[27] *Archives parlementaires*, vol. 29, p. 331.
[28] Emphasis added.

The idea that election for a period of time should be the only mechanism of authorisation of supreme power – the legislative – qualifies the position of the abbé in 1791 as perfectly republican.[29]

It is true, however, that Sieyès did not make his speech at the Assembly in August 1791 and that, furthermore, he published, in the *Moniteur* of 16 July 1791, a reply to Thomas Paine[30] which gained a certain popularity and which was even translated into German in 1792 with the title *Über den wahren Begriff einer Monarchie* ('On the true concept of monarchy')[31] – a text which apparently was much appreciated by Kant.[32]

But let us go back to Sieyès: his reply to Paine was a minor masterpiece of political ability. It shows, incidentally, that the abbé was by no means a doctrinaire, as it is often claimed, but a politician capable of finding compromises between theory and practice.

The problem for him in this particular case was how to avoid betraying his principles while at the same time supporting the Feuillants after the ill-fated flight of the king, which would inevitably radicalise the revolutionary movement and hinder the realisation of a new constitutional order. As Patrice Gueniffey shows above in this volume, it was after Varennes that the pass-word *republicanism* began to appear with a certain frequency, especially in debates in the press:[33]

If they ask me – and I suppose I shall be asked – what I think of the heredity of the monarch, I shall reply without hesitation that in good theory it is wrong to

---

[29] I do not need to cite here the speech of September 1789 against the royal veto, which is sufficiently well known, and is consistent with the manuscript cited here.

[30] *Moniteur*, no. 197 *bis* (vol. 9, pp. 137–9); cf. the issue of 8 July 1791. Paine had asked Sieyès to take a public stance against the monarchy and in favour of a representative republican system.

[31] *Neues Göttingisches historisches Magazin*, vol. 1 (1792), pp. 341–9.

[32] See the article 'Republik' by W. Mager, in O. Brunner *et al.*, eds., *Geschichtliche Grundbegriffe*, Stuttgart, 1984, vol. 5, p. 608. Kant distinguishes, in any case, the idea of 'Republikanismus' from that of the opposition to monarchy: 'Republikanismus ist das Staatsprinzip der Absonderung der ausführenden Gewalt (der Regierung) von der gesetzgebenden.' The same disjunction can also be found in Robespierre; see Mager, 'Republik', p. 596 (speech of 13 July 1791): 'Le mot république ne signifie aucune forme particulière de gouvernement: il appartient à tout gouvernement d'hommes libres, qui ont une patrie. Or, on peut être libre avec un monarque comme avec un sénat. Qu'est-ce que la constitution française actuelle? C'est une république avec un monarque.' (I do not need to stress that for Rousseau the 'republic' is a form of non-representative state – 'tyranny' being the delegation of sovereign power, i.e. legislative power; 'monarchy' on the other hand is simply a form of government – of executive power.)

[33] See the dispute between Laclos and Brissot: the former wrote 'De la monarchie et du républicanisme' in *Journal des Amis de la Constitution*, no. 33, 12 July 1791, as a reply to Brissot's article 'Profession de foi de P. Brissot, sur la monarchie et le républicanisme', in *Patriote français*, nos. 696 and 697, 5 and 6 July 1791. Both texts are republished in Laclos, *Œuvres complètes*, ed. by L. Versini, Paris, 1979, pp. 680–93.

imagine that the hereditary transmission of any public office might be reconciled with the principles of true representation.[34]

Undoubtedly, he adds, it would be possible to apply 'to the first public function' an electoral mechanism capable of combining 'all the advantages of election without any of its disadvantages'. However, in the summer of 1791, the abbé was 'far from thinking that the circumstances [were] favourable to a change in the established constitution on this particular point' (p. 138). Such was the public position stated by Sieyès at a time when the essential political task seemed to be that of ending the revolution.[35] This shows, I believe, convincingly enough that his monarchism of reason never led him to renounce his republican principles.

[34] *Moniteur*, no. 197 *bis* (vol. 9, p. 138). This entire sentence, which is of crucial theoretical importance, is omitted in the German translation cited above.

[35] For a detailed analysis of Sieyès's response to Paine, see my 'Introduction' to the Italian edition of Sieyès's political writings: E. Sieyès, *Scritti politici*, Milan, 1993, esp. pp. 52–5.

6 The Thermidorian republic and its principles

Biancamaria Fontana

I

The years of Thermidor, from the fall of Robespierre in July 1794 to the coup that brought Bonaparte to power in November 1799, were dominated by an atmosphere of political instability and ideological confusion which makes it difficult to see them, even from a distant historical perspective, as a moment of theoretical elaboration. Predictably the attention of historians has been focused upon the conspiracies, the trials, the wild fluctuations in public opinion and the difficult functioning of the political system designed in the Constitution of the year III (22 August 1795), while intellectually Thermidor remains a transitional period, with no clear identity of its own, apart from its practical and ideological opportunism.[1]

In particular the Thermidorian experience can hardly be taken to illustrate the triumph of republican institutions in France: on the contrary, it displays their fragility, their shaky foundations, their tenacious authoritarian vocation inherited from the monarchy of the *ancien régime*. Yet it is in this period that the republican government created by the revolution became for the first time the object of a serious retrospective assessment which clarified its content and implications, setting it against previous historical experiences and intellectual traditions. Until 1794 the fortunes of the French republic were closely bound up with those of the revolution: it was only after Thermidor that the republic acquired an

---

[1] For bibliographical information on Thermidor see the appendix to Denis Woronoff, *La République bourgeoise de Thermidor à Brumaire, 1794–1799*, Paris, 1972 (Nouvelle histoire de la France contemporaine, vol. 3). Cf. also George Lefebvre, *La France sous le Directoire (1795–1799)*, new edn by J. R. Suratteau, Paris, 1977; A. Meynier, *Les Coups d'état du Directoire*, 3 vols., Paris, 1928; Donald M. G. Sutherland, *France 1789–1815, revolution and counterrevolution*, London, 1985; B. Baczko, *Comment sortir de la Terreur – Thermidor et la révolution*, Paris, 1989 and 'L'Expérience Thermidorienne', in C. Lucas, ed., *The political culture of the French revolution*, 3 vols., Oxford, 1987, vol. 2, pp. 341–70; Lynn Hunt, David Lansky and Paul Hamson, 'The failure of the liberal republic in France, 1795–1799: the road to Brumaire', *Journal of Modern History*, 1979, pp. 734–59.

identity of its own, as a political system which must survive the passing of the revolutionary phase.

The views discussed in this essay were, in the main, outlined by Germaine de Staël in her *Des circonstances actuelles qui peuvent terminer la révolution et des principes qui doivent fonder la république en France*, a text seemingly drafted between May and October 1798 and revised (with the assistance of Benjamin Constant) in the course of 1799.[2] The text of *Des circonstances* did not necessarily express the 'official' position of a particular party or faction within Thermidorian politics: it did, however, reflect the shared beliefs of a group of intellectuals and politicians – connected with Staël's salon and the Cercle Constitutionnel – who supported the Directory and the republican government against the threats of a monarchical restoration or a return of Jacobinism. After the coup of Brumaire, which she and her friends saw as a last chance to stabilise the shaky republican institutions, Staël apparently decided to set aside her work, now overtaken by the rapid authoritarian evolution of Bonaparte's regime.

If the short-lived Thermidorian republic seemed to make little impact upon subsequent French historical events, the political model set forth by its supporters exercised a decisive influence upon the future of European democracies. The 'modern' republic, suited to large territorial states and advanced commercial societies, founded upon a wide popular electorate and constitutional guarantees, radically distinct from the republics of classical antiquity, would emerge in the end as the most successful and durable legacy of the revolution.

II

In a series of recollections dictated towards the end of his life, in 1828, Benjamin Constant gave a vivid and illuminating account of the political atmosphere reigning in Staël's salon in the Rue du Bac after the return of the Ambassadress of Sweden from her Swiss exile in the spring of 1795. The salon, he related, was populated at the time by four or five different 'tribes'. There were members of the existing government, whose favour the hostess was trying to court; there were émigrés who had returned to France, whom she was both flattered and embarrassed to receive; writers who had been persecuted by the Jacobins and had now regained some

---

[2] Germaine de Staël, *Des circonstances actuelles qui peuvent terminer la révolution et des principes qui doivent fonder la république en France*, ed. by Lucia Omacini, Geneva, 1979, cited from now on as *DCA*; see in particular the 'Introduction' by Lucia Omacini for further details on the history and structure of the text. This work was rediscovered only at the turn of this century; see Paul Gautier, 'Mme de Staël et la république en 1798', *Revue des Deux Mondes* (1 November 1899).

influence, and diplomats abjectly obsequious towards the Committee of Public Safety while actively plotting against it.[3]

The conversations, the actions, the intrigues of those tribes greatly puzzled my innocent republicanism. When I talked to the members of the victorious republican faction I heard them say that the anarchists should be guillotined and the émigrés shot without trial; when I approached the small group of the surviving terrorists in disguise, I heard that the new government, the émigrés and all foreigners must be exterminated; when I was seduced by the moderate and edulcorated opinions of those writers who preached the return to morality and justice ... they soon began to insinuate that France needed a king, an opinion which I found singularly shocking ... In short I did not know what to say and especially what to do about my enthusiasm for the republic.[4]

In the same text Constant described Staël's political position by stating that she was 'all for the republic and for reaction at the same time': for the republic because the republican system was closer to her ideas and also because she was afraid of being banned as a royalist; for reaction because she was disgusted by the crimes committed by the terrorists who had killed or exiled all her friends.[5] Unlike Constant, who had been able to cultivate his republican beliefs at a safe distance from the French border, Staël had been too directly involved in the revolutionary events, in the collapse of the monarchy and the death and ruin of so many of her family's friends, to feel immediately attracted to republican ideals. The daughter of a minister of the king of France and the wife of an ambassador of the king of Sweden, she had initially shared the preference of her father, Jacques Necker, for a constitutional monarchy of the English type. Her ideological emancipation from her father's views and her conversion to the republic at the time of her return to Paris in 1795 had been received by the old minister with mild scepticism and irony. In a letter to a family friend he commented:

My daughter has arrived in Paris after a long journey but without accident. Monsieur Constant has been her travel companion: they are both wonderfully filled with republican ideas and hopes and a little too inclined to forgive the means employed by the present government in view of its aims. I am far from seeing things in the same way ...[6]

Staël's 'conversion' to republicanism was less superficially 'emotional' and founded upon more solid persuasions than her disapproving parent was prepared to recognise. Like Constant and other supporters of the

---

[3] After the execution of Robespierre in July 1794 a purged Committee of Public Safety remained in charge until the establishment of the Directory on 31 October 1795.

[4] Benjamin Constant, *Ecrits et discours politiques*, ed. by O. Pozzo di Borgo, 2 vols., Paris 1964–5, vol. 1, pp. 8–9.

[5] *Ibid.*, p. 7.

[6] Necker to Meister, 2 January 1796; quoted in Henri Grange, *Les Idées de Necker*, Paris, 1974, p. 462.

Thermidorian government she based her allegiance to the republic in the first instance upon a historical rather than a theoretical judgement. The central argument set forth in *Des circonstances* for maintaining the republican government in France was not that it was, in principle, better than any other, but that it was already in existence. Its establishment had cost the nation an extraordinarily heavy price in sufferings and violence: a change of regime would inevitably entail a new wave of conflicts, persecutions and injustices. Those who believed that the restoration of the monarchy could be effected peacefully, without struggle and revenge, were deluding themselves. The monarchy could be restored only by violent means and in its most despotic form. A limited or constitutional monarchy, perhaps under a new dynasty, was the solution which had the least chance of succeeding, since it would attract the active hostility of republicans and legitimists alike.[7]

This judgement on the prospects of a restoration had as its premise the progressive character of historical development. Ideally the natural evolution should have been from an absolute monarchy to a limited one, and only at a later stage from a limited monarchy to the republic. Ten years of constitutional monarchy, Staël argued, would have sufficiently educated public opinion to the practice of political freedom to bring about the republic by general consent.[8] But in France the constitutional compromise of 1789 between the king and the assembly had not survived, and the transition to republican institutions had been a sudden and violent one.

As Constant suggested in his pamphlets of 1796–7, the political institutions of a nation must develop in pace with the progress of its socioeconomic conditions and with the expectations of public opinion. Whenever institutions were too backward (as in the last stages of *ancien régime*) or too advanced (as the legislative ambitions of the Jacobins had wanted them) there would follow a violent adjustment in the form of a revolution or counter-revolution. The short-term objective of the Thermidorian government must be to stop the unsettling fluctuations of revolutionary action and reaction by consolidating French political institutions at the level which, for better or for worse, they had reached: the republic. 'The republic is a destination; the revolution was a route; it is time to look away from that route to see finally where we have come to.'[9]

The argument that the republic should be sustained for the sake of peace and stability even by those who were opposed to republican principles was primarily addressed by Staël to the royalists of good faith, who

---

[7] Cf. B. Constant's work of 1798, *Des suites de la contrerévolution en Angleterre*, Paris.
[8] *DCA*, p. 35.
[9] B. Constant, *De la force du gouvernement actuel* . . ., ed. by Philippe Raynaud, Paris, 1988, p. 47.

must sacrifice their love of the monarchical cause to save France from further destruction and ruin. The royalists, she argued, could not overturn the republic, but they could render a major service to the mother-country by renouncing their aspirations, backing up the government and thus keeping the republicans from the temptation of arbitrary measures.[10] If expediency was the line of argument on which the contending parties could be more readily expected to agree, the claim made in favour of the Thermidorian republic in *Des circonstances* was much stronger than a mere consideration of opportunity: this claim was that the form of government existing in France at the time reflected more faithfully than any other the needs and feelings of public opinion at large; that it was the one best suited to France such as it had become: a modern nation, a large territorial state with an advanced commercial economy.

Like most Thermidorians, Staël had some reservations about the Constitution of the year III, which was generally seen as a temporary and somewhat imperfect political design – reservations which were retrospectively reinforced by the ready surrender of republican institutions to Bonaparte's ambitions in 1799. These reservations, however, focused upon legislative technicalities, upon the specific shape and functioning of the single institutions; they did not question the basic principles upon which the constitution itself was founded. The definition of these principles – the 'principles on which must be founded the republic of France', to which the title of Staël's work referred – implied a double confrontation. The Thermidorian model must be compared with the political foundations of the fallen monarchy; more crucially, it must also be set against the republican experiment of the Jacobins of which the Directorial government remained unquestionably the direct heir.

III

When discussing the general features of the Thermidorian model, Staël referred to it as 'representative' rather than 'republican' government (a choice of terms which was also adopted by Constant in his later works). The implication was that its distinctive character was representation, not the absence of any hereditary magistrature. In countries with different historical experiences and traditions (England was the obvious example), representative government could, under certain conditions, be compatible with those monarchical institutions which France could no longer tolerate.

The first requirement of representative government was the estab-

[10] *DCA*, p. 79.

lishment of political equality. Other revolutions had been inspired by the desire to eject a foreign power – as in Holland or Switzerland; by religious dissent – as in the case of England; or by a colony's aspiration towards independence – the American experience. The central idea, the leading impulse behind the French revolution was the 'hatred of privilege' and the 'love of equality'.[11] The existence of hereditary distinctions was in conflict with the 'natural inequality' of men: instead of acknowledging merit and allowing the most enlightened, honest and distinguished citizens to emerge and be promoted to public offices, it left to the hazard of birth the choice of those who should exercise the greatest influence upon the community. The idea that anyone should be debarred from prominent positions and public employment merely on the ground of birth was an archaic prejudice which in the eyes of modern public opinion would soon appear as obsolete and unacceptable as the practice of slavery.[12]

This rejection of aristocratic privilege focused in particular upon the rigid exclusion of commoners which had dominated French *ancien régime* society. It was not equally hostile to forms of hereditary distinction of a purely nominal and honorific kind and it could tolerate an 'open' aristocracy prepared to absorb and promote distinguished commoners within its ranks. In this respect it was possible to imagine some form of representative government in the context of a limited monarchy: this system would be ideally less 'perfect' than a republican one, but it could be made desirable by the advantages of tradition and greater social stability. When during the Restoration Constant was reconciled to the existence of an hereditary chamber he could do so without contradicting these earlier positions.[13]

The demand for political equality did not aim at abolishing all natural and social distinctions: Staël insisted on this point since the 'partisans of heredity' would discredit their opponents by presenting their views as a request for radical social and economic levelling, in particular for the abolition of property.

How can we prove that the preservation of property is not an error like hereditary privileges? ... What is the aim of all society? The happiness of the greatest number. Hereditary privileges (if, as I believe, they are not necessary to public

[11] *DCA*, p. 270.
[12] Cf. Constant, 'Fragments d'un ouvrage abandonné sur la possibilité d'une constitution républicaine dans un grand pays', Bibliothèque Nationale, Paris, Mss N.a.f., 14363, fo. 5: 'the struggle of which we have been the witnesses and often the victims has always been in essence the struggle of the elective system against the hereditary one. This is the most important question of the French revolution, and one might say the question of the century.' Since I first wrote this essay the manuscript has been published: ed. by Henri Grange, Paris, 1991.
[13] B. Constant, 'Entre la monarchie et la république' (1830), ed. by E. Harpaz, *Studi Francesi* (1987), pp. 427–33.

order) are to the advantage of some against all. Property instead is equally useful to proprietors and non-proprietors. The sharing of fortunes would initially benefit the majority, but the constant and forced equality of fortune would result in general poverty ... Property is the origin, base and bond of the social pact: heredity derives from conquest and is maintained through servitude.[14]

Addressing a public opinion which two years before had been deeply shaken by the 'uncovering' of Babeuf's conspiracy and the renewed threat of expropriation, Staël insisted that economic inequality was an essential component of the fabric of civilised society and a condition for general prosperity. The difference of fortunes might in some extreme cases prove offensive to our sense of justice and humanity, but these defects could not be corrected by artificial levelling.[15] Reasonable economic inequality did not affect the position of the citizen towards the government and the law. Aristocratic privilege was unacceptable in the context of representative government because this government presupposed a homogeneous political community, in which no individual or group had interests *a priori* distinct from those of the community as a whole. Here Staël restated an argument which had been originally set forth by Sieyès in his *Essai sur les privilèges* of 1788: why were the aristocracy (and, *a fortiori*, kings) unfit to be the depositories of the power of the nation? Because their interest was different from the national interest.[16] Being privileged meant by definition having a separate set of interests and therefore being excluded from the social body.[17]

The direct consequence of the establishment of political equality and the creation of a homogeneous political community was that each citizen had the right to contribute to the formation of the laws that governed him.[18] Representative government was based upon the recognition of the principle of popular sovereignty: a crucial point in the French context, since as late as 1814 in the Royal Charter the Bourbon monarchy denied it, making appeal instead to the divine authority of the king.[19] Sovereignty belonged to the nation, not to the monarch. Moreover the meaning

---

[14] *DCA*, pp. 46–7; cf. B. Contant, 'Fragments', Ms fos. 11–12: 'Property is born from labour and is maintained by justice; heredity stems from superstition and is maintained by iniquity.'

[15] Cf. J. Necker, *Réflexions philosophiques sur l'égalité*, in *De la révolution française*, 4 vols., Geneva, 1796.

[16] *DCA*, p. 17. Cf. J. E. Sieyès, *Essai sur les privilèges*, Paris, 1982.

[17] The use of the term 'interest' in *DCA* remains quite ambiguous; Staël seems to use it meaning simply interests in the community, of individuals or social groups; she is not talking of a society structured by orders, and she does not use the term, as Constant will, to refer to the functions of different bodies or powers within the constitution.

[18] *DCA*, p. 18.

[19] J. Godechot, ed., *Les Constitutions de le France depuis 1789*, Paris, 1979, p. 217; 'La Divine Providence ...', etc.

of popular sovereignty was not merely a symbolic one, and its exercise could not be delegated for once and for all to a king or to a body of magistrates. It was the nation at large that must exercise its sovereignty through the free and regular election of its representatives.

The argument traditionally set forth to deny the viability of republican institutions in a large state had been the impossibility of direct democracy (*démocratie pure*) over a vast territory and in numerous political associations.[20] Staël agreed with the notion that ruling a large state was not compatible with the kind of democracy which had characterised the life of the Greek cities. There were, she argued, two ways of thinking about constitutions: either as the theory of 'the most unlimited rights of man', or as the 'wise application' of this theory to the local circumstances of each nation. Representative government could in fact grant a high degree of freedom; but if you wanted to enjoy 'perfect liberty' you could not expect to do it in a society where thirty million people were represented by seven hundred and fifty deputies.[21]

However, belonging to a large political community brought advantages – in terms of the variety and enjoyments of life – which were well worth the sacrifice of direct political participation, and modern Frenchmen would gladly accept the practice of representation, imperfect as it might be, rather than returning to the tribal, frugal and secluded life-style of the ancients:

A Frenchman would never give up all he derives in glory and enjoyments from his large association to obtain in exchange perfect liberty in a small space, away from the eyes of the world and the pleasures of wealth. This view, which I believe is very reasonable, forces us however to reduce the exercise of liberty from the right to decide about everything, to the power to choose a man out of a thousand to act in the name of the nation in all its interests.[22]

The necessity of representation was not at this stage a controversial issue – though undoubtedly the myth of direct democracy had played a significant role in the dynamics of the Jacobin movement.[23] The question was what form representation should take, which institutional framework would best ensure that the interests and will of the nation were adequately served by her deputies. In *Des circonstances* Staël did not commit herself

[20] Cf. Simonde de Sismondi, *Recherches sur les constitutions des peuples libres*, ed. by M. Minerbi, Geneva, 1965.

[21] *DCA*, p. 158.

[22] *DCA*, pp. 159–60.

[23] Isser Woloch, *Jacobin legacy: The democratic movement under the directory*, Princeton, N.J., 1970; F. Furet, 'Révolution française et tradition jacobine', in C. Lucas, ed., *The political culture of the French revolution*, vol. 2, pp. 329–39; K. Tonnesson, 'La démocratie directe sous la révolution française – les cas des districts et sections de Paris', *ibid.*, pp. 295–307.

to a specific institutional setting, to a detailed programme of constitutional engineering. Although she acknowledged the defects of the Constitution of the year III, and made suggestions for its improvement, she was aware that the priority at the moment was the consolidation of the existing institutions rather than their perfection.[24]

Instead she stressed those features of the 1795 Constitution which in her view reflected the more basic and widely applicable principles of representative government. These features were:

1 the popular election of the two legislative assemblies, the Councils of the Cinq-Cents and of the Anciens;
2 the absence of any hereditary magistracy as dictated by the principle of political equality;
3 the separation of executive power, exercised by the five members of the Directory, from the legislative power of the two Councils.

On the question of popular election, Staël did not discuss the issue of the extension of the suffrage. In the Constitution of 1795 the condition for an adult male to become an elector was the ownership of capital or taxable property of the value of 150 to 200 days' labour: a more exacting condition than the three days' worth of labour of the (never applied) Jacobin constitution of 1793, but one which still allowed for a wider electorate than any of the constitutions of the Empire and the Restoration.[25] Elections were still in two stages, and took place through the clumsy and ill-designed mechanism of the electoral assemblies. In *Des circonstances* it was simply taken for granted that the franchise should be restricted on the basis of property: 'The preservation of property in a country such as France demands also the sacrifice of the metaphysical principle of liberty, since, in order to preserve it, it is necessary to place power in the hands of the proprietors.'[26] This was not intended as a permanent feature of representative government, but it was one that was demanded by the conditions of France – where the advent of the republic was 'fifty years in advance' of the state of society and opinion – in order to preserve public order, at least in the short term. The truly controversial point in the Thermidorian context was not who should be allowed to vote (though of course the return to the Constitution of 1793 was a recurrent theme in Jacobin propaganda) but whether there should be free elections at all.

While Staël was writing, the Directory had already intervened twice to

---

[24] Cf. the article seemingly by Constant in the *Echo des Cercles Patriotiques* cited in A. Mathiez, 'Saint-Simon, Lauraguais, Barras, Benjamin Constant et la réforme de la Constitution de l'an III', *Annales historiques de la révolution*, vol. 6 (1929), p. 11.
[25] *Titre* IV, Art. 35; cf. J. Godechot, ed., *Les Constitutions de la France*, p. 107.
[26] *DCA*, p. 160.

annul the results of a national election: on the occasion of the election of the two-thirds of the legislative body in March 1797, which had been favourable to the royalists and had been quashed by the coup of Fructidor; and at the meeting of the electoral assemblies in April 1798, when the Jacobin majority had been overruled by the coup of Floréal. In both cases the Directory's interference – through the joint agreement of the two Councils – had been within the terms of the constitution, but it had been accompanied by the extensive arrest and deportation of representatives of the two electorally successful parties under accusation of conspiracy.[27]

Staël had ambivalent feelings about this course of action (as she would have later on in relation to the coup of Brumaire): on the one hand she was prepared to believe that the dangers of counter-revolution and popular insurrection were real ones, and that the Directory had been justified in resorting to extraordinary measures to stabilise their power; on the other hand (quite apart from her personal interventions to obtain clemency for the victims of the coups) she was deeply convinced that the only hope of survival for the republic was to abide by legality and the respect of constitutional forms.

To a large extent the judgement turned on the evaluation of the means used by the opponents of the government on both political sides: conspiracy and sedition called legitimately for police measures; the legal and peaceful expression of opinion could not be dealt with in the same way. An electorate of proprietors could not be regarded as a seditious minority: it represented the opinion of the nation, and institutions could not be stabilised by silencing opinion. Free elections at regular intervals were an essential prerequisite of representative government. If the institutions were sound, the expression of dissent and the electoral process would not unsettle them. The difficulties which had led to Fructidor and Floréal were in fact the product of defects in the functioning of the institutions themselves.

Staël approves of the effort made by the Thermidorian legislators to share the legislative and executive powers amongst the two Councils and the Directory. As Necker had repeatedly stressed in his retrospective assessments of the revolutionary experience, it was the concentration of these powers in the National Assembly which had led to the Jacobin dictatorship.[28] Staël was aware, however (and here again she could rely

[27] J. R. Suratteau, 'Les Elections de l'an IV', *Annales historiques de la révolution française*, 1951, pp. 374–93 and 1952, pp. 32–62; 'Les Elections de l'an V au conseils du Directoire', *ibid.*, vol. 5, (1958), pp. 21–63.
[28] J. Necker, *Du pouvoir exécutif dans les grands états*, 2 vols., Strasbourg, 1792.

on Necker's views on the subject,[29] of a number of technical difficulties
which accompanied the new structure. The two legislative chambers, the
Councils of the Cinq-Cents and of the Anciens, both elective, could not
function effectively as two separate bodies with distinct powers and
functions, when the only difference between them was the age required for
their membership, and the irrelevant condition that the Anciens should be
married men. Staël believed that this problem could be solved, without
resorting to an hereditary chamber, by turning the Anciens (at least for
that particular generation) into a life magistrature, of which the retired
Directors should also be part, recreating a kind of aristocracy of merit
and distinction.

The separation of executive power, vested in the Directory, from the
legislative power of the Councils, was a vital condition for the preservation of liberty under representative government; but this division of
powers must be accompanied by some co-ordination between them: if
they acted in complete independence, they would end up hindering or
fighting one another. Staël argued that the complete separation of executive and legislative power was almost as bad as their unification and
confusion in a single agent or body.

More specifically the problem in the Thermidorian context was that the
Directory did not have adequate powers, and had consequently been
forced to act illegally to perform its executive functions. The Directors
should have a right of suspensive veto on legislative measures they
disapproved of; moreover there should be a mechanism that allowed them
to resign (as could the British prime minister) when their conflict with the
Councils could not be solved. An additional condition was that ministers
should be chosen from amongst the members of the legislative assemblies
and continue to be part of them. Staël knew that these suggestions would
be perceived as an encouragement to a 'dictatorship' of the Directory but
maintained that the establishment of a functioning executive was the only
possible bulwark against the temptations to act outside the law.[30]

Unsympathetic commentators, like Mathiez, have construed Staël's
reading of the Thermidorian constitution as an authoritarian dream in
which enhanced power for an entrenched assembly of large proprietors
and *notables* would follow the paralysis of democratic activity, a dream
finally come true on 18 Brumaire.[31] This however is a misrepresentation

---

[29] J. Necker, 'Examen de la Constitution de l'an III'; this text, which is an abstract from *De
      la révolution française* of 1796, was republished as a separate pamphlet in Paris in 1798 on
      Staël's suggestion.
[30] *DCA*, pp. 155–207.
[31] Cf. A. Mathiez, 'Saint-Simon ... et la réforme de la Constitution', pp. 14 and ff. See also
      Basil Muteano, *Les Idées politiques de Mme de Staël et la Constitution de l'an III*, Paris,
      1931.

of the real intellectual and political concerns expressed by *Des circonstances*.

No doubt Staël had learnt – from Montesquieu and De Lolme and, more immediately, from her father and from her political patron Sieyès – of the importance of the separation of powers and the smooth functioning of the executive as a prerequisite for a free moderate government. It is also true that she saw the political community as a citizenry of proprietors, though her use of this category was in fact sociologically wider than some of her critics implied. But her reflections on the institutional shape of the republic described merely the means through which, in a situation of crisis, representative government could be realised and allowed to function. The true depository of power, the force that inspired its decisions and gave it its distinctive character, the aim of republican government, was not the political elite to which power had been entrusted in difficult times: it was civil society at large.

IV

Des circonstances did not simply state the principle that 'public opinion must be the sovereign power of representative government'.[32] It offered an extensive analysis of the character of opinion in Thermidorian France, of the beliefs, fears and expectations which, in Staël's argument, were shared by the nation at large. This analysis had a sharp critical edge which was essentially directed against the conception of the ends and means of republican government advocated and practised by the Jacobins in the years of the revolution.

Staël began by arguing that public opinion must not be confused with the views and behaviour of the active political minorities militating respectively in the republican and royalist camp. Political unrest, revolutionary activity, were always led by a minority, while the mass of the population, though inevitably affected by current events, did not really participate or care except in so far as their life was being disrupted:

Here is the opinion of that mass: it has been sufficiently enlightened by the writers of the revolution to be totally indifferent to royalty; but it is not sufficiently enthusiastic to want the republic at the price of its own tranquillity. It is not interested in the privileged castes since it does not belong to them and has never received any benefit from them, yet it does not hate them enough to wish to persecute them, because it knows that persecution troubles the quiet life of those who are neither persecuted nor persecutors, and this mass of the nation wants peace above all. Agriculture and commerce, the public debt, taxes, peace and war, here is what it is preoccupied with, since all it desires is peace and tranquillity.[33]

[32] *DCA*, p. 21.
[33] *DCA*, p. 107.

It was impossible to rule the country, let alone lay the foundations of republican government, without taking into account this silent majority and their need for well-being, peace, safety and justice.[34] No doubt these people could be frightened into acquiescence, intimidated by rigorous political measures. But they could not be 'forced' to identify with the government and rally around it in a moment of crisis, if they felt that the republic had nothing to offer them; and without their support no regime could hope to last, least of all a new republican one, which did not have on its side the strength of tradition.

In their eagerness to give expression to their factional passions, the French revolutionaries had ignored the true feelings and expectations of this passive majority and had therefore misunderstood a number of important features which characterised the mentality and attitude of the citizens of a modern state. I have mentioned how Staël believed that the advantages of belonging to a large political community would make a subject of modern France unwilling to surrender his opportunities for living a diverse, free and comfortable life in order to enjoy full political participation within a restricted and archaic society. More generally, the citizens of modern states would be disinclined to sacrifice their independence and way of life for the sake of a collective purpose.

The interest of Rome summed up all the interests of the Roman citizens. Enthusiasm was created by sacrificing personal interest to the general one – not because the Romans were more generous than we are, but because the individual sphere mattered less to each citizen than what he derived from the *res publica*. But in France the reverse is true, it is the respect of individual existence, of private fortune that alone can generate the love of the republic. The liberty of the present times is all that guarantees the independence of the citizens against the power of the government.[35]

During the revolution, this concern for personal independence had been stigmatised as lack of virtue and patriotism, and no doubt some at least of the revolutionary leaders had been in good faith. However, this 'modern' attitude towards the collectivity (quite apart from being the product of inescapable historical circumstances) must be judged not as a rhetorical effect, but in term of its practical consequences. The desire to live quietly and be protected from violence may not seem very patriotic, but it inspired in people a concern for justice and respect for human rights that during the revolution had been only too easily set aside in the name of the national interest and 'public safety'.

Here Staël drew a firm line, distancing republican government from the policy of arbitrariness and terrorism with which it had become inevitably

[34] *DCA*, p. 22.
[35] *DCA*, p. 111.

associated in the French experience. Contrary to what was suggested by the very name of the all-powerful executive committee of the Jacobin government, the safety of the people was not the supreme law: the supreme law was justice. The salvation of the republic could not be obtained at the price of a single abuse, of one innocent life, without opening the road to endless persecutions and crimes. The notion of public utility, Staël observed, was an ambiguous one, and it was always easy to convince the men in power that an injustice offered political advantages, and consequently that, as citizens, they had the duty to violate the rights of man.[36] And yet: 'In any country where it will be accepted as a principle that the safety of the people is the supreme law, justice and humanity will never be respected, and consequently the nation will be very unhappy on account of the sacrifices made in its alleged interest.'[37]

A condition of insecurity, in which individuals knew that they could be sacrificed at any moment to some alleged national interest, undermined all sense of public morality, all confidence in the law. Thus for example the revolutionary propaganda had preached austerity and frugality, denouncing as anti-patriotic the indulgence in wealth and luxury and the corruption of mores. But had this propaganda succeeded in turning France into a virtuous nation? On the contrary, 'there had never been greater corruption': the political climate of insecurity and suspicion could hardly improve people's moral character. In a country where everybody lived in fear of a public crisis or individual proscription, money inevitably appeared 'the only means of independence, the chief source of happiness, the only hope of salvation' since it could buy protection and grant the possibility of escape to another country.[38] The random denunciations, the activity of spies and informers violated the most sacred bonds of friendship and family ties; people were encouraged to break their duties and obligations and were punished for their loyalty to their loved ones who had become the victims of persecution.

Staël was very decisive in denying any intrinsic association between republican government and the horrors brought about by arbitrary measures during the revolution. As Constant had stressed in his pamphlet of 1797, *Des effets de la terreur*, it was not the practice of terrorism which had saved the republic and the achievements of the revolution: the republic had survived in spite of the destructive effects of terror.[39] The whole design of *Des circonstances* aimed at the definition of a political

---

[36] *DCA*, p. 242.
[37] *DCA*, p. 261.
[38] *DCA*, p. 324.
[39] B. Constant, *Des effets de la terreur*, in *De la force du gouvernement*, ed. by Philippe Raynaud, p. 167.

system founded upon the limitation of power and legal guarantees. But the author was also aware that this was the most delicate and controversial point in the Thermidorian project. The Machiavellian tradition, which identified the republic as a political model both internally conflictual and externally bellicose, had found in the French experience an apparent confirmation which it would be extremely difficult to dislodge from contemporary imagination.

V

The dimension in which the peaceful aspirations of the citizens of modern states and the nature of republican government seemed to be more at odds with one another was the role that the war against the coalition had played in the short life of the French republic. Staël recognised that the experience of war had contributed to undermining the sense of justice and human values as much as that of domestic violence and terrorism:

In recent times people have acquired entirely false notions about courage. All Frenchmen at war, the victims on the scaffold, the revolutionaries in political debates, have displayed the most perfect indifference towards life, but they have carried this strength of character to the point of being insensible to death in general. Here is another social bond broken, another moral sentiment destroyed! Valour is a virtue because it is connected with the idea of an effort and a sacrifice. When courage derives from contempt for one's life, you are very close to despising the life of others in the same way, and you will just be a man of instinct, not a hero ... There is no valour but for him who loves and praises life; there is glory only in purpose, not in danger.[40]

The experience of war and terrorism had been closely interconnected, and yet, unlike terror, war could not be dismissed altogether as a form of political degeneracy. When in 1791 France began the hostilities with Austria and Prussia, Staël had acknowledged the right of the nation to defend itself against the illegitimate interference of foreign powers in its domestic political affairs. Like the Girondins and the constitutionalists, she had in fact welcomed the war as an opportunity to control political extremism, turning social unrest and revolutionary pressures against the foreign enemy and thus averting a civil war.

It was in the framework of this hope of securing domestic peace and consolidating constitutional monarchy that she had successfully canvassed for the nomination of (her then lover) the Count of Narbonne to the post of Minister of War, with the ultimate design of offering the supreme command of the French army to the 'liberal' Duke of Brunswick. On the occasion of Narbonne's nomination on 7 December 1791, Marie

[40] *DCA*, pp. 345–6.

Antoinette had written to Count Fersen: 'What glory for Mme de Staël, what joy for her to have the whole army at her disposal . . .',[41] a characteristically bitchy remark which however captured the association of Staël with the project of a military solution. The constitutionalists' hopes of controlling the war had soon collapsed, together with the monarchy itself. But the calculation that the war effort would strengthen domestic unity had proved only too right: the war, fought largely by an army of volunteers and conscripts against foreign mercenaries, had failed to stop the revolutionary process, but it had sustained the revolutionary regime, and with the regime the republic.

Events had given further confirmation to the old Machiavellian vision of the republic as a political form especially attuned to military expansion when the French revolutionary army had gradually progressed from defence of the national territory to conquest. The legitimate protection of national political independence had thus turned into a crusade to export the ideas of the revolution to other countries: these had justly reacted by resisting a freedom imposed upon them by a foreign army, while local republicans and sympathisers of the revolution had been placed in an impossible position of conflict between their political ideals and their national loyalties.[42]

In her pamphlet *Réflexions sur la paix* written after the fall of Robespierre in 1794, ostensibly addressed to Pitt and the forces of the Coalition, Staël had pleaded for peace precisely on the ground that, unless the war stopped, the expansionistic ambitions of the republic would never come to an end. By continuing the fighting, the forces of the Coalition would obtain as a result only the spreading of national conflicts to other European countries, leading to an interminable total war.

The whole of Europe, turned upside down, will prolong the internal disorder of France; the echoes of democratic factions of Germany, of Holland, will reach Paris, and no government will ever be able to establish itself there. It will take centuries before the European empires cease to subvert one another, and maybe some day this devastated part of the world will be similar to the deserts of Africa or the abjection of Asia.[43]

To stop this process of general mobilisation it was essential not only to reach a negotiated solution to the conflict, but to disperse as fast as possible the French popular armies by 'encouraging agriculture, restoring

---

[41] Quoted in J. C. Herold, *Mistress to an age*, London, 1959, p. 105.
[42] Staël was most concerned with the case of Switzerland – see below; cf. also Pagden on the Neapolitan republic, ch. 7 in this volume.
[43] *Œuvres complètes de la Baronne de Staël*, 17 vols., Paris, 1820, vol. 2, pp. 82–3. It is interesting to compare Staël's views with a similar line of argument adopted at the same time by Choderlos de Laclos to advocate the continuation of the war. Cf. his Memoir addressed to the Directory in the first months of 1795, during the negotiation of the

the freedom of trade and undertaking large and useful public works',[44] thus absorbing the soldiers within the body of the civil population.

If in 1794 Staël had been very eloquent in her appeal for peace, the question that she confronted in *Des circonstances*, in the light of the renewed successes of the revolutionary armies and the increasing influence of military leaders on the political scene, was how to envisage a peaceful future for the republican government in France when the republic was crucially dependent on the war effort for its survival.

Staël's argument was that the presence of a conquering popular army undoubtedly constituted a support for the republic, but an 'artificial' one, which prolonged the exceptional circumstances of national mobilisation and prevented the government from ever reverting to a 'normal' situation in which political institutions had to subsist on their own strength. Moreover, 'kings' hatreds [died] with them, national quarrels [were] eternal'.[45] In this protracted state of war fuelled by national sentiment the government would feel that it could dispense altogether with the consent of public opinion. The militarised republican regime would fail to put down roots in the only durable source of power for a free representative government, the civil population, and it would make no efforts to educate the people politically, confining itself to the exploitation of their patriotic feelings.

The first basis of a republic is national patriotism. Now, as long as the French government makes appeal to circumstances to resort to revolutionary means, the spirit of a free people will never be formed. In France, while the continuation of the war will force six hundred thousand men to remain in arms, the government will never need public opinion, and public opinion will never regain strength. France will be governed in a hundred years' time as it is now and the nation will never become republican. There will still be a republican party, but this party will agitate, give orders, dominate, make revolutions all by itself, while the nation will take no part.[46]

Unfortunately Staël did not develop the topic of conquest, as she had planned, in a separate chapter of her work. In the sketchy outline she left, as in other passages in the text, it is possible to recognise some of the themes which would be illustrated by Constant in his work of 1813 on the *Spirit of conquest*: the opposition of war and commerce, the military class (like the priesthood) as a separate body within the nation, the corruption

Treaty of Basle, 'De la guerre et de la paix', in *Œuvres complètes*, ed. by L. Versini, Paris, 1979, pp. 701–18.
[44] *Œuvres complètes de la Baronne de Staël*, vol. 2, p. 82.
[45] *DCA*, p. 365.
[46] *DCA*, p. 321.

of the values of civic morality in a prolonged war.[47] In Constant's work, however, the identity of the spirit of conquest had become that of imperial tyranny, while the republic had disappeared in the background. When Staël was writing this transition was far from clear.

A political class of proven survivors, greedy, compromised, could laugh at Bonaparte playing Alexander amongst the pyramids and prepare to negotiate with the Coalition. But they knew that they must negotiate from the vantage point of victory: a defeat of the revolutionary army would deprive the former regicides of all support and pave the way for the restoration of the monarchy. Unsurprisingly, Staël's draft chapter was full of references to Machiavelli's *Discorsi* and the fate of the Roman republic.

Moreover, it was the booty of the Italian campaigns which kept the Directory's cash flow healthy, averting the danger of economic collapse.[48] It would have been difficult for Staël to reject her own political upbringing – steeped in natural jurisprudence and political economy – in which the peaceful nature of commerce, and the belief that wars never pay in the end, were basic and uncontested precepts. But the short-term economic advantages of Bonaparte's victories were hard to deny, and the only hope was that his military exploits might be finally brought under the control of civil administration by promoting the conquering general to high political magistrature.

The impossibility of disentangling the revolutionary and republican heritage from the military fortunes of the nation surfaced again in 1813 and 1815, when Napoleon confronted the Coalition in the two decisive battles of Leipzig and Waterloo. In spite of their long struggle against the Emperor, which had resulted in prolonged exile for both of them, neither Constant nor Staël could bring themselves to hope for the victory of foreign armies against France. Constant chose to believe in Napoleon's good faith in accepting constitutional guarantees and supported his cause during the Hundred Days; Staël canvassed to place an exiled Frenchman (Bernadotte in 1813, the Duke of Orleans in 1815) at the head of the Coalition. On 23 January 1814 she wrote from London to Constant:

One must not speak ill of France when the Russians are at Langres! May God banish me from France rather than let me return with the aid of foreigners! ... What a combination of circumstances, that we must tremble at the defeat of such a man! ... Has not France two arms, one to punish the enemy, the other to overthrow tyranny?[49]

[47] See, in *DCA*, the note 'Des conquêtes', pp. 364–6 and pp. 289–90: 'nothing is more contrary to liberty than the military spirit ...'

[48] Florin Aftalion, *L'Economie de la révolution française*, Paris, 1986.

[49] J. C. Herold, *Mistress to an age*, p. 436.

After Napoleon's abdication she wrote to her son Auguste: 'The blow is cruel. All London is drunken with joy' and reported how people congratulated her on the possibility of returning to France after her long exile, while she was 'in despair'.[50] Significantly, in a retrospective assessment of the circumstances which had brought Bonaparte to power, written shortly before her death in 1817, she would refer to him as *ce fatal étranger* – 'that fatal foreigner' – thus attempting for the last time to sever the link between the conquering dictator and the French republic.[51]

VI

Des circonstances is in many ways a fragile, problematic work. It was conceived and written in the middle of an acrimonious debate, in the course of which its author had been denounced by the Jacobin press as the 'divinity of the oligarchs', the 'patroness of the émigrés', the '*sultane* of the king of Blankenbourg [Louis XVIII]';[52] branded by royalist pamphleteers as an 'infernal slut' and a 'hermaphrodite ... discrediting both sexes at once';[53] and finally described by the liberator of France general Bonaparte (incautiously saluted by Staël herself as 'the best of republicans') simply as 'that madwoman'.[54]

It was a work celebrating no triumphs or certainties, which addressed itself explicitly to the survivors of a catastrophe, and aspired to reconcile 'the theoretical opinions of the victors with the feelings of the vanquished'.[55] It was, moreover, a bold attempt at theorising about a political situation so fluid and unstable, that in the few months Staël spent drafting her text circumstances had changed too dramatically to allow for its publication. Probably its most significant impact at the time was the use that Constant was allowed to make by the author of extensive abstracts from the text which were later incorporated into his own political works.[56] Yet the relevance of *Des circonstances* was not merely that of documenting a transitional phase in French political history, and

[50] *Ibid.*, p. 437.
[51] *Considérations sur la révolution française*, in *Œuvres complètes*, vol. 13, p. 239.
[52] Ghislain de Diesbach, *Mme de Staël*, Paris, 1983, p. 204.
[53] J. C. Herold, *Mistress to an age*, pp. 173–7.
[54] *Ibid.*, p. 172. Cf. also Henri Guillemin, *Mme de Staël, Benjamin Constant et Napoléon*, Paris, 1959.
[55] *DCA*, pp. 4–5.
[56] It is difficult to establish to what extent Constant had contributed in the first place to the text of *DCA*, which he revised and which was undeniably the product of a close intellectual collaboration; cf. Lucia Omacini, 'Introduction' to *DCA*, pp. lxxii–lxxxiv. More recently it has become clear that some of his markings on the text were indications to a copyist to prepare a selection of passages which he later reproduced in his own works. It seems to me that the use of passages from *DCA* in the 'Fragments' (written around 1800) is unmistakable.

the draft contained a number of theoretical insights of a value as universal and durable as the author had hoped them to be.

The first of these insights was the definition of representative government, of a limited power founded upon popular sovereignty and electoral participation and bounded by constitutional guarantees. In spite of the accusations of conservatism, Staël's work showed how much a generation educated on Montesquieu and De Lolme had actually learnt from the experience of the revolution, how much closer these components of the political tradition had come to historical reality and legislative practice. Certainly Staël had the uncommon advantage of possessing both a fine intellect and a direct experience of the exercise of power. But she made full use of these advantages, combining her sense of theoretical commitment and continuity with a sharp political realism – a realism hardly disproved by an error of judgement, Brumaire, which she shared with the French political class at large.[57]

The second important element of Staël's text was the portrait she presented of French and European civil society such as it had emerged from the revolution. The attention she paid not only to economic constraints, but to feelings, private identities and personal aspirations shows how she had made a more intelligent political use of her reading of Rousseau and of eighteenth-century sentimentalist writers than many of her contemporaries. Staël understood that the notion of a peaceful commercial community bent on its own private enjoyments went against the grain of a deeply rooted French tradition, in which the republican models of classical antiquity combined with the aristocratic '*étique de la gloire*' of absolute monarchy to sustain an heroic conception of individual as well as national achievements.[58]

This 'heroic' national identity had been slowly eroded by the process of social and economic transformation; but it was the experience of the revolution, civil war and Terror which, by cutting away at the festering wounds within it, had finally opened a space for those 'milder' bourgeois virtues without which the new republic could not survive. Significantly, in the pages of *Des circonstances* the true modern commercial republic was not France, but America, free from the bonds of tradition, economically

[57] Several years later she wrote: 'In all the circumstances of my life the mistakes I committed in politics were always caused by the idea that men would ultimately be receptive to the truth, if this were presented to them with sufficient force', *Œuvres complètes*, vol. 13, p. 204.

[58] On the impact of classical models on French *ancien régime* and revolutionary culture cf. H. T. Parker, *The cult of antiquity in the French revolution*, Chicago, Ill., 1937, the more recent but disappointing work by Claude Mosse, *L'Antiquité dans la révolution française*, Paris, 1989, and François Hartog, 'La Révolution française et l'antiquité', *La Pensée politique*, no. 1 (1993), pp. 30–61; on aristocratic ethos see Paul Benichou, *Morales du Grand Siècle*, Paris, 1948.

flourishing and protected by geographical distance from the territorial ambitions of European powers.[59]

Finally, *Des circonstances* pointed at another significant area of reflection. On 28 January 1797, Staël had stood next to her father on the balcony of their *château* of Coppet, watching the French troops on march to 'liberate' the Vaud. Although French intervention in Switzerland had allegedly been requested to assist the local revolutionary movement, the sight of a free republic engaged in the military occupation of another proved profoundly traumatic.[60] By bringing to an end the international balance reached by the European powers in the course of the eighteenth century, the revolution had set in motion unforeseen forces, the identity of which was no longer adequately captured by the old constitutional categories of monarchy and republic. In this context Staël's work on the history of European literature and German romanticism, to which she dedicated herself in the years of exile following Bonaparte's rise to power, was not an escape or deviation from political themes, but the natural continuation of a line of reflection which led from the new republic and its future to the intractable issues of national culture and national identity.

[59] *DCA*, pp. 394–5. Cf. the position of Pagano – see Pagden, ch. 7 in this volume.
[60] *Considérations*, in *Œuvres complètes*, vol. 13, pp. 208–15, 'Invasion de la Suisse'.

7   Francesco Mario Pagano's 'Republic of Virtue': Naples 1799

Anthony Pagden

I

The 'Repubblica Partenopea' lasted only a few months from 24 January 1799 until 13 June when it was destroyed by the royalist forces of Cardinal Ruffo with the assistance of an English fleet under Nelson. Although proclaimed in the name of liberty and equality, and in the interests of the entire people, it was unique among eighteenth-century republics in having been made possible only by foreign arms against a popular army which, insofar as it had any discernible political identity, was monarchist, conservative and Catholic. The republic was – as Vincenzo Cuoco, its historian, and one of its few active members to escape with his life, said of it – 'a revolution which was intended to create the happiness of a nation, but instead has brought about only its ruin'.[1]

Shortly before Christmas 1798 Ferdinand IV fled from Palermo (on one of Nelson's ships) abandoning the government into the hands of Francesco Pignatelli, Prince of Strongoli. Pignatelli, faced with the seemingly invincible army of the French general Jean Etienne Championnet, destroyed both the royalist fleet and the artillery to prevent these from falling into French hands. On 15 January the people, convinced that the government had no intention of resisting the 'unholy French', took up arms, in the name of their absent king and against the urban nobility and the government whom they believed to be in league with the 'Jacobins'. The struggle which ensued was bitter and bloody. It amply fulfilled the fears of the ideologue Joseph Dominique Garat, ambassador to the city who, in November 1798, had written to Talleyrand, 'I tell you, general, that the idea of a revolution made in Italy by the Italians fills me with horror. Wherever one stops one sees only passions and ignorance.'

Championnet, victorious after days of street fighting, told the people of Naples he had just defeated, 'You are finally free, your liberty is the only

[1] *Saggio storico sulla rivoluzione di Napoli*, Milan, 1806, p. 21.

price which France demands for its conquest.'[2] The blood of St Gennaro duly liquefied, a provisional government was established, composed mostly of members of what, in Naples, had for long been known as the *popolo civile* – the legal and administrative class – most of whom had already been exiled for their opposition to the Bourbon regime. This was, to use Cuoco's phrase, a 'passive revolution'. It was a revolution made against, rather than by the people, and it was a revolution which, despite subsequent claims that the programme of reform devised by the republic had won it widespread popularity, never achieved any popular support.

II

In this essay I shall be concerned with the ideas of Francesco Mario Pagano, the most articulate of the Neapolitan revolutionaries and the probable architect of the constitution of the republic. Pagano was the most influential member of the legislative assembly of the provisional government. He had been a lawyer, *Avvocato dei poveri* of the 'Consolato di mare', between 1789 and 1796. In this capacity he had done his best to make judicial procedures more accessible to the poor, and to free the Neapolitan fish trade from government restrictions. He was imprisoned in 1796 for his hostility to the government and banished in 1798 when he fled, like many of his countrymen, to republican Rome. He returned to take his place in the provisional government on 1 February 1799. He was the author of a number of works, most importantly – for my purposes – the lengthy preamble to the *Progetto di costituzione della repubblica napoletana* (*Project for a constitution for the Neapolitan republic*) and, so far as we can tell, of most of the *Progetto* itself. He also wrote a treatise – *Considerazioni sul processo criminale* (*Considerations on the criminal law*) – which was translated into French in 1789 and was much praised by the *Moniteur de la révolution française*,[3] a number of legal tracts urging the abolition of torture and the simplification of Naples's Byzantine legal system, several rather turgid dramas in verse, and a number of poems. But his best known work, and the one which provided much of the theoretical and historical structure for the republic's constitutional programme, is a long, sometimes rambling, study, entitled *Saggi politici de'principi, progressi e decadenza della società* (*Political essays on the origins, progress and decadence of society*), first published in 1783. It is in part a continuation of, and heavily indebted to, Giambattista Vico's *Scienza nuova*, with

---

[2] *Monitore napoletano* for 22 January 1799, in *Il monitore napoletano*, ed. by Mario Battaglini, Naples, 1974, p. 18.

[3] See Gioele Solari, *Studi su Francesco Mario Pagano*, ed. Luigi Firpo, Turin, 1963, p. 322. This is still the most detailed study of Pagano and his work.

echoes of Robertson, Ferguson, Boulanger and Pluche. For all its inherent bagginess it is an attempt to give a political shape to the aspirations of at least three generations of Neapolitan reformers, from Vico himself, to Gaetano Filangieri, the jurist who became, in Pagano's words, the revolution's 'tutelary genius'.[4] For despite its frequent claims to be modelled on the French republic, and the indebtedness of its constitution to the French constitution of 1791 and the (never applied) Jacobin constitution of 1793, despite the decision to begin the republican era on 22 September 1792 – when, of course, Naples was still a monarchy[5] – and the description of France in the first number of the *Monitore napoletano* (itself, of course, a copy of the *Moniteur*) as 'la Madre Repubblica' of which all Neapolitans were 'her little sons'[6] – despite all this, the Repubblica Partenopea was, for most of the members of its provisional government, a far less radical affair than the French republic. It was, in effect, a prolongation by other means, and in a slightly modified language, of the reform programme which had been in progress since the first decade of the century. Pagano himself would, probably, have preferred a reform movement guided by an enlightened prince, a Neapolitan version of the Archduke Peter Leopold, architect of the famous Tuscan constitution of 1779, which he referred to as the 'envy of all true republics'. But by the 1790s the movement of history, which, he insisted, followed laws as exact as those of the planets was, he believed, all set for catastrophe. Reform could no longer be guided by hereditary monarchs. It had to be *made* by those with the political will, which all hereditary monarchs, even Peter Leopold, clearly lacked, and it could now be made only in the form of a republic.

For Pagano, as for Vico, as for Genovesi, Grimaldi, and Filangieri, familiar as they were with the writings of Vico's 'jurisconsul of mankind', Hugo Grotius, it was axiomatic that all societies were the product of needs. 'Society', wrote Pagano, 'which precedes every imaginable social pact, tacit or express, was the creature of needs'.[7] But since the satisfaction of needs changes the animal by creating new needs, it is 'the idea of our needs' which drives our spirits.[8] In this early state man was an innovative individualist. On this account culture precedes society, for 'the first social link [between men]', Pagano argued, 'was public religion and

[4] Quoted in Solari, *Studi su Francesco Mario Pagano*, p. 319.
[5] *Progetto di costituzione della repubblica napoletana del 1799, con le note di Angelo Lanzelotti*, Naples, 1820, p. 419.
[6] *Monitore napoletano* for 2 February 1799, p. 7.
[7] *Considerazioni di Francesco Mario Pagano sul processo criminale*, Naples, 1825, p. 1.
[8] *Saggi politici de'principi, progressi e decadenza della società*, 2nd edn, 3 vols., Milan, 1800, vol. 2, pp. 28–30.

public custom'.[9] But with the growth of society there grew 'the force of habit, that insuperable moral inertia, which is established by example, fortified by imitation and corroborated by use'.[10] Men became what most are still today, the 'slaves of habit', who 'at the mere mention of change either laugh or shudder'.[11] And it is this 'moral inertia', which, by replacing the concept of justice by a notion of order, and reason by sentiment, allows some men, in pursuit of power, to prevent others from satisfying their needs. The structure of custom holds together the order of classes. This is a relationship based upon power; yet it is a power which is exploited not through force, but through what Pagano, in the *Saggi politici*, calls 'trust', *fede*. (This is to be distinguished from 'la buona fede' which for Pagano, as for Genovesi, is the sole basis of commerce.)[12] Like Vico, Pagano believed that this form of trust had its origin not in the membership of a community which allowed for the rational calculation of the possible behaviour of all its members – but in the protection provided by the strong to the weak. Trust and the vocabularies which sustained it (Vico had claimed that the Italian word 'forza' derived from the term *fides*) was what underpinned feudal relations, not relations between free men.[13]

There existed then an inescapable tension between the structure of custom and of class, on the one hand, and the natural needs of men on the other. There existed a conflict between the kind of society – labelled 'feudalism' – which sustained unreflective custom, and that – the true republic – in which the legitimate needs of all men would be expressible and could be satisfied. The true republic will, of course, be based upon liberty and rights, those liberties and rights guaranteed by the Declaration of the Rights of Man, which were summarised in the preamble to the Neapolitan constitution. Given such a view of the origin of society it was little wonder that Pagano, like Filangieri before him, laid so much stress on the need to sustain justice and the well-ordered society through civic education.

The 'philosophical history'[14] which Vico had created offered, so

---

[9] *Ibid.*, pp. 109–11.

[10] *Ibid.*, vol. 1, pp. 20–1, and see *Ragionamento sulla libertà del commercio del pesce di Napoli diretto al regio tribunale dell'ammiragliato e consolato di mare*, Naples, November 1789, p. 17.

[11] *Considerazioni*, p. 91.

[12] *Ragionamento*, p. 26. On Genovesi's use of the term see Anthony Pagden, *Spanish imperialism and the political imagination*, New Haven, Conn., and London, 1990, pp. 65–89.

[13] *Saggi politici*, vol. 2, pp. 64–5.

[14] *Ibid.*, vol. 1, p. 67. Pagano placed Vico within a genealogy which ran from Thucydides to Tacitus to Machiavelli, but, he concluded, 'niuno avea della storia formato filosofia' except Vico.

Pagano believed, the basis for those 'moral laws which are as constant and necessary as are the laws of physics'.[15] And from Vico, Pagano drew another history, one which would provide him with an argument for the *kind* of society the 'just republic' had to be. In the beginning men lived of course solitary lives. The first communities were barbarous ones in which individual rights were sustained by private rather than public force. It was from these early monarchical bands that the first republics developed. They, too, were communities of private individuals, 'despotic feudal aristocrats, to whom the plebeians were enslaved and sovereignty resided only with the nobility'. Despite their names, the republic of Rome, which was, in any case, little more than a military encampment, and the republic of Athens, were merely limited monarchies.[16] These were communities of fierce individualists and 'could flourish only in those times when men had not entirely lost their love of independence'.[17] The people were united only in each individual's relationship to the oligarchs, a relationship of 'servants, clients and companions', a relationship which was military, and essentially private. The occupation of these early republics was civil war and even the Roman Law, which Pagano saw as Europe's highest civil achievement, was an imperial structure, which had grown out of the republican code covering the rules of duelling.[18] The crucial element of this dismal picture of the ancient republics is not, however, the point, so familiar to Montesquieu and later to Constant, about the restrictions such societies place upon private liberty, nor the limited nature of the citizen body – a modern republic, in Pagano's view, should have an equally limited governing elite – nor even the necessary presence in the midst of all ancient republics of a large slave class. It is rather that there is, in fact, precious little structural difference, in Pagano's account (and, indeed, in Vico's), between the ancient republic and the Gothic feudal monarchy. The monarchical element (*pace* Aristotle) was, Pagano claimed, missing in these early republics, but it required only the elevation of a war-lord to the status of *dux* to complete the transformation of the heirs of Brutus into the sons of Alric.

There is, of course, nothing very original about this link between ancient republics and feudal monarchies. But whereas earlier, and indeed most later, critics, including Constant, had identified the contractual nature of the relationship between the community and its ruler as the link between the two, for Pagano feudal monarchies and ancient republics

---

[15] *Contro Sabato Totaro, reo dell'omicidio di Giuseppe Gensari in grado di nullità, Aringo secondo*, Naples, 10 November 1784 (Naples, Biblioteca Nazionale, Coll. Bass. III D. 65): 'Le leggi morali son così constanti e necessarie come le fisiche sono' (p. 32).

[16] *Saggi politici*, vol. 2, pp. 130–45.

[17] *Ibid.*, vol. 1, p. 98.

[18] *Ibid.*, vol. 2, p. 150.

shared a common character as societies based on clientage, war and the monopoly of the ruling elite on property. There were features of the ancient republics – most notably, as we shall see, the Spartan ephorate and the Roman censors – which Pagano applauded and which he attempted to incorporate into the Neapolitan constitution. But it was clear that not only would ancient republicanism not do as a political model, it was, itself, indistinguishable in its essentials from precisely that form of government which had, for centuries, been the curse of the Neapolitan people.

Ever since the Spanish occupation of the kingdom in 1504 the power of the feudal barony had been steadily growing. Why and how is part of another story. But for all the reformers of the eighteenth century feudalism was identified with an earlier form of barbarism, an outmoded historical type, and equated with a monarchical despotism[19] long since abandoned by those modern republics, England and Holland, and even by pre-revolutionary France. Feudalism had come to denote a general category in which, broadly speaking, political power, sovereignty, is indistinguishable from possession. For Felice Capella, Moses, David and Solomon were all feudal lords, and feudalism was the common lot of the Syrians, Macedonians and Egyptians, as well as of the Spaniards and, of course, of the poor Neapolitans. 'Feudal government and monarchical government ... differ only in name', one member of the provisional government, Gennaro Cestari, told the legislative assembly on 9 April 1799 (discussing the abolition of feudalism).[20] Feudalism, said Pagano addressing the same assembly, was 'a part of the booty which the prince–assassins granted to their clients'. It was the 'chain which ran from the hand of the tyrant, linked the barony to him, and from the barony extended to the people'.[21] And not only did feudalism transform civil relations into property, it also established monopolies on all real property, and, as Pagano pointed out, 'monopoly is that common vice, which has now become inherent in our political constitution'.[22] Monopolies limit the growth of wealth. In the feudal monarchy the commercial counterpart of the fief was the guilds and leasing companies. Monopolies, as Pagano observed, had been 'the seeds of that fatal division' sown by the viceregal government. 'All these colleges', he moaned. 'How many small groups there are in the city of Naples. And what delight, what energy, what loyalty men have to these bodies, while there is no attachment, no zeal for the community or the public good.'[23]

[19] See *Considerazioni*, p. 13.
[20] *Monitore napoletano*, p. 383.
[21] *Ibid.*, pp. 385–6.
[22] *Ragionamento*, pp. 14–15.
[23] *Ibid.*, p. 22.

In a true civil society property could, of course, be 'only that which derives from the natural right common to all humanity'. It could, that is, only be *private* property. Sovereignty, in Pagano's account, extends to the right to impose taxes, but feudalism entails the sale and purchase of that right, and that 'is a violation of sovereignty itself'. Hence the insistence in Pagano's constitution on ownership as that 'sacred and inviolable right'.[24] It is also unsurprising that the definition of private property given in both the *Saggi* and in the *Progetto* should be that of Locke, 'the only one', as Pagano put it, 'to have described the true principle of the right of property'.[25] For, of course, only Locke's definition, summarised in the preface to the *Progetto*,[26] could escape from any prior conditions of ownership. Only rights based essentially on labour, and the parallel claim that all men have the right to the fruits of that labour,[27] could be truly natural ones, and thus the only rights the new republic could accept. It was also the case that only private property, 'the dominion and possession of those things which are ours', has the power in a civil society to assure us of our identity, of our – as Pagano put it – *nostreità*.[28] Feudalism, which is a form of monopoly on property,[29] therefore deprives men not merely of their right to meet what they are legitimately entitled to regard as their needs, it also deprives them of the one moral faculty they all share in common. By doing that it deprives them of their capacity to resist oppression and hence of their capacity to create civil communities. And because of this, it destroys their natural capacity for creative thought. Italy, claimed Pagano, which in antiquity had been home to the intellectual leaders of Europe, the *praeceptores Europae* whose passing Machiavelli had lamented, had, under its Gothic rulers, collapsed into ignorance. Only under the Florentine republic had there been some hope of a return to past glories, but, said Pagano, 'political science was born again and died with the Florentine Secretary like those animals whose graves are next to their cradles'. Similarly poor Naples, too close to the 'ruinous court of Rome' and subjected to three centuries of viceregal rule,

---

[24] *Progetto di costituzione ... del 1799*, p. 125, art. 402.
[25] *Saggi politici*, vol. 2, pp. 146–7.
[26] *Progetto di costituzione della repubblica napolitana presentato al governo provvisorio dal comitato di legislazione* (this is the preamble to the constitution), in Franco Venturi, ed., *Illuministi italiani*, vol. 5, *Riformatori napoletani*, Milan and Naples, 1962, p. 910: 'L'uomo impiegando le sue forze su di una porzione del comune patrimonio di tutti, sulla terra io dico, dandole nuova forma colla sua industria e col suo lavoro, fa passare in quella le sue facoltà personali.' Cf. John Locke, *Second treatise of government*, ch. 5, para. 28 (original emphasis): 'Whatsoever then he removes out of the State that Nature hath provided, and left it in, he hath mixed his *Labour* with, and joyned to it something that is his own, and thereby makes it his *Property*.'
[27] *Ragionamento*, p. 19.
[28] *Saggi politici*, vol. 2, p. 144.
[29] *Ragionamento*, p. 14.

had had to wait for Vico 'to open a breach in the wall and shown the way'.[30]

In Pagano's philosophical history, the collapse of Gothic rule is followed by those modern enlightened monarchies where 'humanity and sweetness of customs' – unknown either in the state of nature or in the ancient republics and their feudal heirs – are allowed to develop, societies in which torture no longer should or need be practised,[31] societies which are, potentially at least, reforming.[32] Since, however, such polities are necessarily dependent upon a single individual, they are highly susceptible to corruption. And when they finally become terminally corrupt, as Naples had done under Ferdinand IV, the only possible solution is their replacement by a modern commercial republic.[33]

This, the true *respublica*, is defined by Pagano in familiar terms as that society where the laws are sovereign and every citizen acts in the common good. 'Laws and civil discipline', he said, 'constitute all republics'.[34] *Modern* republics, however – and in this Pagano's model more closely resembles the United States than it does revolutionary France – are commercial and pacific. Modern republics, he claimed in the preamble to the *Progetto*, are based on a code of the Rights of Man,[35] not on those privileges, feudal concessions, guild monopolies and their like, which are the common feature of all clientalist societies, be they ancient republics or feudal monarchies. They are based on free trade, because freedom of trade, he had argued (in his pamphlet on the Neapolitan fish trade in 1789), was a natural human right when applied to foodstuffs, since these belong to the category of simple needs and consequently, 'the quantity of the needs will establish what is the just price'.[36] Freedom of trade is also a natural right because all men have the right to the fruits of their labour, particularly when their trade is as labour-intensive as fishing. Furthermore free trade is the means by which

good faith (*buona fede*) will be re-born, something which, for so many reasons, is rare among our people. The advantages of the exercise of virtue will be redis-

---

[30] *Saggi politici*, vol. 1, pp. 6–7.
[31] *Considerazioni*, pp. 83–7.
[32] *Saggi politici*, vol. 1, p. 98.
[33] For Pagano commerce was the natural activity of those not directly involved with the monarch, and this means not only 'the people', but also, in most cases, the aristocracy (*Saggi politici*, vol. 2, pp. 177–8). Pagano's image of the modern republic is of an aristocratic – although not an oligarchic – one, and he constantly, both in the constitution itself, and in his addresses to the assembly, attempted to incorporate the Neapolitan barony into the republic, even to the extent of exculpating them for any blame in the feudal system which they, in fact, had sustained.
[34] *Politicum universae Romanorum nomothesiae examen*, Naples, 1768, p. 103.
[35] *Progetto di costituzione*, in Venturi, ed., p. 909.
[36] *Ragionamento*, p. 6.

covered ... Good faith will by its own interest animate the numerous classes among our people, good faith will become for them a deep well from which they will be able to draw the security which they require.[37]

Commerce, because it involves exchange, also favours change. It not only makes men 'sweet' as Montesquieu had famously argued,[38] it also makes them conscious of the worlds in which they live, and only men who are conscious in this way can be modern citizens. 'Those peoples', Pagano observed in the *Saggi*, 'who do not have commerce are little given to changes in customs and government, which is why Sparta closed its ports to traders'.[39] All warrior societies remain closed, static, whereas the merchant 'carries culture with his produce', and brings 'the light of culture and of liberty'.[40] Free trade, then, was guaranteed by article 399 of the constitution.[41]

III

The various kings, the Trastamara, the Habsburgs, the Bourbons, who had ruled Naples had, however, done little to create the conditions out of which a modern *respublica* could be formed. If a modern commercial republic was to be established in Naples it had to be done *ex nihilo* on the back of the French army, one of those 'external moral forces' which in Pagano's account sometimes serve to accelerate the process of historical transformation.[42] It could be sustained only by the force of law, by, that is, a radical reform of the legal system which in Pagano's terms meant the abolition of feudal rights and privileges and the imposition of Roman Law, a written constitution, and public civic instruction.

The Neapolitan republic, declared the opening paragraph of that constitution, is based on the Rights of Man, which can be summarised as each man's right to act in order to meet his needs, his crucial, 'sacred and

---

[37] *Ibid.*, p. 26.
[38] *De l'esprit des lois*, Book XX, ch. 1, in Montesquieu, *Œuvres complètes*, ed. by Roger Caillois, Paris, 1951, vol. 2, p. 585, and see Albert O. Hirschman, *The passions and the interests. Political arguments for capitalism before its triumph*, Princeton, N.J., 1977, pp. 61–3.
[39] *Saggi politici*, vol. 1, p. 91. Russo made the same point – only he ran the argument the other way – when he demanded that Naples should also deny the status of citizen to merchants in all but the most basic goods (as he claimed the ancient republics had done) because true republics – in his view, that is *ancient* republics – are communities of producers not traders: Vincenzo Russo, *Pensieri politici*, Naples, 1894, pp. 113–14 and *Monitore napoletano*, p. 312.
[40] *Saggi politici*, vol. 1, p. 79.
[41] *Progetto di costituzione ... del 1799*, p. 125.
[42] *Saggi politici*, vol. 1, pp. 78–9.

inviolable'[43] right to private property, and his right to resist all those – including the state – who seek to deprive him of those rights.[44] He is also, of course, bound by the corresponding duty to observe the law. Liberty is, conventionally, the right to exercise one's natural faculties without restraint, and virtue is the 'energy of that faculty'. But although all natural rights are to be upheld, equality is 'not a right but a relationship, and rights are faculties'.[45] Pagano, and even Russo who had argued for the abolition not only of trade but also of private property, both agreed with Filangieri that *natural* equality was as much a contradiction in human as it would be in physical terms. Equality, indeed, was one of the features of savagery. It was only man's failure to develop his natural properties that made him equal with all his fellows.[46] All men, Pagano argued against Rousseau, 'have the right to civil liberty, that is to the tutelage of personal rights, but not all have a right to government, that is to legislation and command'.[47] Like many modern republicans Pagano recognised the paradox that not only, as Montesquieu had argued, *could* a true republic be created under a monarchy; but that in a sense the well-ordered republic of both Cicero's and Machiavelli's imaginations could be constituted *only* under the kind of all-powerful central authority which monarchies had formerly been. Pagano, for all his belief in the moral sovereignty of *virtù*, had a firm grasp on the contemporary realities of power. He had read Grotius (if not Hobbes) with as much care as Vico, and like Grotius was prepared to accept that 'all the rights of man derive from the one fundamental right of self-preservation'.[48] If, with the sole and transitory exception of Peter Leopold, the hereditary monarchs and their corrupted aristocracies had failed to re-direct their energies into the creation of virtuous states, then they had to be replaced by some other form of government. But that government would exercise no less power than the monarchy had done. In Pagano's conjectural history, as we have seen, true civil society, the truly *modern* republic, was a natural evolution from absolute monarchy.

Naples, then, was not to be, as Russo hoped it might become, a virtuous Roman republic. For Pagano it was to be an aristocratic society based on merit, the government, as he described it in the *Saggi*, 'of the

[43] *Monitore napoletano*, p. 386.
[44] *Progetto di costituzione ... del 1799*, pp. 29–31.
[45] *Progetto di costituzione*, in Venturi, ed., p. 909.
[46] See, for instance, the observations of Filangieri's contemporary, Francesantonio Grimaldi, *Reflessioni sopra l'ineguaglianza tra gli uomini*, in *Illuministi italiani*, ed. by Franco Venturi, Milan and Naples, 1958, vol. 5, p. 562.
[47] *Saggi politici*, vol. 2, p. 144.
[48] *Progetto di costituzione*, in Venturi, ed., pp. 909–10.

optimati by virtue'.[49] Although article 396 of the constitution limited distinction between citizens to that which was 'relative to their public function',[50] it restricted citizenship itself – defined as the faculty to create the constitution – to those whose involvement in the society placed them 'at risk through their own true interests'. This explicitly excluded both the 'plebeians absorbed by ignorance and degraded by slavery' and the 'cancerous part of the aristocracy'.[51] (The legal qualifications for citizenship provided by the constitution was: those over 23 – in the French constitution of 1795 the age was 21; those who pay direct contributions to the state; those who exercise a profession; those who know how to read and can recite their 'republican catechism'.)[52] There was, Pagano said, no name for this group in any modern language but, in practice, it seems to have corresponded pretty closely to the older *popolo civile* – the administrative and mercantile class under the viceroyalty – and to the liberal members of the barony. There was to be freedom of the press and freedom of speech (article 398) and a greater degree of access to government and of public accountability. This meant the abolition of that public secrecy which had characterised government under the *ancien régime*, and which had, since at least the late seventeenth century, been regarded as the main source of all the kingdom's political ills. In the new republic all men were encouraged to exercise what Pagano described as 'the faculty of opinion';[53] but for the mass of the people this was to be passive since there was to be no representative assembly – that much, at least, it shared with the ancient republics. Articles 406 and 407 of the constitution thus banned all political parties and restricted all kind of political activity to the constituent assemblies[54] (the members of those assemblies were to be elected, but only from among those persons chosen by the assemblies themselves).

The legislature was to be divided into an upper and a lower house. These, too, were to share with 'the ancient republics' their small size (the upper house was to be composed of fifty members, the lower of 120) and the fact that all their members were to be 'men of mature age, since the drafting of laws is more the effect of cold analysis than of ardent genius'.[55] The executive power was entrusted to a five-man body chosen by the legislative assembly and to be called the 'Archonate' (*Arcontato*), although, as Angelo Lanzelotti, who published the text of the constitution in 1820 (on the eve of another uprising against the monarchy), observed,

---

49 *Saggi politici*, vol. 2, pp. 164–5.
50 *Progetto di costituzione ... del 1799*, p. 122.
51 *Progetto di costituzione*, in Venturi, ed., pp. 910–12.
52 Quoted in Solari, *Studi su Francesco Mario Pagano*, p. 305.
53 *Progetto di costituzione*, in Venturi, ed., p. 909.
54 *Progetto di costituzione ... del 1799*, p. 125.
55 *Progetto di costituzione*, in Venturi, ed., p. 913.

this owed more to the *Directoire* than it did to any feature of the republic of Athens.[56] The meetings of criminal courts were also to be restricted to four sessions with five judges each. The purpose of this limitation on the size of the political machine was precisely to prevent those 'noxious delays' in government, which for Pagano were, like the long delays in court procedure (such as that created by article 219 of the French constitution of 1795 which allowed for the transfer of appeals to a separate court in a neighbouring *département*),[57] another mark of feudal despotism. Since in true republics the government operates in the interests of its people it does not need to hamper its leaders' capacity to act.

Pagano had for long been concerned about the proper structure of the modern republic. Like Montesquieu, he recognised the importance of the separation of powers. But, he argued, since it was 'the natural tendency of every power to enlarge itself', if the two powers were too closely linked then one would eventually come to absorb the other. This, he believed, is what had happened under the French constitution of 1793, in which the executive power had been made too heavily dependent on the legislative; this had finally 'allowed the assembly to become despotic'. If, on the other hand, they are too far apart then 'the political machine' is in danger of becoming 'inactive and languid'.[58] Like Montesquieu, he believed that the model of the mixed English constitution – particularly since England was just the kind of monarchy Peter Leopold's Tuscany had been intended to be – was the best possible government. But with his Vichian (and Machiavellian) preoccupation with processes over time, he feared that the perfect balance of interests might lead to what he called the 'inattentiveness' of the opposing forces. Perfectly balanced societies are slow to respond to change, and as a consequence are more susceptible to the ever-present threat – indeed, Pagano believed, the inevitability – of corruption. With Nelson's ships cruising along the Neapolitan coast, he might be forgiven for thinking that England had long since ceased to be the 'republic that hides under a monarchy' of Montesquieu's imagination. Similarly, although a series of forces in constant opposition might make for a stable constitution, they also ultimately weaken each party, since opposition becomes their only role, 'and each wishing to preserve the right of usurpation will merely abuse their respective right to veto'. And this, too, must inevitably lead to divided, corrupt government, 'uncertain in its outcome and slow to operate'.

The solution to this problem provided in the *Saggi* is the creation of a chamber which has 'no function, neither legislative, nor judiciary, nor

[56] *Progetto di costituzione ... del 1799*, p. 66.
[57] *Progetto di costituzione*, in Venturi, ed., pp. 913–15.
[58] *Ibid.*, p. 917.

executive' and which, because it has none of these powers, will become 'the bulwark of the constitution, the supreme tribunal of power, the guardian of the line which none of those who exercise sovereign power should ever pass'.[59] Just how such a body would work he does not say. But in title 13, article 350 of the constitution this middle chamber became the 'ephorate', an elected assembly with one member from each of the departments of the republic which, like the United States Supreme Court, was to act as the custodian of the constitution, and which alone would have the power to modify it.[60]

Thus protected from both the inertia and the potential corruption of its own members and, crucially, made able to respond rapidly to changes in the outside world, the republic was set to provide the best possible existence for all its members. But in order to make this compelling for a people who had, for the most part, seemed to prefer the old despotic feudal order, the republic had first to modify those 'moral laws which are as constant and necessary as are the laws of physics'.[61] Under their feudal rulers the people of Naples had been kept in a state of permanent civil ignorance. As Lisetta, the heroine of Pagano's verse drama *L'Emilia* – discovered by her father reading the *Spectator* – angrily observes, 'Prison, force and hypocrisy do not produce virtue.'[62] The ignorant are far more prone to the winds of passion, and to disorder, whether sexual or political, than are the educated. Like the Neapolitan women of the drama, the Neapolitan people must be instructed in the values of liberty. For liberty, Pagano declared in the preamble to the constitution, was under threat, 'not only from the usurpation of constitutional power, but also from private citizens and public corruption'. Like Filangieri before him, Pagano believed that a true political society could be created only through the ultimate transformation of a people's customs. This was why the Neapolitan constitution had to lay greater emphasis on the need for moral education than the French had done, French society, in his view, having been traditionally more concerned with the intellectual education of its citizens.[63] The modern republic was to be pacific and commercial, but the need to discipline such people as the Neapolitans in civic virtues demanded, initially at least, some of the sterner ways of the ancients. This was to be achieved by two means. The first was the provision 'in every commune [of] public places and gymnasia set aside for various gymnastic and war-like exercises' and the creation, on 12 February, of a *Sala*

[59] *Saggi politici*, vol. 2, pp. 167–9.
[60] *Progetto di costituzione ... del 1799*, p. 112.
[61] *Contro Sabato Totaro, reo dell'omicidio*, p. 32.
[62] *L'Emilia, commedia di F. M. Pagano*, Naples, 1792, p. 4.
[63] *Progetto di costituzione*, in Venturi, ed., pp. 916–17.

d'istruzione pubblica established in imitation of the Jacobin clubs (although these had, of course, been suppressed in France itself in 1794). This met in the university and, according to article 298 of the constitution, was to comprise all children over the age of seven who, on every feast day, were to learn their republican catechism. The second was the creation of a five-man tribunal of censors – the 'priests of the patria' as Pagano called them – to look after public and private morality. All those, declared article 307 of the constitution, 'who do not live democratically, that is to say all those who lead a dissolute and voluptuous life, who give a vicious education to their family, adopt arrogant and insolent manners ... shall be deprived by the censors of their active and passive rights of citizenship'.[64] Religion itself, however, which Pagano described in the *Saggi* as being born of fear and hierarchy, and on whose dependency upon the vocabularies of force he makes some interesting observations,[65] was to play no role in the new state. The Catholic church was too closely associated with the Bourbon regime ever to be capable of transformation into a civil creed.

Pagano's republicanism owed, in fact, very little to French revolutionary models, and nothing at all to the Jacobinism of which his monarchical enemies accused him. Although he was indebted to Montesquieu for many of his constitutional ideas, he only ever mentions Rousseau to refute him, and never refers to the revolutionary constitutionalists at all. Pagano had been the pupil of Genovesi, a close friend of Filangieri, and his most sustained intellectual project was a continuation – in, as he claimed, a more accessible language – of Vico's *Scienza nuova*. It was from them that he had learnt to recognise the startling absence of anything which could be described as civil society in Naples, a recognition which led to an attempt to re-direct the older structures of power – and in particular the old tripartite society of orders – into new, more civil, directions, through legal and educational reform. The republic fell, as it had arisen, through force of arms and, despite the claims of the *Monitore napoletano* that it had won most of the people to its cause, it remained the liberal dream of a small group of enlightened professionals and aristocrats. In the end Cuoco may have been right in implying that any new society had to be grounded in 'the needs and customs of the people, and by an authority which they believed to be legitimate and national'. True republics could be founded only where there already existed 'the memory of some earlier better government, like that Magna Carta which has been the compass for all the English revolutions'.[66] Without the prior existence

---

[64] *Progetto di costituzione ... del 1799*, p. 138.
[65] *Saggi politici*, vol. 1, pp. 160–1.
[66] Cuoco, *Saggio storico sulla rivoluzione di Napoli*, p. 117.

of the kind of civil society which, in Pagano's eyes, Naples so evidently lacked, the reformer was forced to rely upon the agencies of the state, and in this case those agencies could be called into existence only by a foreign army of occupation.

8 Kant, the French revolution and the definition of the republic

Gareth Stedman Jones

As the task of this volume has been defined, the major problem of 'modern republicanism' after Hobbes and Montesquieu is 'how to link the idea, the project of a moderate, limited, non-despotic government with that of a popular/national sovereignty and of juridical equality (in a society without a king and aristocracy)'. Such a task was confronted by Montesquieu, Madison and Sieyès, as Pasquino and Manin have demonstrated, and arguably by Benjamin Constant and Madame de Staël, as Fontana has revealed. But as the earlier discussion has shown, there has been a real difficulty, historically, in making post-eighteenth-century theorists answer the questions that a modern republican theorist might wish to put to them. As might be expected, the forms of republicanism thrown up by the French revolution possessed, in practice, little direct precedent in theory. Furthermore, if we move outside the frontiers of France, it becomes particularly important to disentangle what it was in the complex sequence of events that sympathisers sympathised with – a problem made more difficult by the ubiquitous term, Jacobin, used and often accepted to describe all who expressed sympathy with the revolution. And it is a difficulty which particularly arises in the case of Kant, both at a superficial and at a deeper level.

At the superficial level, we have the testimony of his friends and contemporaries and of his European reputation in the 1790s. According to his friend Jachmann, he remained hostile to the anti-revolutionary crusade throughout the 1790s.[1] According to Abegg, Kant didn't blush in 1798 to be called a Jacobin. If an anecdote of Varnhagen is to be believed, after the declaration of the republic, and the Terror, although he deplored its excesses, he was said to have exclaimed, like Simeon, 'Lord let your servant depart in peace, for I have lived to see this remarkable day',[2] while another friend, Nicovius, claimed, 'he said that all the horrors which had taken place in France were nothing beside what France had

---

[1] See J. Droz, *L'Allemagne et la révolution française*, Paris, 1949, p. 158.
[2] *Ibid.* The reliability of this report has been questioned in G. Vlachos, *La Pensée politique de Kant*, Paris, 1962.

suffered from the fact of despotism and that the Jacobins were probably right in all their actions'.[3] Certainly, there is nothing in his published writings or unpublished notes to support these claims. However, it may be that these contemporaries did not mishear him, but misunderstood the basis upon which such statements might have been made. Jachmann was nearer the mark in stating of his sympathy, that 'it was the impersonal sympathy of a citizen of the world and of an independent philosopher who observes the construction of a state on the basis of reason, exactly in the same way as a scientist observes an experiment destined to confirm his hypothesis'.[4] When speaking of the French revolution in 'The contest of the faculties', Kant stated that

The occurrence in question is not a phenomenon of revolution, but ... of the *evolution* of a constitution governed by natural right. Such a constitution cannot itself be achieved by furious struggles – for civil and foreign wars will destroy whatever *statutory* order has hitherto prevailed – but it does lead us to strive for a constitution which would be incapable of bellicosity i.e., a republican one.[5]

It was because of his support for republican institutions and in particular because of the distinction he made between a republican form of sovereignty and a republican mode of government (put forward most unambiguously in 'Perpetual peace' in 1795, and rapidly translated into French) that Kant's name was associated particularly with that of Sieyès.[6] The association was made most clearly by the German Girondin

[3] Droz, *L'Allemagne*, p. 158.
[4] *Ibid.*, p. 156.
[5] I. Kant, 'The contest of the faculties', in H. Reiss, ed., *Kant's political writings*, Cambridge, 1970, p. 184. (Henceforth, emphasis is original unless stated otherwise.)
[6] Kant's distinction between republic as a form of sovereignty and as a mode of government built upon an article by Sieyès, which originally appeared in the *Moniteur*, 8 July 1791, and which was translated in *Neues Göttingisches historisches Magazin*, vol. 1 (1792), pp. 341ff. In this piece Sieyès argued:

> in my opinion, every social constitution in which representation does not constitute the essential principle, is a false constitution; whether it be called a monarchy or not. Every collection of men who wish to organise themselves into a state and where not all at the same time can attend to the Commonwealth, has no other choice than that between representatives and rulers, between a lawful government and a despotism.

What mattered according to Sieyès was not whether the executive power was entrusted to a monarchical or republican government, but whether the governemnt was tied to a representative principle. If 'republic' meant representative government, then both parties – monarchists and republicans – were striving for a republic. The difference between them, whether the state should culminate 'in a point' or a 'platform', was not a question of legitimacy, but of fitness. See W. Mager, 'Republik', in O. Brunner *et al.*, eds., *Geschichtliche Grundbegriffe*, Stuttgart, 1984, vol. 5, pp. 607–8. According to Sieyès, both a monarchic and a polyarchic government were compatible with a republican position. His own preferred solution appears to have been that of an elective monarchy and in 1799, after the coup of 18 Brumaire, Sieyès proposed that France choose a 'great elector'. See M. Forsyth, *Reason and revolution. The political thought of the abbé Sieyès*. Leicester, 1987, pp. 178, 181.

sympathiser living in Paris, Karl Oelsner. Oelsner was a fervent admirer of Sieyès and, according to Jacques Droz, was chiefly responsible for Sieyès's fame in Germany. Sieyès, in Oelsner's view, was not only a promoter of liberty, but also the creator of a new social system. By the light of this system man was not on earth for the satisfaction of the prince, but as an end in himself. Sieyès's achievement, Oelsner wrote, was to have preserved authority without sacrificing liberty, through his insistence on the jury system and on the separation of powers, and he was particularly admirable in observing and then rejecting the idea that the rights of man could not be preserved in a monarchy. In the language of Sieyès, the term – monarchy – designated only 'the character of the executive power', not the essence of the regime, which even under a monarchy could remain republican. In re-establishing this distinction, Oelsner went on, Sieyès was Kant's equal. Friends of the truth would learn with joy that 'The citizen of Fréjus and the philosopher of Königsberg had created a continuous chain of thought which stretched from the shore of the Mediterranean to the shores of the Baltic.'[7] It was mainly on the basis of this affinity that Sieyès, who was acquainted with Kant's 'Perpetual peace' through Reinhardt's translation, dispatched an ex-Prussian and now French diplomat, Charles Theremin, to consult with Kant in January 1796. Kant should put himself at the service of the republic, according to Theremin, since 'the study of this philosophy by the French would be a complement of the revolution', and, as he stated in a pamphlet at the same time, 'Europe today has reached the point where it could only be governed by philosophers'.[8] Kant refused to advise, on the grounds that he should not become involved in the affairs of a foreign country. But the rumour persisted, fuelled by the revelation in the *Königsberger Zeitung* that Sieyès had asked for Kant's advice on the republic's constitution, that Kant was destined to become the law-maker of France.

On the surface, the reasons for Kant's sympathy with the revolution and the republic were expressed clearly enough. They are stated in 'The contest of the faculties':

Firstly, there is the *right* of every people to give itself a civil constitution of the kind that it sees fit, without interference from other powers. And secondly, once it is accepted that the only intrinsically *rightful* and morally good constitution which a people can have is by its very nature disposed to avoid wars of aggression (i.e. that the only possible constitution is a republican one, at least in its conception), there is the *aim*, which is also a duty, of submitting to those conditions, by which war, the source of all evils and moral corruption, can be prevented.[9]

---

[7] Droz, *L'Allemagne*, p. 75.
[8] *Ibid.*, p. 160.
[9] Kant, 'The contest of the faculties', pp. 182–3.

But when looked at more closely their clarity as the basis of modern republicanism tends to dissolve. Firstly, it is not simply that Kant is in agreement with Sieyès that republican institutions are compatible with a monarchical form of sovereignty: he further emphasises these institutions to the point where the best republic appears to be a monarchy governed 'in the spirit of republicanism'.[10] In 'Perpetual peace' Kant is most concerned to distinguish a republican constitution from a democratic one. His argument is as follows: states can be classified either according to the different persons who exercise supreme authority, or according to the way in which the nation is governed by its ruler. The first classification – form of sovereignty – can take three forms: autocracy, aristocracy or democracy. The second classification – form of government – 'relates to the way in which the state, setting out from its constitution (i.e. an act of general will whereby the mass becomes a people), makes use of its plenary power. The form of government, in this case, will be either *republican* or *despotic*.'[11] Republicanism, in the sense that Kant wished to identify himself with the term, is that principle 'whereby the executive power (the government) is separated from the legislative power'. By contrast, despotism 'prevails in a state if the laws are made and arbitrarily executed by one and the same power, and it reflects the will of the people only in so far as the ruler treats the will of the people as his own private will'. On this criterion, as a form of sovereignty 'democracy in the truest sense of the word is necessarily a despotism'. The democracy that Kant had in mind was clearly of the direct kind, for his objection was that 'it establishes an executive power through which all the citizens may make decisions about (and indeed against) the single individual without his consent, so the decisions are made by all the people and yet not by all the people', which meant that the general will was in contradiction with itself and hence with freedom.[12]

Any form of government which was not representative was *an anomaly*, because one and the same person could not be both the legislator and the executor of his own will. The 'anomaly' was akin to that in logical reasoning, in which a general proposition could not at the same time be a secondary proposition subsuming the particular within the general. Autocracy and aristocracy, Kant conceded, could also leave room for despotic government but in those cases it was at least possible that the form of government might accord 'with the *spirit* of a representative system'. From there Kant confidently went on to conclude that 'the smaller the number of ruling persons in a state and the greater their powers of

[10] *Ibid.*, p. 184.
[11] Kant, 'Perpetual peace', in Reiss, ed., *Kant's political writings*, p. 100.
[12] *Ibid.*, p. 101.

representation, the more the constitution will approximate to its republican potentiality'. For this reason, it was more difficult in an aristocracy than in a monarchy 'to reach this one and only perfectly lawful kind of constitution'.[13] But even this minimal definition of a republic as a mode of government appeared too constricting. Kant did not specify any institutional or procedural mechanisms whereby powers might be separated. 'Spirit' means no more than that. Thus the republican mode of government might be one in which 'the state would be administered by a single ruler (the monarch) acting by analogy with the laws which a people would give itself in conformity with universal principles of right.'[14] It is not surprising that on this basis Oelsner could consider that Prussia also possessed a republican mode of government, while England, in Kant's opinion, conversely, possessed all the hallmarks of despotism.[15]

The extent of these qualifications would also appear to diminish the force of Kant's international proposals for perpetual peace. The emphatic and apodeictic character of Kant's association between international peace and republic, Vlachos notes, seems to be closely related to the declaration of non-aggressive intentions made by the French governments in 1792 and 1793.[16] But the explicit justification given in 'Perpetual peace' links it very firmly to a representative form of government:

If, as is inevitably the case under this constitution, the consent of the citizens is required to decide whether or not war is to be declared, it is very natural that they will have great hesitation in embarking on so dangerous an enterprise ... But under a constitution where the subject is not a citizen, and which is, therefore, not republican, it is the simplest thing in the world to go to war. For the head of state is not a fellow citizen, but of the owner of the state ... He can thus decide on war, without any significant reason ...[17]

Lurking in the interstices of this analysis is an interesting blend of old and new republican conceptions. The old association of republican *vivere civile* with *grandezza*, and hence with war, is now displaced by an equation of civil participation with peace. For the reason why a true republic would not engage in war is that for the citizens it would mean 'Calling down on themselves all the miseries of war, such as doing all the fighting themselves, supplying the costs of war from their own resources, painfully making good the ensuing devastation, and as the crowning evil, having to take upon themselves a burden of debt which would embitter peace

---

[13] *Ibid.*
[14] Kant, 'The Contest of the faculties', p. 184.
[15] *Ibid.*, p. 186–7.
[16] Vlachos, *La Pensée.*
[17] Kant, 'Perpetual peace', p. 100.

itself.'[18] Conversely, a rich corrupt state like eighteenth-century Britain, by using a mercenary army instead of a militia, and by employing the national debt to support its external affairs, was associated with 'ease in making war'.[19] Kant's discussion of the British case further clarifies his emphasis upon the *spirit* of republican government. Despite a constitution in which the will of the monarch was limited by the two houses of parliament, the people of Great Britain lived in reality under an absolute monarchy: 'A mendacious form of publicity deceives the people with the illusion that the monarchy is limited by a law which emanates from them, while their representatives, won over by bribery, secretly subject them to an *absolute monarch*.'[20] 'The monarch of Great Britain', Kant added, 'has waged numerous wars without asking the people's consent'. Kant's model of republican government, so far as its features could be discerned in phenomenal form, clearly had little to do with Montesquieu's picture of monarchy, but nor – apart from its endorsement of a militia – did it share any of Rousseau's nostalgia for classical republics. Kant was dismissive of the Romans and unsentimental towards fashionable German fantasies about the Greeks. 'The so-called "republics" of antiquity ... invariably ended in despotism', because they lacked a representative system.[21] On the other hand, an allegedly representative system like that of Britain was, in fact, an absolute monarchy because it lacked 'publicity'. The truly republican form which Kant had in mind would 'only be achieved by a laborious process, after innumerable wars and conflicts'. In the meantime, it was 'the duty of monarchs to govern in a *republican* (not a democratic) manner, even though they may rule autocratically'. 'In other words', wrote Kant, 'they should treat the people in accordance with principles akin in spirit to the laws of freedom which a people of mature rational powers would prescribe for itself, even if the people is not literally asked for its consent'.[22] Since, however, philosopher kings were the exception rather than the rule, a true rather than 'mendacious' form of publicity was essential to assist development towards its desired end. The only group who might be claimed to possess 'mature rational powers' were 'the free teachers of right, i.e. the philosophers'. Such a group was often decried as a menace to the state, but this was mistaken, 'for they do not address themselves in familiar tones to the *people* (who themselves take little or no notice of them and their writings), but in *respectful* tones to the state,

---

[18] *Ibid.* The role of the military in a republican form of government would be purely defensive. Citizens would undertake 'voluntary military training from time to time in order to secure themselves and their fatherland against attacks from outside', p. 100.

[19] *Ibid.*

[20] Kant, '.The Contest of the faculties', p. 187.

[21] Kant, 'Perpetual peace', p. 102.

[22] 'The Contest of the faculties', p. 187.

which is thereby implored to take the rightful needs of the people to heart.'[23]

This brief analysis of the meaning of republicanism in Kant's late political writings ('Perpetual peace' and 'The contest of the faculties') naturally raises the question, in what sense the French revolution affected Kant's political philosophy, and whether his 'republicanism' depended at all upon the events in France. For, as will be clear, the tendency to extend moral liberty towards civil and political liberty was present in Kant's writings before the revolution, and his enthusiasm for the French experiment was in no way incompatible with his public claim to remain the king of Prussia's 'most loyal subject'. But so as to elucidate and situate the effect it did have, it is first necessary to say something of his antecedent philosophical evolution and of the place of politics within it.

In order to understand what distinguished the republicanism of Kant from that of Jacobinism, it is best to start not with Montesquieu but with Rousseau – an inspiration in common to both, but developed in wholly discrepant directions by them. In the thread that connected Rousseau with the Montagnards, 'conscience speaks the language of nature, which everything has caused us to forget'.[24] The culprit was history. History had blocked justice by carrying man away from nature into a fatal spiral of demand and satisfaction, spreading mastery and slavery in its wake. This corruption – civilisation – had somehow been superimposed upon the natural life-cycle of the people, modelled upon the biological career of the individual. On the basis of this phylogenetic analogy, as portrayed for example in *Emile*, this viciousness could only have been surmounted, had man received a different upbringing from the one which civilisation had actually accorded him. The outlook was bleak, but Rousseau conceded that men and peoples were sometimes accorded a second birth: Sparta and Rome among them. It was upon this basis that, according to Montagnard understanding, France might be returned to 'nature', and to a second birth. 'If nature created man good', declared Robespierre, 'he must be allowed to return to nature'. 'The French people, that large industrious class ... is untouched by the causes of depravation which doomed those of superior condition.'[25] France might be returned to the condition of Rousseau's 'Corsicans' and from there start afresh.

Kant also was profoundly impressed by Rousseau. Rousseau's conception of liberty as self-enacted law became the basis of Kant's conception of transcendental freedom. Rousseau was the 'Newton of the moral

[23] *Ibid.*, p. 186.
[24] J.-J. Rousseau, *Emile*, London, 1972, p. 254.
[25] See G. A. Kelly, *Idealism, politics and history: sources of Hegelian thought*, Cambridge, 1969, pp. 70–1.

world'. Kant was struck by Rousseau's observation that 'thanks to conscience, we are able to be men without being scholars'[26] and that thought was embodied in Kant's conviction that theoretical reason was useless in teaching men how to act. *The critique of practical reason* with its premise of equality in moral intuition was elaborated upon this insight. But Kant sharply dissented from Rousseau's association between nature, origins and infancy. If Kant accepted Rousseau's uncoupling of knowledge and morality, he did not see them as antitheses. Moreover, he firmly rejected Rousseau's tendency to link the ethical and the customary; there was nothing to be learnt from the Corsicans, a position which strongly distinguished Kant from other adherents of German Rousseauism, such as Möser or Herder. Civilisation was not the opposite of morality, but rather a mediating term, between nature and morality. The state of nature was akin to a Hobbesian state of war, and the social contract was not a quasi-historical act by which civil society might have originated, but rather an idea to which legal–political order would tend in a moral universe.[27] In his 'Idea for a universal history' Kant agreed with Rousseau that 'We are *cultivated* to a high degree by art and science. We are *civilised* to the point of excess in all kinds of social courtesies and proprieties. But we are still a long way from the point where we could consider ourselves *morally* mature.'[28] However, 'the idea that morality is indeed present in culture' was obstructed by the 'vain and violent schemes of expansion' on the part of political rulers. Moreover, nature aided humanity in forcing 'our species to discover a law of equilibrium to regulate the essentially healthy hostility which prevails among the states and is produced by their freedom. Men are compelled to reinforce this law by introducing a system of united power, hence a cosmopolitan system of general political security.'[29] Humanity was only 'at a half-way mark in its development'. It was only if 'this last stage which humanity had to surmount' was left out of account, that Rousseau's preference for the state of savagery might be accepted. In Kant's hands, Rousseau's *Emile* no longer signified what man might have become, if God had led him from nature to society, rather than abandoning him.[30] It became, instead, a paradoxical vision of human advance under the mysterious moral tutorship of nature. In place, therefore, of Rousseau's despairing and impossible 'second nature', Kant

[26] Rousseau, *Emile*, p. 254.
[27] Kant, *On the old saw: that may be right in theory but it won't work in practice*, trans. by E. B. Ashton, Philadelphia, Pa., 1974, pp. 69–70; I. Kant, 'Groundwork of the metaphysic of morals', in Reiss, ed., *Kant's political writings*, p. 143.
[28] Kant, 'Idea for a universal history', in Reiss, ed., *Kant's political writings*, p. 49.
[29] *Ibid.*
[30] Kelly, *Idealism*, p. 50.

speaks of the creation of 'a second nature out of the material supplied to it by actual nature'.[31]

There are many commentators who claim that the French revolution had only the most superficial effect upon Kant's philosophy or even that it was irrelevant. Some claim that in political terms his philosophy remained one of enlightened absolutism both in the 1780s and in the 1790s. Others, such as Cassirer, saw the more explicitly liberal writings of the 1790s simply as further exploration of consequences implied by the gospel of freedom propounded in the field of ethics.[32] The precise relationship between the evolution of Kant's thought and the occurrence of the revolution is made difficult to determine with any certainty because 1789 coincided with Kant's construction of his Third Critique, the *Critique of judgement*, whose purpose was precisely to ascertain in what way freedom could find effect in the phenomenal world, and it is arguable that that hopeful but cautious work might have taken the same form even if the revolution had not occurred. From the point of view of the immediate impact of Kant's writings, however, this position seems implausible. Wittingly or unwittingly Kant was immensely influential in setting up an intellectual framework within which Germans came to judge the revolution, and in this sense contributed considerably to a debilitation of republican thinking in nineteenth-century Germany. Thought of a republic became inextricably linked with the problem of the relationship between ethical freedom and political right, and pragmatic problems of constitutionalism became mired in a prior framework of moral pedagogy. Thus neither 1848 nor 1918 found Germans prepared with an armoury of republican solutions.

To see why this was so, we must go back to Kant's writing of the 1780s, in order to understand why his reaction to the revolution proved so decisive. What was clear at that point is that he had no more precise idea than Rousseau had had of how his developing conception of freedom could make itself effective in the historical and political world. His 'Idea for a universal history' and 'What is enlightenment?' illustrate this point. On the one hand, they could be taken as endorsements of enlightenment absolutism. Freedom was the long-term destination of the species, but for the moment political discipline and intellectual freedom were what was required. 'Man is an animal who needs a master ... to break his self-will and force him to obey a universally valid will under which everyone can

---

[31] I. Kant, *The critique of judgement*, trans. by J.C. Meredith, Oxford, 1978, p. 176. Kant continues there: 'by this means we get a sense of our freedom from the law of association (which attaches to the empirical employment of the imagination), with the result that the material can be borrowed by us from nature in accordance with that law, but be worked up by us into something else – namely, what surpasses nature.'

[32] E. Cassirer, *Kant's life and thought*, trans. by J. Haden, New Haven, Conn., p. 407.

be free.'[33] The conjugation was between a strong monarchy and spiritual and intellectual freedom. Such a framework was explicitly preferred to that of a republic. As Kant stated in 'What is enlightenment?': 'But only a ruler who is himself enlightened and has no fear of phantoms, yet who likewise has at hand a well-disposed and numerous army to guarantee public security, may say what no republic would dare to say: *argue as much as you like and about whatever you like, but obey!*'[34]

Nevertheless, the schema within which the Frederickian state is endorsed is only a temporally limited one. For the long-term plan of nature is that man should develop his faculties, happiness and perfection solely through the efforts of his own reason; and, even if the initial stage of man's release from his self-incurred immaturity is compatible with absolutism, that destiny will take him way beyond it. It would certainly put into question the position of the master who breaks man's will, for the master himself was also an animal needing a master.[35] Moreover, the position of the master was being weakened in other ways, too. Kant reversed the usual procedure of granting freedom to private opinion, but enforcing restrictions upon the public expression of views, by stating that while 'the private use of reason may often be very narrowly restricted without hindering the progress of the enlightenment', on the other hand 'the public use of one's reason must always be free'.[36] As this freedom of thought worked back on the character of the people, they would become 'capable of managing freedom', and it would become an advantage to the govenment to treat 'man, *who is more than a machine*, in a manner appropriate to his dignity'.[37] Already, the customary natural law justification of the absolute ruler was being weakened at a crucial point: the ruler's 'law-giving authority rested on his uniting the general public will in his own'. But this procedure is no longer taken as axiomatic, for it is qualified by the statement that 'something which a people may not even impose upon itself can still less be imposed on it by a monarch'.[38]

The latent conflict between freedom and authority in these writings is mainly evaded by maintaining the pitch of discussion at the level of the species rather than at that of individuals.[39] The destiny of the species is

---

[33] Kant, 'Idea for a universal history', p. 46.
[34] I. Kant, 'What is enlightenment?', in Reiss, ed., *Kant's political writings*, p. 55.
[35] 'But where is he [man] to find such a master? Nowhere else but in the human species. But this master will also be an animal who needs a master.' Kant, 'Idea for a universal history', p. 46.
[36] Kant, 'What is enlightenment?', p. 55.
[37] *Ibid.*, p. 60.
[38] *Ibid.*, p. 58.
[39] 'In man (as the only rational creature on earth), these natural capacities which are directed towards the use of his reason are such that they could be developed only in the species, but not in the individual.' Kant, 'Idea for a universal history', p. 42.

freedom, but the effectiveness of the moral freedom of individuals in the phenomenal world is not discussed. Individuals use freedom to be above nature and yet, in terms of historical explanation, they conform to it. The moral destiny of man was that his works, when perfect, would become nature. Nature, in endowing man with reason as well as with instinct, could be considered to possess a moral purpose. Thus human history as a whole could be regarded 'as the realisation of a hidden plan of nature' in which nature guided man through antagonisms to the rational end of a 'perfect political constitution', as the only possible state within which all natural capacities of material can be developed.[40] It produced the transformation of 'the primitive natural capacity for moral discrimination into definite practical principles'; 'the pathologically enforced social union is transformed into a *moral* whole'.[41]

The problem, though, was how it did so. For, far from being the result of the incursion of freedom into nature, it seemed to employ exclusively Mandevillian techniques. History was placed in the realm of nature; the place of moral freedom was not discussed except through its putative empirical effects which were too dispersed to be knowable. It was only conceivable in an indirect sense of a system of nature which gives an external regulative organisation to internally unplanned activities of the whole species.[42] History was a source of natural knowledge, not a field for the demonstration of the effects of men's moral action.

Part of the interest of these effects lies in what they did not explore. For in the earlier *Critique of pure reason*, Kant had thrown out various hints about the possible bridges that might be built between morality and experience. In that work, Kant had drawn a sharp line between knowledge and action, between experience and things-in-themselves, between nature and freedom, the theoretical and the practical. The main point about action, freedom and things-in-themselves was that they were not knowable. But, if transcendental ideas of reason had supersensible objects which were not knowable, they could still be validly employed as heuristic principles: statements which assumed an 'as if'. These were 'regulative principles of reason' and could in that capacity possess 'practical power', they could supply a moral standard and thus 'form the basis of the

[40] *Ibid.*, p. 50.
[41] *Ibid.*, p. 44–5.
[42] 'The only way out for the philosopher, since he cannot assume that mankind follows any rational *purpose of its own* in its collective actions, is for him to attempt to discover a *purpose in nature* behind this senseless course of human events, and decide whether it is after all possible to formulate in terms of a definite plan of nature a history of creatures who act without a plan of their own.' ('Idea for a universal history', p. 42.)

possible perfection of certain actions'.[43] One such idea was that of nature itself. For theoretical reason's vain search for ultimate unity makes it 'evident that the ultimate intention of nature in her wise provision for us, had indeed, in the constitution of our reason, been directed to moral interests alone'.[44] Thus, these regulative ideas systematise knowledge in such a way as to indicate the susceptibility of experience to purposive action. They do so, however, only by supplying an organising unity to empirical facts; they do not suggest an authority for action. Most important in this respect was Kant's resolution of the antinomy of causality, by turning it into a regulative idea. In so doing he considered that he had not and could not prove the reality of freedom, but had established that 'causality through freedom is at least not incompatible with nature'. Once placed securely in the world of practice rather than knowledge, the laws of morality were no longer 'a mere idea', but 'at the same time a practical idea which really can have, as it also ought to have, an influence upon the sensible world, to bring that world, so far as may be possible, into conformity with the idea'.[45]

The world of spirit became pure act and the political corollary of this ethical sphere would be the establishment of a 'constitution allowing the greatest possible human freedom in accordance with laws by which the freedom of each is made to be consistent with that of all the others'.[46]

In the 1780s not only did Kant not extend these connections between morality and experience further, as the political writings of the mid-1780s testify, but in his 'Groundwork of the metaphysic of morals' and the *Critique of practical reason*, he pushed them further apart. The point of both works was to establish an absolute separation between the rational and empirical side of ethics. 'Is it not of the utmost necessity', Kant asked, 'to construct a pure moral philosophy which is completely freed from everything which may be only empirical and thus belong to anthropology?'[47] The moral society prescribed by the categorical imperative and its various derivatives seemed like the provision of an ethical foundation for a political constitution. But the ruler of this democratic kingdom of ends was God, and the employment of political language – a figure of speech. No bridge was offered between this noumenal realm and politics, for politics – like history – had been left mainly in the realm of nature and nothing based on experience could be a source or basis of moral action.

[43] I. Kant, *Critique of pure reason*, trans. by N. Kemp Smith, London, 1950, p. 486; and see on this L. Krieger, *The German idea of freedom*, Chicago, Ill., 1957, pp. 95–7.
[44] *Ibid.*, p. 632–3.
[45] *Ibid.*, p. 637.
[46] *Ibid.*, p. 312.
[47] I. Kant, 'Groundwork of the metaphysic of morals', cited in Krieger, *The German idea*, p. 99.

It was the French revolution which breached this divide between the realm of nature and the realm of morals. The occurrence was both a phenomenon and 'something moral in principle'. As he reflected in 'The contest of the faculties':

A phenomenon of this kind which has taken place in human history *can never be forgotten*, since it has revealed in human nature an aptitude and power for improvement of a kind which no politician could have thought up by examining the course of events in the past. Only nature and freedom, combined within mankind in accordance with principles of right, have enabled us to forecast it.[48]

What most especially impressed Kant was not so much the drama of political reversal itself, as the 'attitude of the onlookers'. 'They openly express universal yet disinterested sympathy for one set of protagonists against their adversaries, even at the risk that their partiality could be of great disadvantage to themselves.' Their reaction showed that 'man has a moral character, or at least the makings of one'. Their disinterested sympathy could not have been caused by anything other than 'a moral disposition within the human race'.[49] This position was echoed in the *Critique of judgement*, whose theoretical ambition was to construct a bridge between the First Critique and the Second: judgement lay at a midway point between reason and understanding; judgement was that which thinks the particular in terms of the universal. The key concept was reflective judgement which hypothesises a universal causality as analogous to the production of individual actions by an intelligent being like man, i.e. as components in a series directed to a certain end. The teleological hypotheses of the reflective judgement are definite analogies whose basic principle links the particular in man's natural experience with the individual in his moral action, and consciously attempts to organise man's knowledge of the natural world on the standards of the moral world, thereby preparing experience for the reception of his freedom. Physical teleology as a mere subjective hypothesis brings no authority and does not, therefore, supersede the mechanism of real natural laws. What it does, is indicate that in nature, in addition to mechanical causality, there is the possibility of a causality analogous to that of men in their moral action. It is thus suggestive of the way in which 'the concept of freedom is meant to actualise in the sensible world the end proposed by its laws'.[50]

The consequence of this for Kant's conception of history was indicated in his section on culture. In the 'Idea for a universal history' the end to which nature strove was a condition in which men could develop their

---

[48] Kant, 'The Contest of the faculties', p. 184.
[49] *Ibid.*, p. 182.
[50] Kant, *Critique of judgement*, p. 14.

natural faculties, an end which still envisaged man as part of nature and kept the whole plan within the frame of nature. Now, however, this end seemed ambiguously to prepare an end beyond it: for now it might be possible to discern 'nature striving on purposive lines to give us that education that opens the door to higher ends than it can itself afford'.[51] The arts and sciences of culture would 'prepare the way for sovereignty in which reason alone shall hold sway'. The status of the plan of nature changed, from being a regulative idea which brought system into the knowledge of human history, to a concept of reflective judgement which organised human experience so as to show the possibility of effecting his freedom within it through action.[52] The implication was that if the world was viewed via natural laws as physically interchangeable entities moving physically through time, then the role of freedom was to inject dynamism into certain of these entities, giving them self-movement and a vital inter-relationship of parts. His example was that of an organism, the only natural being to which a physical end could be ascribed. In an organism the parts and the whole produce each other, both as ends and as means. Thus an organism was a 'self-propagating formative power', which could not be explained solely by mechanical movement. Organism was then in turn used as the basis of an analogy to the free civil constitution of 1789. 'Organisation' could be used to describe the constitution of this state in the constituent assembly, 'For in a whole of this kind certainly no member should be mere means, but should also be an end, and seeing that he contributes to the possibility of the entire body, should have his position and function in turn defined by the idea of the whole.'[53]

This analogy provided the basis upon which Kant attempted to think the effectiveness of freedom in the phenomenal world in his political writings in the 1790s. Individuals acting according to the laws of freedom could not fashion the world simply in their image within the temporal political realm, but they could supply the dynamic and cohesive elements amid the machinations of natural political entities.

Perhaps the most obvious example of this is in 'Theory and practice', where Kant constructed a constitutional structure whose independence was based upon a moral analogy, but whose reference was to the world of experience. The aim was to show that *a priori* legislating reason embodying principles of freedom was compatible with the order established by the natural laws of political experience. The main point was to establish constitutional principles not based upon experience. Laws and rights had nothing to do with men's natural purposes, which would have brought

[51] Kant, 'Critique of teleological judgement', in *Critique of judgement*, p. 97.
[52] Krieger, *The German idea*, p. 110.
[53] Kant, 'Critique of teleological judgement', p. 23.

back happiness as a goal. On the contrary, right was 'the limitation of every man's freedom so that it harmonises with the freedom of every other man in so far as harmonisation is possible according to a general law',[54] and law was the coercive rule which ensured the possibility of that harmony. From right three *a priori* principles follow: the freedom of every member of society as a man, the equality of each member with every other as subject, and the autonomy of each member of the commonwealth as a citizen. In other words the normative principle of right could be inferred (with the addition of coercion) from the categorical imperative outlined in the 'Groundwork of the metaphysic of morals'.

But there we return to the point where the analysis began, for when applied to the present phenomenal world, these principles became diluted to the point where they no longer conflicted with the structure of existing states. The autonomous political rights of citizens were given the subjunctive status. The criterion of judgement of laws was whether 'they could have originated in the original contract'. 'The inalienable rights' which people had against the head of state could not be coercive and the limitation which the three principles imposed on the head of state 'obviously applies to the law maker's judgement only, not to the subject's'.[55] There was, on the other hand, nothing subjunctive about the statement 'the people never have any right of coercion (any right to be refractory in word or deed) against the head of state'.[56]

At the beginning of this chapter, the problem confronting modern republican thought (i.e. after Hobbes and Montesquieu) was defined as that of linking the idea or project of a moderate, limited, non-despotic government with popular or national sovereignty and juridical equality in a society without a king or an aristocracy. In a broad sense, Kant's political writings certainly did attempt to address this sort of question. His failure to produce a solution which looks theoretically plausible or has proved historically workable only highlights how difficult it was to provide a rigorous and systematic answer to the question.

Despite what now seems the naivety, unrealism or unattractiveness of much of Kant's political thought, his starting point has as much claim to modernity as that of other major political thinkers in the eighteenth century. Even before the French revolution, his political writings presupposed a society based upon exchange, civil equality and the absence or imminent disappearance of a privileged aristocracy. Kant was in accord with writers like Hume and Smith in believing that the political precondition of the viability of such a society depended upon the presence or

[54] I. Kant, 'Theory and practice', in Reiss, ed., *Kant's political writings*, p. 58.
[55] *Ibid.*, p. 55.
[56] *Ibid.*, p. 70.

absence of despotism, rather than the more pragmatic and classical question about the three forms of state. It was mainly for this reason that he so emphasised the importance of a republican manner of governing. In modern parlance, Kant's republican state was simply what most people now call a liberal state. It was explicitly anti-paternalist and eschewed all organic metaphor or any appeal to tradition of the kind appealed to by Burke and his German followers. Similarly, Kant broke entirely with the nostalgic conceptions of the ancient republic, whether Greek or Roman. His rigorous separation of ethics and politics distinguished sharply between the laudable aims of the 'moral politician' and the mystifying confusions of the 'political moralist'. He was thus unsentimental about 'honour' and 'virtue', and equally scathing about the more modern version of the same confusion, i.e. that the purpose of the state was to promote happiness. The state for Kant was a precarious artificial entity; its role was to organise, not happiness or virtue, but right or justice. Its arrangements could be validly applied even to a 'race of devils'. As Kant argued in 'Theory and practice',

If the supreme power makes laws which are primarily directed towards happiness (the affluence of the citizens, increased population etc.), this cannot be regarded as the end for which a civil constitution was established, but only as a means of *securing the rightful state*, especially against external enemies of the people ... The aim is not, as it were, to make the people happy against its will, but only to ensure its continued existence as a commonwealth.[57]

Where Kant departed from the more familiar path of liberal republicanism was in his inability to incorporate a genuinely pluralist notion of power within this state. Kant's relationship with Hobbes was mediated by Rousseau rather than by Locke and Montesquieu. As a result, the notion of civil equality was more heavily underlined and the idea of representation assumed a quite different meaning from that current in England, France or America.

Kant was Hobbesian in his acceptance of the indivisibility of sovereignty and the association of political authority with a unitary will buttressed by force. Antagonism was the fruitful natural progenitor of progress; 'unsocial sociability' described the character of civil society. For these reasons, man was an animal that needed a master. Outside the state, there was no 'people', only anarchy and the mob. There could thus be no question of a right to resistance or a right to rebellion, however tyrannical a state might be.

But, on the other hand, a Hobbesian position was inadequate in its simple equation between legitimacy and force. In addition, 'There must

57 *Ibid.*, p. 80.

also be a *spirit of freedom*, for in all matters concerning universal human duties, each individual requires to be convinced by reason that the coercion which prevails is lawful, otherwise he would be in contradiction with himself.' There were also more pragmatic grounds for building in a notion of consent: 'Obedience without the spirit of freedom is the effective cause of all *secret societies*.'[58]

In the Anglo-French tradition deriving from Locke and Montesquieu, the problem of consent was resolved through representative institutions and institutional devices to ensure an effective separation of powers between legislative, executive and judiciary. So far as these devices were purely technical – mechanisms like bi-cameralism to ensure delay in decision-making, for instance – Kant showed little interest in them. But, in so far as they were associated with the empirical example of Great Britain, such solutions were unacceptable. Either such arrangements, tacitly or explicitly, contravened the presupposition of juridical equality by smuggling in quasi-sociological conceptions of the aristocracy as an intermediary force; or, at the very least, they tended to undermine the assumption of the indivisibility of sovereignty, the presupposition upon which civil freedom was based. The problem was that if there were to be 'a universally valid will under which everyone can be free', then man required a master to break his self-will and to force him to obey it. This 'master', as Kant admitted, would also be 'an animal who needs a master', but the 'master' of this latter 'master' could not take on the form of representatives of the people in an ordinary parliamentary sense since the role of the representative of the sovereign will of the people was already performed by the monarch or holder of supreme power.[59]

It was this position that divided Kant from the constitutional theories of republicanism developed from the writings of Montesquieu, Madison or Sieyès. In Kant's theory, the executive is not juxtaposed to the legislative, but rather to the sovereign power which resides in the person of the legislator. This originating sovereign power was the 'people', but not the people as an empirical or historical aggregate, only the people as an idea of reason. Kant strongly opposed any notion of the social contract as a historical event, not simply because it was unlikely that such an event had ever occurred, but because, in his thinking, the contract as the rational basis of a republic was not the origin, but the goal of the state, the rational norm to which the state would gravitate. The movement towards this goal could come only from the ruler who would govern in a republican manner. The separation of powers was not between ruler and ruled, but between the executive power and the rational will of the people as

[58] *Ibid.*, p. 85.
[59] 'Idea for a universal history', in Reiss, ed., *Kant's political writings*, p. 46.

sovereign – in other words, the sovereignty of the law. The possibility of the greater participation of the actual people in the actual business of government depended upon the people first learning to accept this sovereignty of law. The direction of history was from arbitrary origins to rational form, a movement through which the spirit and letter of republican government would approximate more and more closely to one another. As Kant put it in the 'Groundwork of the metaphysic of morals':

The old empirical (and statutory) forms, which serve only to effect the *subjection* of the people, should accordingly resolve themselves into the original (rational) form which alone makes *freedom* the principle and indeed condition of all *coercion*. For coercion is required for a just political constitution in the truest sense, and this will eventually be realised in letter as well as in spirit.[60]

In practice, what Kant's position meant was that no institutional constraint was placed upon the operation of the executive. The three powers (*trias politicas*) discussed in the 'Groundwork of the metaphysic of morals' and elsewhere were only normative constraints, which the ruler might impose upon himself; the only aid available to the monarch in the observation of such norms would be the existence of freedom of discussion among philosophers – the guardians of the purity of the idea of the noumenal republic.

Thus, in place of any paternalist or organic conception of the state, Kant substituted a pedagogical idea, which generated the question – persistent within the German tradition down to 1918 – of whether the people were yet ready to assume their awesome moral responsibility. Political reform was not to be the cause, but the consequence of the progress of enlightenment, pushed forward under the aegis of the alliance between monarchy and philosophy. It was the failure to follow this pedagogical sequence which came to be seen as the reason for the calamitous climax of the French revolution. As Schiller put it, as early as 1794:

The fabric of the natural state is tottering, its rotting foundations giving way, and there seems to be a physical possibility of setting law on the throne, of honouring man at last as an end in himself, and making true freedom the basis of political associations. Vain hope! The moral possibility is lacking and a moment so prodigal of opportunity finds a generation unprepared to receive it. Man portrays himself in his actions. And what a figure he cuts in the drama of the present time. On the one hand, a return to the savage state, on the other, to complete lethargy. In other words, to the two extremes of human depravity, and both united in a single epoch.[61]

---

[60] In Reiss, ed., *Kant's political writings*, p. 163.
[61] F. Schiller, *On the aesthetic education of man*, trans. by E. M. Wilkinson and L. A. Willoughby, Oxford, 1982, p. 25.

Kant was saved from this sort of pessimism only by the glimmer of hope that he discerned in the evidence of disinterested sympathy which he sensed all over Europe in the 1790s. But that position was too fragile to be sustained among his followers. Among Kant's immediate successors, either the delicate distinctions between politics and ethics were preserved, or politics would cease altogether to be a priority – in which case, the actuality of republican government would be relegated to a remote future after the aesthetic education of mankind had taken place.

9 French historians and the reconstruction of the republican tradition, 1800–1848

François Furet

The idea of the Old Regime did not disappear from France with that first 'ending' of the Revolution that was the Napoleonic regime. No doubt, the Consular reorganisation effectively neutralised the historical content of the Old Regime by drawing liberally upon many of its elements within the context of a post-revolutionary edifice, beginning with the appropriation of the political authority by a single individual. All that the Bonapartist monarchy retained of the 'before' and 'after' 1789, helped the French to forget their taste for, and even their memory of, the great rupture. Moreover, the French responded by giving a quasi-unanimous approval to the new administrative state, which they would not renounce during the nineteenth or twentieth centuries. Nonetheless, even as emperor, Bonaparte remained a vulnerable sovereign; the offspring of his own genius and his military victories, he was infinitely more fragile than the state he had created. On the day in 1814 when he laid down his arms before the European coalition, his son disappeared with him and his ephemeral realm. But he had expected this, had even proclaimed it in 1813, at the beginning of his ruin: 'After me, the Revolution, or rather the ideas that made it, will recover their course. It will be like a book from which one takes the marker, to resume reading the page at which it had been closed.'[1]

It was the Restoration which recreated or rediscovered the opposition between Old Regime and Revolution. The French king took up his script at the very place where his brother lost his thread in 1789. He dated the Charter from the 'nineteenth year' of his reign: an inevitable extravagance given that his power was hereditary, but a dubious symbol, since the French had other memories. Although he did not restore the Old Regime, he was constrained to rule as if he had succeeded it, which was enough to place him outside of the national memory. Had he wanted to, he could not have restored the world in which he came of age, precisely because the Old

---

[1] In a speech by Mathieu Molé receiving Tocqueville to the Académie Française, 21 April 1842. The same statement is also reported in Marquis de Noailles, *Le Comte Molé*, Paris, 1922, vol. 1.

Regime died in 1789. Thus, what so many French hated as a 'return' was nothing more than a belated invention of the restored monarchy which, like all of France since 1789, was condemned to innovate. This 'Old Regime', reputedly returning to the France of 1814 like some kind of revenge or curse, had never existed in the national history. It was a figure of the past that had been transformed and renewed by the Revolution: neither the aristocratic monarchy, the alliance of throne and altar, the clerical obsession with repentance, nor the fear of the common people belonged to the pre-1789 repertoire. Rather, they created an image of the Old Regime that was antagonistic to the Revolution, and consequently inseparable from the break of 1789.

However, to reign securely, the monarchy had to exorcise this break and reunite the two histories of France around the throne. Such was the advice that the two greatest writers of the period, Germaine de Staël and René de Chateaubriand, gave to Louis XVIII at about the same time. Together their voices persisted vainly, if in different registers, in trying to reunite what had been separated in 1789. Each, in its own way, testified to the irreparable nature of the break.

What did Mme de Staël say to the successor of the Bourbons as he returned to the throne of his ancestors?[2] Exactly this: that he must forget his friends and even his recollections, in order to fix his attention upon the constraints of the present and upon a monarchic past that was older than his own memory. His friends, his recollections inevitably drew him to the last thirty years at Versailles and the subsequent exile, thus providing his own particular idea of the Old Regime and his condemnation of what crushed and followed it. Mme de Staël, on the contrary, sought to reconstruct a national history common both to the monarchy and the Revolution. She wished to give back to the restored king an ancient heritage he had forgotten, and a more recent heritage he detested: the pre-absolutist monarchy and the Constituent Assembly. On the one hand, she sketched the image of a monarchy that was, between the fourteenth and sixteenth centuries, surrounded by constituted bodies that moderated that crown's power through the intermediary of the Estates General. This aristocratic and feudal liberty had led, at the end of the sixteenth century, to the guarantee of religious freedom by the Edict of Nantes. On the other hand, Necker's daughter returned to the point at which the events of 1789 had overcome her father, in order to recover their liberal inspiration and associate them with the English model of representation. In this way, she

---

[2] I am commenting here on the posthumous work by Mme de Staël, published in 1818 by her heirs, her son Auguste and her son-in-law Victor de Broglie: *Considérations sur la révolution française*, reprinted Paris, 1983, with a preface by Jacques Godechot which discusses the circumstances of its composition.

kept the best elements of Old Regime and Revolution. Even *émigrés* could find something useful in 1789; even revolutionaries could picture their origins in the Old Regime.

By the same means, however, no one truly recovered his own tradition: because each was cut off from its antagonist, neither tradition was recognisable. In that world of survivors of the Old Regime and of the Revolution in which the baronne de Staël lived, no one could find his own past in the history that she recreated, neither king, nobility, church, nor any of the French who served or fought under republic or empire. The nobility, the clergy, and the brother of Louis XVI had experienced the same preceding quarter-century as had the revolutionaries, but from the opposite side. At the very least, they shared the conviction of the men of 1789 and 1793, a conviction inscribed in their own lives and inseparable from them, that French history had irremediably broken with them. How and why reunite these two parts if they would always remain opposed in memory?

Unlike Mme de Staël, Chateaubriand was not born a 'modern'. From his childhood in Combourg, he clung to the Old Regime as if it were a part of himself. His birth, his family, his women, his service in the army of the Prince de Condé, the very essence of his character and emotions, wed him to the past. With the return of the king and his last loyal followers in 1814, Chateaubriand found himself face to face with the France of his childhood, a France which he judged as severely as did Mme de Staël, but with greater tenderness because it was a part of himself. In fact, there was no significant disagreement between him and Staël on the essentials of their political visions: both favoured 'representative government', in other words, the Charter. It was their memories which separated them rather than their ideas.

Chateaubriand did not treat Louis XVIII as the key element to the working of a free government. In this old king, the survivor of such great misfortune, he celebrated the offspring of a family inseparably bound to the national history. To exorcise the regicide of 1793, he did not argue for divine right but for the most ancient memory of the French, for their customs and traditional fidelities, for the poetry and the honour of the past. The church? Chateaubriand restored it with the *Génie du christianisme*. The nobility? He was of their number and spoke the language of the Ultras to the point that, like them, he deplored the king's dissolution of the *chambre introuvable* in September 1816.[3] If he wanted a representative government it was because he saw in it the occasion for a great role,

---

[3] François-René de Chateaubriand, *De la monarchie selon la Charte*, 1816, post-scriptum; republished in Chateaubriand, *Mélanges politiques*, 2 vols., Paris, 1827, vol. 2, pp. 253–65.

under his tutelage, for the old nobility, once more aristocratic as during the heyday of the monarchy.

The problem was that, in wanting to put the national history at the centre of his conception of the Charter, Chateaubriand instead placed the Old Regime, along with his childhood, at the very heart of his literary work; the same writer who celebrated the past as indispensable to the institutions of the present believed, more than did any of his contemporaries, in the irremediable disappearance of that past. Moreover, he buried it beneath the powerful charm of his art far more effectively than did any of those who professed to hate it. The Old Regime remains a powerful presence in the work of Stendhal while it dies endlessly for Chateaubriand, who builds the magic of his literature upon the feeling of loss. 'The writer', wrote Maurras in one of his best essays, 'orchestrated a secret but unvarying condition of mourning into a funereal music; he required that his dirge be sustained, that his sadness be nourished by substantive disaster, by consuming and definitive unhappiness, and by falls without hope of redemption. He did not expend sympathy and eloquence upon partial misfortunes. His subject must be stricken to the very heart.'[4] Thus, Chateaubriand ceaselessly mingled his political theory with funereal undertones that announced its failure in advance. What he sought in the France of the past was less a plan of action than the substance of his art: in return, the past could offer him only the vanity of reminiscence. Far from providing the Old Regime with a link to the present, Chateaubriand mourned what the Revolution had forever banished. Here lay the source of his profound complicity with the republican left. The man who never missed an opportunity to deplore the tragedies of the legitimist monarchy (1793, 1820, 1830) could not, in the end, conceive of anything else; while he put his principles to rest, he also destroyed them. After 1830, he would be closer to Armand Carrel than to Guizot.

As for Guizot, he had none of this nostalgic taste for the past. He came from an altogether different world: the son of Protestant bourgeois, he belonged to a new generation which, not having lived through it, sought more eagerly to interpret the revolutionary rupture. We can better understand Guizot by comparing him not to Chateaubriand, with whom he had nothing in common, but to his fellow Protestant, Germaine de Staël, upon whose last work he commented.[5] A year after her death, in 1818, when he annotated her *Considérations*, Guizot praised her for having grasped the essential nature of the revolutionary event: the Revolution was not an

---

[4] Charles Maurras, *Trois idées politiques: Chateaubriand, Michelet, Sainte-Beuve*, Paris, 1898; republished as *Essais politiques*, Paris, 1954, pp. 64–8.
[5] François Guizot, in *Archives philosophiques, politiques et littéraires* (June–July 1818), vol. 3, no. 12, pp. 386–409 and vol. 4, no. 13, pp. 63–85.

accident, but an 'epoch' in the social order which had been prepared, almost defined by the centuries that preceded it. Nonetheless, behind the honours that he bestowed upon Staël for having so impartially reconstructed the ineluctable progression of events, stood the reproach of her rather too marked weakness for the unprincipled republicans of the Directory, who bore the guilt of having opened the way to Napoleonic despotism.

Guizot was never a republican and, even after Thermidor 1794, he saw nothing in the republic but the 'spirit of revolution' which he loathed and which he ultimately identified with democratic anarchy. Writing her *Considérations* at the beginning of the Restoration, Staël had had to pay her respects to the legitimist monarchy; but her notion of 'representative government' was not necessarily incompatible with forms of executive power other than that of a king, as she had made clear between 1794 and 1799. For Guizot, on the contrary, constitutional monarchy was the only viable form of representative government for the great European nation-states. True, this monarchy was not necessarily embodied in France by the elder branch of the Bourbons, as July 1830 would prove. But the hereditary power of a single individual was, if not necessary, at least sufficient for the organisation of a public authority that was favourable to liberty. To the same extent that the historian Guizot treated the monarchy, even the 'absolutist' monarchy of the seventeenth century, more favourably than did Staël, he judged the feudal aristocracy with much greater severity. Guizot despised the authority of the *seigneur* over the peasant, the sheer force of one individual's power over another, while what he admired in the development of the monarchy was its affirmation of a public authority legitimately imposed upon all. In this sense, absolutism prepared the way for 1789 by creating a political arena that had been made necessary by social developments: the men of 1789 crowned his evolution by endowing it with what had hitherto been missing – liberty.

In this way, Guizot effectively bridged the rupture between the Old Regime and the Revolution. The object of his hatred in the old France was more the aristocracy than the monarchy: this is quite apparent in his pamphlets of 1820–2 against the Ultras who, in his eyes, represented the party defeated in 1789.[6] But because this aristocracy had been ruined by the crown before it was destroyed by 1789, there was a continuity between the Old Regime and the Revolution. Staël argued that it was aristocratic liberalism which prefigured democratic liberty, which left two centuries of despotism between absolutism and representative government. For

---

[6] *Du gouvernement de la France depuis la restauration et du ministère actuel*, Paris, 1820 and *Des moyens de gouvernement et d'opposition dans dans l'état actuel de la France*, Paris, 1821; reprinted Paris, 1988, introduction by Claude Lefort.

Guizot, on the contrary, the absolute monarchy and the Revolution of 1789 were products of the same progressive movement of society and they were called to serve the same task, the birth of bourgeois society. In the end, the Revolution only completed what had been done before its advent: 'It is necessary', he said during his course at the Sorbonne in 1820–1, 'to date revolutions from the day upon which they break out: that is the only precise time we may assign them; but it is not the time in which they act. The shocks that we call revolutions are less the symptoms of something that is beginning than they are the signs of what has already taken place.'[7]

July 1830 only confirmed what July 1789 had already demonstrated, just as 1688 in England closed the English Revolution: forty years later the need for revolutionary adjustment could finally be separated from the anarchic spirit that was also part of revolution. Hence, July 1830 opened the way to the necessary synthesis between Old Regime and Revolution: the *trois glorieuses* inaugurated the reconciliation of two distinct histories. The Orleanist regime, born of a Parisian revolt that Guizot sought to forget and to efface with the argument of 'quasi-legitimacy',[8] had no foundation other than that which could be drawn from the Old Regime and the French revolution together. Unlike Bonapartism, the Orleanist monarchy, did not make use of a legend or of acquiescence to despotism to hide the juridical poverty of its origins. Consequently, it was forced to place itself at the very point at which the two traditions that had been purged from the national history – the reforming monarchy and the liberal revolution – still met and intermingled. It was necessary to carry out what Guizot had written, that is to say to refound 1789, but as a link between the past and the future, and no longer as a line of partition or as the stakes in a civil war. Louis-Philippe restored the Château of Versailles to make it a museum of national pride, and he also brought the emperor's tomb to the Invalides. The history of France became the quintessential arena of legitimation for the new monarchy, which doted upon it as upon a favoured child: consider, for example, the extraordinary efforts to conserve and enlarge the architectural and archival patrimony.

But February 1848 sounded the death knell for the monarchy of 1830, bringing to an end the first systematic effort to bridge the chasm that had opened between Old Regime and Revolution in 1789. Before serving as its head, Guizot had been the theoretician, indeed the inventor of this regime. Thus, the Revolution of 1848 destroyed not only a monarchy, but the very ideas from which it had issued; it brought back to life, with still greater force, all that these ideas had tried to avert. With the February

---

[7] François Guizot, *Essais sur l'histoire de France*, 2nd edn, Paris, 1824, p. 16.
[8] Paul Thureau-Danguin, *Histoire de la monarchie de juillet*, 7 vols., Paris, 1884–92, vol. 1.

days in Paris, it reappropriated the fundamental heritage of French politics, its founding principle, which was rooted in the desire to reconstruct a new society on the ruins of the old. In fact, the democratic construct may never have known finer days than those in Paris during the late winter of 1848; utopian socialism was combined with the revolutionary tradition, as almost every thinking person held forth on 'the best of all possible societies'. It was a comic, or a touching, spectacle, according to one's inclinations. In the first register, Flaubert was unrivalled,[9] but we may also appreciate the liberation of the social imagination that was effected by the imaginary effacement of the past and by the abstract prefiguration of the future. In this sense, February 1848 not only replicated 1789, but gave it extraordinary variety by infinitely multiplying providential events and happy coincidences. Its great difference from 1789 was that future happiness now conjured away past curses. In other words, the 'Old Regime' of 1789, already reconquered in 1830, could not be recalled to service endlessly: no longer a presence or a threat, it had become a memory. The future, on the other hand, had more than ever to be reinvented because the 'social question' was so much more pressing than the issue of government.

Hence, the particular force of the 1848 Revolution in the national history does not derive from its unique trajectory, nor from the talent of its political leaders, nor from its brilliant achievements, but from what it revived and restored to the great foundational stage of French politics: the revolutionary rupture. In retrospect, July 1830 was nothing more than the makeshift construct of politicians, while February 1848 was meant to be the reincarnation of the mighty ancestors. A comparison between the great historians of 1830 and those of 1848 underscores this: the former, Guizot foremost, but also Thierry, Mignet, Barante, wanted to recreate a 1789 that could encompass both Old Regime and Revolution; the latter, foremost amongst them Michelet, but also Quinet, Louis Blanc, and even Lamartine, wished above all to recommence the Revolution.

We need only consider how the idea of temporal rupture underlies, even dominates, Michelet's history of the French Revolution.[10] Michelet served both Bourbons and Orleans without any great commitment. Very early associated with Victor Cousin, he was an established Orleanist after 1830, holder of an important post in the National Archives, and a professor at the Collège de France by 1838. He began his *History of France* during these years, covering the Christian middle ages as the first

9 Gustave Flaubert, *L'Education sentimentale*, Paris, 1870, 2 vols.
10 The best work on the subject is still that by Gabriel Monod, *La Vie et la pensée de Jules Michelet, 1798–1852*, 2 vols., Paris, 1923 (nos. 235 and 236 of the Bibliothèque de l'Ecole des Hautes Etudes).

moment in which the France nation was called to its civilising mission. But he could not wait upon the natural progression of the centuries to arrive at the Revolution; current events demanded that he treat it. Moreover, his teaching at the Collège de France brought him face to face with students who were eager for discussion of contemporary debates, which were soon dominated by the opposition between university and church over the issue of lay education. He freed himself, probably after the marriage of his daughter Adèle in 1843, of what remained of his Catholic faith as if shaking free a part that still enshrouded him: now he was ready to fight to free a future that Louis-Philippe and Guizot held tight in their aged hands.

The mood of the early 1840s was one of novelty and radical rupture. The founding idea of political and intellectual Orleanism – to put an end to the French Revolution – was in pieces: it was necessary to begin again. Not only did Michelet know and feel this, but he incarnated the somewhat mysterious shift that prepared the way for the events of February 1848. France remained that country in which intellectuals kept their eighteenth-century predecessors' privilege of anticipating the future: a privilege perhaps less mysterious than it seems if we remember that these intellectuals, in acknowledging the ability of their predecessors, tended to attribute it to themselves and to convince the public of their capacities. Enlightenment *philosophes* did not believe themselves to be, nor did they wish to be, prophets; but in declaring them to be such after the fact, their successors placed them in a role that the national history had already confirmed by its intermediaries. Thus, in the nineteenth century, French writers seemed to foresee events because of their doggedness in predicting them. Michelet had already considered, in 1841, leaving his great history of France at the end of the middle ages, in order to write about Napoleon. 'All has vanished for me', he noted in his journal in August 1841, 'antiquity, the middle ages; I feel profoundly modern at this moment'.[11] Nonetheless, he continued his history of France from Joan of Arc to Louis XI, since volume 6 appeared at the beginning of 1844, but his teaching had already veered toward the Revolution.

He arrived there via the two distinct but convergent paths of religion and nationality. As Gabriel Monod has shown, he interrupted his course of 1842–3 halfway through the middle ages.[12] He devoted the first semester, autumn–winter 1842, to the rise of cities in the twelfth century, and when he began the second half of the academic year, on 27 April 1843, it was with a visceral attack upon the Jesuits: he entered into a battle that was already raging around him and joined his voice with that of Quinet.

[11] *Ibid.*, vol. 2, Book III, chs. 5 and 6.
[12] *Ibid.*, Book IV, ch. 1.

So was born the second and final Michelet, the adversary of the Catholic church as a form devoid of living matter, the accuser of the Jesuits as eternal plotters of counter-revolution, the admirer of the eighteenth-century *philosophes* as the annihilators of a dead religion. From that moment, he rediscovered the true life of men and history in the Revolution. In the notes that remain from his first lesson of 1845, 16 January, we read:

there is no legality outside the Revolution, so that in treating the Revolution, I place myself upon the base, the very foundation of law itself. I set my back against that foundation to face an army of lies and from that position I will seek the true friends of liberty. I have shown that the Revolution swept away ruins, less than ruins ...[13]

The Orleanists, historians above all, wanted to reincorporate the France of 1789 into their past. The Michelet of 1845, who had been one of them, could conceive of nothing other than a new foundation.

France was, would be, must be the missionary of this foundation: Michelet did not separate the idea of revolutionary universalism from that of French nationalism. Like so many writers of the period, he had an exceptionally powerful sense of the immortality of nations which, to persist, must incarnate an idea or principle, or risk collapsing into the alien, the borrowed, the imitative (as had the France of Louis-Philippe which wanted to mimic the English). France had the finest role: that of forging the path for humanity and acting as the universal nation. Thus Michelet, from the outset, held together in his powerful hand the two separate threads of the revolutionary age, universalism and nationalism. It was all the more necessary that the 'people' know their past and their future, so that they might be equal to the great task that faced them: such was the objective of his book of 1845,[14] which carried exactly that title – *Le Peuple* – and through which the historian became prophet. This, it seems to me, is a key work in the intellectual development of Michelet: it makes clear all that shifted in his universe between the (provisional) end of the *History of France*, and the first volume of the *History of the French Revolution*, published in 1847.

At the end of this intellectual voyage, the *History of the French Revolution* opens with that magnificent and magisterial introduction whose goal is, precisely, to define that against which 1789 occurred, all that to which the Revolution put an end, in order to open wide the doors upon the future. Michelet refashioned the Old Regime from all of those Catho-

---

[13] *Ibid.*, ch. 6.
[14] Jules Michelet, *Le Peuple*, Paris, 1845; reprinted Paris, 1974, introduction and notes by Paul Viallaneix.

lic centuries in the history of France. Catholic: this is indeed the keyword because, at the same point at which the men of 1789 called feudalism and monarchy into question, the republican historian fifty years later named a third party, which was the source of those two calamities: the church. Certainly, the church did not reign over France in exactly the same way throughout the course of the centuries: there was the religion of the middle ages and the theocratic–political monarchy of the Bourbons. But both periods were characterised by the same principles of original sin and the arbitrary nature of divine grace, while the Revolution of 1789 was the dawning of justice and law. Because there was an affinity between fraternity and Christianity, the former could be realised only in the wake of the destruction of the church and its institutions, and by the extinction of all transcendence: the French Revolution had necessarily to become its own religion. Because the Revolution did not fully understand this truth that it only glimpsed, it could not accomplish it, so leaving the task to posterity.

The essential shift in the idea of the Old Regime during this period, arose from its having taken a religious turn. Although the French revolutionaries of the later eighteenth century had been able, especially after 1792, to associate the church with the curse that weighed upon the national past, they had never placed it at the centre of their attacks. In the mid-nineteenth century, with the legitimist monarchy once more defeated, the great struggle of French democracy found its target in the church, which returned blow for blow after having so indiscreetly sided with the restored Bourbons between 1814 and 1830. The stakes of the *tabula rasa* of 1789 were displaced without losing any of their radicalism: on the contrary, enveloped in religion, the opposition of two incompatible societies became clearer than ever, rendering all the more imperative the uprooting of the society of the past.

For Quinet as well,[15] Michelet's comrade for his years at the Collège de France, the Old Regime was a dead religion that had too long hidden from Christians the path to their true future. The royal monarchy, modelled upon the pontifical monarchy, appropriated the spirit of Christianity, which in turn remained crushed under this dual oppression for centuries until the Revolution unwittingly freed it; in this way the French made a great political and social revolution before having accomplished, as had the English, the Dutch, and the Americans, a religious revolution. This made 1789 a unique, and almost monstrous event: for Quinet, the religious dimension overshadowed the political one, and kept possession

---

[15] The lectures by Edgard Quinet at the Collège de France which I am discussing are those of 1845. They would be published the following year, in 1846, under the title: *Le Christianisme et la révolution française*. Cf. my book *La Gauche et la révolution au milieu du XIX siècle*, Paris, 1988 pp. 17–27.

of the ultimate secrets of human history. Michelet saw the Revolution as a religious event. Quinet, on the contrary, saw in it a religious failure because of the inability of the men of the time to found new beliefs. The opposition between these two conceptions of the Revolution, visible in the writings of the two friends that dated from their courses at the Collège de France in 1845–6, was probably not as marked as they themselves later believed because religion, for Quinet, was inseparable from history, so that its external manifestations also varied between peoples and periods. But this also meant that, for Quinet, the separation between the old and the new, between the living and the dead spirit, became all the more rigid. The French Revolution was a failure, but it was a prodigious failure because through its universalism it was able to represent to the world that something radically new was in the process of being born, even if it could not yet be definitively heralded.

In the nineteenth century, the idea of the Old Regime drew its strength, almost its very existence, from the notions of 'epoch' and 'historical period' that it had helped to create. To the extent that historicism replaced *jusnaturalisme* in the interpretation of the Revolution, the division of history into chronological blocks that were defined by their dominant ideas favoured the summary definition that the French of 1789 gave to their past. In a sense, this collective rejection of the Old Regime helped to shape historical and political thought. Constant, as early as 1796,[16] conceptualised the history of Europe as the gradual realisation of the idea of equality, and 1789 as the transition from the world of nobility (or, to use his words, of 'heredity') to one of careers open to talent. Restoration intellectuals were obsessed with what had died just before their time, and with what was being born before their eyes. One need only compare the work of Jouffroy with that of Quinet[17] to understand the extent to which the future *quarante-huitards* shared this vision and this anguish.

'Twenty years ago', Quinet told his students in 1845, 'we saw how dogmas perish. Watch closely what is occurring before you. You will see how a doctrine, a school dies.' The professor was taking aim at Jouffroy's famous article,[18] 'How dogmas end', published in *The Globe* in 1825. At that time, the young men at *The Globe* were laying siege to the power of the ultra-royalists. Jouffroy offered them a philosophy of historical change permeated throughout by the sequence of Old Regime/

---

[16] Benjamin Constant, *De la force du gouvernement actuel et de la nécessité de s'y rallier*, Paris, 1796; reprinted Paris, 1989, preface by Philippe Raynaud.

[17] Cf. note 15 above.

[18] Jouffroy's famous article has recently been reprinted in *Commentaire*, no. 27 (fall 1984), pp. 146–55.

Revolution/post-revolutionary order which was the obsession of those years and of that generation, shared for example by liberals and Saint-Simonians alike. The events of 1789 had taken place on the ruins of a society of dead ideas; the succession of governments was fostered by the succession of ideas, which were themselves studied more in terms of their social influence than as the products of individual genius. Thus, the Revolution represented the final stage in the destruction of the old beliefs and yet it was unable to replace them with new ones, because the generation that destroyed, having grown up in an age of scepticism, could not be the one that recreated. However, the generation born after the Revolution escaped this negativity and so could begin a process of spiritual reconstruction. This was both the ambition and the philosophy of Orleanism, crowned by what Michelet called the 'spirit of July'.

But ten years after July, everything had to be reclaimed in the name of the same philosophy. The young Quinet had been an enthusiastic reader of *The Globe*; the mature Quinet left his former friends, 'doctrinaires' or 'eclectics' of the Old Regime of dead ideas, and turned, like Michelet, toward a new spirit. Like Michelet and like so many of his contemporaries: one need only think of the flourishing of socialist ideologies in those years to understand the degree to which the idea of the *tabula rasa*, the ambition to construct, the search for new principles, which is inseparable from the negation of the historical past, is constitutive of French political thought. But something else was apparent in Quinet's dialogue across time with Jouffroy: Quinet remained faithful to the intellectual structure of Jouffroy's article, according to which intellectual activity must be related to life's progress, hence to each of its ages. This may explain why, nine years later, he could so little understand the emotional force of Jouffroy's 1825 article, which he had once shared, that he went so far as to repudiate it altogether. To it, he opposed a new eschatology, after having shared in that of the preceding generation. Nothing better reveals the extraordinary force of the revolutionary idea for the nineteenth-century intelligentsia than, on the one hand, the celebrated dissolution of the notion of truth in history and, on the other, the passion for reconstructing, from terribly fragile material, something that might finally escape history. Meanwhile, what was the other friend, Michelet, doing in the neighbouring chair at the Collège de France? Gabriel Monod describes him as obsessed, in his course of 1845, by the idea of revolutionary *foundation*, intervening at the end of an interminable dissolution.[19]

Thus, the idea of the 'Old Regime' acted as a repository in which the post-revolutionary generations continued to bury their disappointed

---

[19] Monod, *La Vie et la pensée de Jules Michelet*, vol. 2, Book IV, ch. 6.

hopes. The Revolution had already set the example as the Constituent Assembly finished by becoming the Old Regime of the Convention. Similarly, the Restoration had become the Old Regime of the Orleanists; and still again, years before it was overturned, Orleanism was reshaped into the Old Regime of what would be February 1848. There was a remarkable passion for discontinuity in nineteenth-century France which subsequent historians, liberal and republican alike, have tried to tame by imposing a narrative of the linear progress of democracy. The political truth of the century is to be found in the long survival of the revolutionary tradition which so many contemporaries commented upon in order to celebrate or disparage it. Like the last ten years of the preceding century, the succession of regimes continued to emphasise the opposition between the Old Regime and the Revolution.

The years 1848–51 introduced an additional repetitive element into this sequence, with the caveat that this period alone constituted a new version of the course of the French Revolution. Drawing analogies between the two events was a commonplace in the contemporary writings of political actors and political commentators, who were often one and the same. The two greats, Tocqueville and Marx, set the tone in different but comparable moods: as the former deplored the resumption of the French Revolution, the latter described it as French farce, and both ridiculed its parodic character.[20] Both men sought to understand the ignoble enigma of the end, of the unworthy nephew who closed the show on 2 December, as the unlikely and yet logical heir to the all-powerful state built by his uncle upon the accumulated ruins of the Old Regime and the Revolution.

The Second Republic resuscitated the great images of the national history in both caricatural and spectacular fashion. No other regime so forcefully revived the idea of the *tabula rasa* – at least during its first months between February and June 1848: this rarefied spring was a period of almost extravagant social invention. It witnessed the blossoming, like so many hot-house flowers, of bouquets of new societies or, better yet, sprays of happy cities. In the fair of utopias that was Parisian political life for this brief period, Flaubert saw only a naïvety that was either touching or ridiculous, according to the disposition of the witness. But there was also the powerful sense of *tabula rasa* that French democracy drew from its origins and which had never ceased to be a source of inspiration: modern artificialism is driven by the continual negation of the past, just as the democratic spirit is driven by the systemic negation of

[20] Karl Marx, *Les Luttes des classes en France (1848–1850)*, *Le Dix-huit Brumaire de Louis-Napoléon Bonaparte*, Paris, 1900; reprinted Paris, 1984; Alexis de Tocqueville, *Souvenirs*, Paris, 1893; full edn Gallimard, 1942; reprinted in vol. 12 of his *Œuvres complètes*, Paris, 1964.

what it has accomplished. The socialist critique reinvented a multiplicity of prospects for a society whose entire political code was directed toward the future.

However, the end of the adventure pulled the French backwards: not only because the Second Empire was the successor of the First, but because of the form of this repetition. The 2 December did not offer any of the justifications that had provided the 18 Brumaire with a half-century of respectability in the eyes of the left, republicans included. No longer the close of a revolutionary epoch transformed into national glory by the most astonishing genius of the time, rather this was the ignominious conclusion of a meeting between a society that feared itself, a centralised state, and a petty despot with a famous name. In losing its excuses, the accession of a second imperial despotism also lost its meaning. It could no longer be understood in terms of civil and foreign war. Made possible and ratified by universal suffrage, it brought the French face-to-face with their own desires. It obliged historians to consider the tyranny of the past over the present. How, then, could they avoid questioning the Old Regime?

It was not enough to seek the key to the Second Empire in the First. Tocqueville understood this quickly, having first considered writing a study of Napoleon I in 1852, and having even begun an introduction. Then from origin to origin, he was dragged upstream to the time before 1789 where he found the true sources of the French penchant for despotism, which became the subject of his famous book of 1856.[21] In exactly those years, Quinet, in exile in Brussels, shared the same obsession: how was one to explain France's welcome for the adventurer of 2 December? He too began by considering a more distant history, indeed a far more distant history, before throwing himself into a history of the Revolution: in the *Philosophy of the history of France*, published in 1854,[22] he went as far back as the defeat of the Vercingetorix as if he were returning to the first defeat of liberty. But what he had in mind was more polemical. He sought to indict all historians who had preceded him – Orleanists as well socialists, Guizot as well as Buchez, Augustin Thierry as well as Louis Blanc – of conspiring with despotism by celebrating the role of the monarchy in the emancipation of the Third Estate and the crowning glories of 1789. He believed that all those who were obsessed by the class struggle between nobles and bourgeois ended by giving priority to equality to the detriment of liberty: hence, their apparent indifference to the issue of political liberty. Even Guizot, the Protestant Guizot,

---

[21] Alexis de Tocqueville, *L'Ancien régime et la révolution*, Paris, 1856, vol. 1; reprinted in *Œuvres complètes*, vol. 2, Paris, 1953, preface by Georges Lefebvre.

[22] Edgard Quinet, *Philosophie de l'histoire de France*, Paris, 1954. See also my commentary in *La Gauche et la révolution*, pp. 30–4.

remained largely indifferent to the reactionary turn taken by French history under the dictatorship of Richelieu, which was quickly followed by the despotism of Louis XIV and the revocation of the Edict of Nantes. According to Quinet, the terrible 'absolutist monarchy' traced into the pontifical monarchy constituted the very essence of the Old Regime and of the inclination to servitude that dominated French history.

Even the Revolution could not long escape this tendency, falling under its spell soon after the Constituent Assembly with Robespierre as the reincarnation of Richelieu. So it was that Quinet, ten years later, wrote a *History of the Revolution* that was imbued throughout with the notion of the Old Regime as the evil curse of the history of France.[23] He made of the concept elaborated by the men of 1789 a vast negation of the national spirit; but unlike the men of 1789, he extended its reach over the entire course of the Revolution and throughout the nineteenth century, up to the moment of his own exile. The Old Regime was the failure of French history, a radical defeat which included even the Revolution, because it was the Revolution itself which was the measure of its extraordinary reach. From Brussels, Quinet yet again saw nothing in France but its grim shadow, more overpowering then ever. This constituted the past and present of the country: taken together, the Catholic church, the 'Byzantine' royalty, Robespierrist and Napoleonic despotism were all successive types of absolutist domination that were characterised by a common abasement of the individual which masked the national passion for unity and equality. Like the men of 1789, Quinet characterised the 'Old Regime' as the negative pole of France's history, but he added two considerations that heightened the force of his condemnation. Firstly, neither the efforts of the revolutionaries nor those of the men of the nineteenth century had saved France from the tyranny of its past. Secondly, what was needed to alleviate that tyranny was not, as the revolutionaries had believed, simply a political solution, but a religious one: it was necessary to shatter the Catholic matrix of despotism and to build a new democracy upon a new Christian cult.

For the exiled historian, the Old Regime was a 'spirit' at work in history which could be annihilated only by the semi-providential appearance of an opposing 'spirit'. For Tocqueville, on the contrary, it was the unusual product of a particular history, French history, which mingled together aristocracy and democracy under the protective wing of the monarchy. Tocqueville would not have known how to oppose 'Old Regime' and 'democracy' within the framework of his analysis. He did not define democracy as a political world in which the free citizen reigned, but rather

---

23 Edgard Quinet, *Histoire de la révolution*, 3 vols., Paris, 1865; reprinted Paris, 1987, preface by Claude Lefort.

as a state of social equality; and it was just such a social state that emerged from the interaction of mores and beliefs, interests and classes in eighteenth-century France under the tutelage, or at least as a side-effect, of the administrative monarchy. Tocqueville, like Quinet, detested Guizot the politician, and for very much the same reasons, but he was a better reader of Guizot the historian. From him, Tocqueville took the idea that French democracy developed within the shadows of monarchic power, upon the ruins of the aristocracy. And it was the history of that 'democracy', of the real conditions of its development, that he attempted to describe in order to enrich, and even transform the concept. His 'Old Regime' represented the place and time in which was already apparent, at the very depths of French society during the last century of monarchic rule, the disappearance of the world of aristocratic dependence; or, more precisely, the particular form of this decline – above all, the growing surveillance of society by the royal bureaucracy which made of the social democratic state emerging in France the forerunner of the revolutionary *tabula rasa*.

What is properly 'old' in Tocqueville's Old Regime is the society that is anterior to the rise of the centralised state, a society which he called indifferently 'feudal' or 'aristocratic' to signify that it was characterised by hierarchic ties of dependence between men and social groups that composed it. Here, political power was not distinct from social superiority and it was distributed all along the pyramid of social positions. But the development of the absolutist state was inseparable from the concentration of political power into a single place, namely into the hands of the king and, consequently, it was also inseparable from the dispossession of others: the aristocracy was the first, but not the only victim of this transformation because the whole social order was upset.

All of the great historians of the nineteenth century had recognised the absolutist revolution. Mme de Staël, and later Guizot, saw it as the period of European history between feudalism and 'representative government'. Michelet used it as the foundation of his idea that the nation was incarnated in the person of the king of France, an enigma of usurpation that the Revolution cut short by replacing the king with the people. But Tocqueville was the only writer to describe absolutism as a sociological phenomenon which, like the Revolution, but before it, subverted the structure of social relations. His Old Regime pulled between opposing principles, was the accumulated corruption of the aristocratic principle and the democratic principle which destroyed in just a few centuries not only all tradition but the very idea of tradition: it could lead only to its own negation. This explains the peculiar idea of the *tabula rasa*: contrary to its own claims, it was a product of history, but of a history that had left nothing but ruins and fictions. As a tradition, the Old Regime left nothing to its successors but the overwhelming desire to obliterate all traces of itself, and the illusion that they possessed the means to do so.

Thus, the singularity of the French experience was that it was composed of a series of revolutions that left no room for liberty: the Old Regime, the Revolution, and the crises of the nineteenth century did no more than disturb national political habits. The young Tocqueville had organised his first book around the opposition between American democracy and French revolutionary democracy, hoping perhaps that the second might in time become more like the first. The Tocqueville of the Old Regime, writing under the reign of a second Bonaparte and after the failure of yet another revolution, was necessarily resigned to examining the singularity of the French experience. The Old Regime, the Revolution, and Bonapartism constituted the national version of democracy; and it was the oldest form of this that had been shaped over the course of the centuries of monarchic rule by intellectual habits and mores.

This was the source of the great success of his book of 1856 amongst the liberal public: that it offered the most extensive explanation of the dictatorship of the second Bonaparte. There was no reliable arena for representative government in a country deprived of intermediate bodies and dominated by a centralised administration; this was as true of the nineteenth century as it had been of the eighteenth. The English comparison which dominated the work of Guizot made no sense to his old adversary. Thus, the Old Regime of Tocqueville triumphed in the end over the Old Regimes of Guizot or Augustin Thierry. It was no longer the engine of historical optimism that allowed the Orleanist historians to portray the administrative state as the necessary precursor to representative government; it was, on the contrary, its lasting opponent which survived its own disappearance. The only 'representation' of citizens that it allowed, in the century of triumphant democracy, was that assured by a single, all-powerful head of state. So disappeared the positive continuity that Guizot and Thierry had posited between the role of the old monarchy and the appearance of representative government. In its place, Tocqueville revealed the dark face of France's history which, along the line that united the Old Regime with modern democratic government, warded off liberty.

And yet, Bonapartism is not the last word of the revolutionary culture of French democracy. The compromise with parliamentary government that Napoleon III sought, and finally found during the latter half of his reign, had already opened a breach in the radical pessimism that was the heritage of Tocqueville's work. Above all, the fall of the Second Empire restored to French politics all of its constitutional indeterminism. The French rediscovered intact the problem of post-revolutionary reconciliation: the episode of the Commune, followed by a final attempt by the royalist right to return the last of the Bourbons to the throne, made clear the continuing opposition between Old Regime and Revolution upon the national state.

In less than ten years, however, moderate republicans, together with an Orleanist party, would offer a solution to the French institutional problem by installing a conservative republic. Jules Ferry and Thiers joined efforts to diminish the tension between the Old Regime and the Revolution. To this end, Tocqueville was of no use to them, because he offered the French nothing more than a hateful Old Regime, followed by a revolution that was still worse. Nor could they take anything from Taine who, in a different philosophical mode, shared Tocqueville's general pessimism. Rather, they returned to the sort of history of France that Guizot and his friends had designed a half-century earlier.

This is not to say that Guizot once more became a historian worthy of the republicans, not even for moderate republicans like these. Between them and Guizot yawned the gap that separated republic from monarchy, and universal suffrage from limited representation. Thiers crossed this gap, but he had always possessed an instinctive rapport with the culture and history of the French Revolution that escaped even the young Guizot, to say nothing of Guizot the minister to Louis-Philippe. Thus, even in 1880, the latter could find no appeal against the verdict delivered against him by 1848: he remained a narrow, bourgeois anglophile, detested by Michelet, Quinet, even Tocqueville.

But his history of France retained its capacity to inspire the history that the victorious republicans would teach to the children of the nation. Those who created a free education for all under the auspices of a Comtiste philosophy of progress were much closer than they realised to Guizot's notion of public sovereignty as the figure of reason. Above all, their history of France, shorn it is true of the English comparison, acknowledged the part due to the Old Regime in the work of the centuries. One need only re-read Lavisse to see the extent to which his vision of the past, which would soon influence all levels of teaching, borrowed its structure from Guizot: a nation slowly created by kings over nobles, and crowned by the emancipation of the Third Estate in 1789. As it took root in the depths of the countryside, the republic had to cloak itself in a tamed version of the revolutionary *tabula rasa* in order to accomplish its project: it persisted in finding its immediate origins in the Revolution, but its history stretched back still further, and even the kings had made their contribution without knowing that they did so. An easy compromise, like that which, during the same period, reigned over the establishment of the institutions of 1875, and which had similar political virtues: it restored to the French all of their history, invested with the dignity of human progress.

10   The republic of universal suffrage

Pierre Rosanvallon

The republican idea acquired new meaning in France after 1830. It no longer designated a particular type of political system by referring only to the memory of 1792, nor by evoking the governments of ancient cities. Rather, it acquired a far more complex significance. Identified with the theme of universal suffrage, reference to the republic neatly concentrated a whole ensemble of social and cultural aspirations into a single word. The republic of universal suffrage implied, above all, the search for a society without divisions. Indeed the central problem of the first years of the July monarchy was that of social division. The onset of industrialisation widened schisms in the social fabric at the same time that the disappointment of the hopes raised by the 1830 Revolution aggravated political tensions. Such was the context in which the figure of the proletarian emerged. 'The proletarian remains excluded', summarised Blanqui in 1832. 'Oh noble bourgeois, cease repelling us from your bosom, for we are men, and not machines', demanded one of the first workers' journals, the *Artisan*,[1] in 1830, while Lamartine wished that the name of the proletariat, 'this base, injurious, pagan word [should] disappear from the language as the proletarian himself must disappear little by little from society'.[2] The demand for universal suffrage, which emerged at the beginning of the July monarchy, was linked to this demand for social inclusion. In 1789, the demand for political equality had derived simply from the primary principle of civil equality: the essential struggle had been waged in the realm of civil rights, around the destruction of privilege and the suppression of legal distinctions between individuals. At that time, suffrage merely extended the new society of equal individuals into the political realm; by 1830, however, social distinctions and differences of status were no longer expressed in the civil domain. The idea of universal suffrage acquired a directly social dimension, while the problem of integration was displaced accordingly: henceforth, the question of

---

[1] Cited by W. Sewell, *Gens de métiers et révolution. Le langage du travail de l'ancien régime à 1848*, Paris, 1983, p. 270.

[2] Cited by I. Tchernoff, *Le Parti républicain sous la monarchie de juillet*, Paris, 1901, p. 203.

equality among men would be played out on the social and the political stage. This explains the centrality of the figure of the proletarian after 1830, just as in 1789 all struggle had been organised around the figure of the individual. But the question of universal suffrage was not only subject to a political shift between these two periods; it was also accompanied by new anxiety about the social. In 1789, suffrage had been understood in terms of the dominant abstract universalism; at the beginning of the July monarchy, on the contrary, it assumed a class dimension. In less than half a century, the emergence of the issue of the workers profoundly altered the terms in which social relations were understood. Those excluded from political rights would in future be identified as a social group. 'Are the powerful and the rich worth more than we are?' asked Achille Roche in his *Manuel du prolétaire*, a question which summarised the basis of his political claim.[3] By 1830–4, reflection on universal suffrage was no longer a general philosophical interrogation of the modern individual citizen, nor *a fortiori* a questioning from above of the relationship between numbers and reason; it was being expressed *from below*.

Throughout the July monarchy, the theme of universal suffrage played exactly the same role as had the demand for civil equality in 1789. Both cases reveal the same struggle against feudalism and the Old Regime. The critique of feudalism and the denunciation of the electoral system functioned in exactly the same way during the two periods, the same words and the same expressions returning to denounce caste and privilege. The 200,000 eligible voters were assimilated to the old aristocrats, just as those who were excluded from the suffrage became a new Third Estate. Now, however, political monopoly had taken the place of the former social privileges. The *Journal du peuple* wrote in 1840, 'Bad legislatures, bad laws, and the anguish of the proletariat are the results of the monopoly. What then is a free people amongst whom only 200,000, out of 30 million, are called upon to name their representatives? There is an anomaly here that must end.'[4] Such words spilled forth from all the pens of the day, repeating *ad infinitum* this condemnation of limited suffrage as a remnant of the old figure of privilege in the new France. Thus, the struggle for universal suffrage is a direct descendant of the revolutionary movement. Moreover, it is striking that this same period witnessed the popular reappropriation of the French Revolution. All republicans and social reformers of the period shared the same outlook. In 1839, Pagnerre, the publisher of all republican causes, significantly republished a cheap edition of Sieyès's *What is the Third Estate?*[5] Cabet's *Popular history of the*

---

[3] A. Roche, *Manuel du prolétaire*, Moulins, 1833, p. 3.
[4] 'Account of a democratic banquet', *Journal du peuple*, 5 July 1840.
[5] This includes an important study of Sieyès by Chapuys-Montlaville.

French Revolution (1839) was enormously successful, and Laponneraye's *History of the French Revolution* was re-issued several times between 1838 and 1840. From the earliest days of the 1830 Revolution, the Society of the Friends of the People, then the Society of the Rights of Man and Citizen, nourished the memory of the great moments of the Revolution. They circulated the works of Robespierre, Saint-Just and Marat, and sold small plaster busts of illustrious deputies to the Convention. Certainly, more radical circles celebrated 1793 and Robespierre's declaration of rights above anything else, but the sense of parallel between the conquest of civil equality in 1789 and the conquest of political suffrage in the 1830s was omnipresent, even in the most moderate circles. The term parallel is almost inappropriate if it implies only resemblance; there was in fact a deeper identity between the two movements: in both cases, the principle at stake was that of social inclusion. Hence, the striking specificity of the history of universal suffrage in France.

This convergence was also the source of the divorce between French society and the monarchy. The monarchical idea in France had been overburdened with an accumulation of negative images until, in the end, it came to be associated with every possible form of inequality and social division: fiscal exemptions, social privileges, inequalities of status, electoral barriers, even economic differences. The divorce was definitively accomplished in the 1830s: the monarchy ceased to be conceived of as a simple political regime whose essence might survive its more- or less-fortunate historical instantiations. Identified with privilege, the monarchical idea would, in the future, represent a totally negative principle, economic as well as social. The image of the monarchy was superimposed on that of the Old Regime just as it was on that of capitalism. The pamphlets and booklets of 1831–5 make this quite clear, in terms that scarcely vary between republicans as moderate as Cormenin and reformers as radical as Laponneraye. The *Lettre aux prolétaires*, which the latter published in 1833, is entirely representative of this Manichean vision, which led to attributing to the republic every conceivable virtue. 'With the monarchy', he wrote, 'there are privileged and proletarians; with the republic there are only citizens who possess equal rights, and all of whom participate in forming laws and electing public officials'.[6] The socialist idea, in turn, remained wholly rooted in republicanism, seeming only to implement it in the specific domains of the economic and the

---

[6] Laponneraye, *Lettre aux prolétaires*, Sainte-Pélagie Prison, 1 February 1833, p. 2. Cormenin used the same language: 'Universal suffrage', he wrote, 'therein lies the entirety of the republic. There will no longer be plurality, sinecures, civil lists, fat salaries, nor pensions ... the budget of expenditures will be reduced to the strictly necessary.' *Les trois dialogues de maître Pierre*, published under the aegis of Aide-toi, le ciel t'aidera, Paris, December 1833, p. 15.

social. This becomes very clear upon leafing through the *Revue républi-caine* (1834–5), the first publication of the Left whose theoretical quality was equal to that of the great liberal reviews. It was in particular Martin Bernard, a printer, who published there two articles with the suggestive title: 'On the means of bringing the republic into the workshop'.[7] He wrote:

It is impossible to deny the analogy of the relationship between today's man of the *workshop* and the former man of the *château*, the *serf*... Prejudice has so distorted the consciousness of the masses that we find the proletarian who well understands that a king is a dispensable cog in the political order, and yet who refuses to believe that the same can be accomplished in the industrial order ... In the eighteenth century, politics displayed the same character as does industry today ... Isn't the workshop a monarchy in miniature?[8]

These brief phrases say everything, prefiguring Ledru-Rollin and Louis Blanc, Marc Sangnier and Jules Guesde. The demand for universal suffrage, in its association with the generic critique of monarchy, formed the original and constitutive basis of modern French political culture. Consequently, in the 1830s the idea of universal suffrage evoked a form of society more than it defined a precise technique of political participation; it was nourished by singularly powerful images and undergirded by violent rejections, while remaining institutionally vague.

Apart from its demand for social inclusion, the theme of electoral reform catalysed a whole ensemble of political and economic claims. Electoral reform played the role of a universal political remedy, which should provide answers to the great problems of the moment: the suppression of corruption, installation of affordable government, respect for the general good, guarantee of social peace. Criticism of the electoral system encompassed and explained all: political monopoly was believed to be the source of all evils and disturbances.[9]

One of the central themes of republican literature under the July monarchy is the association of limited suffrage with corruption. Cormenin ably summarised the argument in his highly influential pamphlet, *Ordre du jour sur la corruption électorale et parlementaire*.[10] Corruption, this scourge that ate away at 'the heart and bowels of France', originated, he believed, in the electoral system. As he saw it, individual disorder and the absence of public morality logically derived from the narrow base of the electoral system: they simply extended the initial corruption of political

[7] *Revue républicaine*, vol. 3 (1834) (first article), and vol. 5 (1835) (second article).
[8] *Ibid.*, vol. 3, p. 296 and vol. 5, pp. 62 and 65.
[9] See the highly representative pamphlet of C. Pecqueur, *Réforme électorale. Appel au peuple à propos du rejet de la pétition des 240 mille*, Paris, 1840.
[10] Eighth edition, 1846. Cf. his *Avis au contribuable* of 1842.

representation. 'Seeking to sweep away corruption without introducing universal suffrage is to attempt a useless exertion', concluded for his part Ledru-Rollin; 'it will restrict evil, but will not eliminate it'.[11] Universal suffrage, wrote the *Journal du peuple*, 'renders corruption impossible or impotent; it will substitute compact masses for this kind of fat bourgeois cliques, for these minorities of privilege'.[12] The people, on the other hand, were essentially incorruptible, in so far as they constituted a social unity. They were not incorruptible in the sense of possessing moral virtue, as Saint-Just and Robespierre understood it, but in a more trivial, economic sense: the broadening of suffrage no longer permitted the distorted distribution of public goods, but led almost automatically to equal distribution. 'Elections are corrupted with crosses and posts, but one cannot buy the masses', said Stendhal.[13] The number of 200,000 electors was often parallelled to that of 200,000 officials, as if the ministry were implicitly accused of having bought each vote with the offer of a job.

The theme of affordable government almost naturally elaborated upon the theme of corruption. Here again, Cormenin gave a classic formulation in his *Lettres sur la liste civile*, published for the first time in 1832. Throughout the July monarchy, republicans were convinced that representative government could be nothing other than economic government. Moderates and radicals agreed in their assessment that bureaucracy was not a natural phenomenon, that it was only a perverse effect engendered by insufficiently democratic power. 'Be republican because under the republic, you will have no more taxes to pay, the rich alone will pay them; because you will elect your deputies and your officials; because you will have an affordable government': Laponneraye used expressions very much like those of Cormenin in his *Lettre aux prolétaires*.[14] The rejection of the monarchy inherent in this approach was of a very different nature from the rejection characteristic of the revolutionary period. Here the monarchy was not only challenged as a political form: it was also denounced as a social form. The consequence of this was the veritable reinvention of the republican idea in 1848. The republic of universal suffrage which emerged at that time was not a direct continuation of Condorcet's rational republic or of Robespierre's avenging republic. It

[11] Speech of 31 November 1847, in *Discours politiques et écrits divers*, Paris, 1879, vol. 1, p. 342.

[12] *Journal du peuple*, 11 July 1841.

[13] *Mémoires d'un touriste*, Bordeaux, 1837. For his part, Lamartine said that one might poison a glass of water, but not a river.

[14] *Lettre aux prolétaires*, p. 4: 'Under the monarchy', he writes, 'there are enormous salaries, and still greater expenditures; there is a dilapidation of the state's funds. Under the republic, salaries are proportionate to the absolute necessities of officials, expenditures are limited, public funds are wisely allocated, because the nation itself oversees the allocation.'

was inscribed in a new understanding of the relationship between the social and the political.

On 5 March 1848 a decree of the provisional government instituted direct universal suffrage. All men over the age of twenty-one would henceforth be called upon to elect their deputies, without property qualifications or restrictions of capacity. One name symbolised the accomplishment of this revolution: Ledru-Rollin. Since 22 February, *La Réforme*, which he advised, had simultaneously demanded Guizot's resignation and the institution of the universal vote. Ledru-Rollin's contemporaries considered him to be the true founder of universal suffrage; Louis Blanc, Crémieux and Victor Hugo would all recall this at his graveside.[15] Throughout the 1840s, he made himself the tireless apostle of popular sovereignty, proliferating pamphlets, petitions and depositions of legislative projects at the very moment that the July monarchy seemed to have disarmed its critics and achieved stability. Ledru-Rollin incarnated an entire generation of progressive writers for whom the republican ideal was inextricably linked with universal suffrage, representing this 'sacred ark of democracy' of which Louis Blanc, Ferry and Gambetta were also singing the praises.

In urging the provisional government to proclaim universal suffrage without delay, Ledru-Rollin only continued his earlier struggle; his role was hardly surprising. More unexpected, however, was the general approval with which the decision was greeted. All doubts, hesitations, objections were swiftly swept away; even as many partisans still believed it to be a proposal for the long term, universal suffrage abruptly imposed itself with the force of truth. Cormenin, charged by Ledru-Rollin with preparing the decree to establish the new electoral system, raised only the question of soldiers' and domestics' rights to vote, but the members of the provisional government swept away his hesitations almost without discussion.[16] Technical objections against the possibility of rapidly reading millions of ballot papers bearing several names each – the principle of the list system had been retained – were quickly dismissed as well. Seizing upon the problem, the Academy of Sciences initially urged caution, calculating for example that the reading of the Paris lists by traditional means would take 354 days! But it later revised its opinion, putting its

---

[15] Cf. their speeches of 24 February 1878, reproduced in vol. 2 of *Discours politiques et écrits divers* of Ledru-Rollin.

[16] Cf. on this point the information provided by P. Bastid, *Un juriste pamphlétaire, Cormenin précurseur et constituant de 1848*, Paris, 1948, and the account by Garnier-Pagès in his *History of 1848*, illustrated edition, Paris, n.d., vol. 2, pp. 2–4. See also the recent analysis by Alain Garrigou, 'Le Brouillon du suffrage universel. Archéologie du décret du 5 mars 1848', *Genèses*, no. 6 (December 1991).

methodological uncertainties to rest.[17] Not a single voice within the public was raised in protest or uncertainty; no questions were asked; the cautious and the critics miraculously disappeared. Reform was no longer the issue: the principle of universal suffrage was immediately evident in all of its simplicity and radicalism. Acceptance and enthusiasm were also universal: no one even dreamed of discussing or commenting upon means to implement the new law. Neither the departmental list system, the abandonment of the second ballot, nor the vote for soldiers was contested: these procedures seemed to be simple details, overshadowed by the magnitude of the event. The dominant sentiment everywhere was that something great had just taken place. Everyone spoke of universal suffrage in lyrical and emotional terms: country *curés* and bishops, petits bourgeois of the towns and great landed proprietors, journalists and intellectuals, conservatives and traditionalists.[18] How are we to make sense of this striking conversion and abrupt reversal? Many historians have described this 'spirit of 1848' as extraordinarily enthusiastic and optimistic, a singular crossbreeding of republican utopias and Christian sentiment; but they have generally done so in order to circumscribe it by squeezing it into the frame of exceptional circumstances, underscoring with a kind of relief the resumption of the 'normal' course of history in May, as political and social conflicts intensified under the pressure of the critical economic conditions. And yet, far from constituting a sort of parenthesis in the history of French democracy, the months of March and April 1848 reveal some of its most deep-seated characteristics.

The *Bulletin de la république*, the provisional government's official newspaper, directed by Ledru-Rollin with the assistance of George Sand,

[17] On 3 April 1848, the Academy of Sciences received a report by Cauchy on the means, proposed by authors of various memoirs, of solving the difficulties presented by counting and registering votes under the new electoral system. Having stressed the technical difficulties, the report noted laconically: 'Must we conclude that it is impossible to provide the electoral procedure with the mathematical certainty that is essential to all important operations? ... We think not.' *Comptes rendus hebdomadaires des séances de l'Académie des sciences*, vol. 26 (1848), p. 400.

[18] There are many echoes of the reception of universal suffrage in local monographs devoted to 1848. Amongst the mass of such monographs consulted on this question, the following stand out: M. Agulhon, *La République au village*, 2nd edn, Paris, 1979; A. Charles, *La Révolution de 1848 et la Seconde République à Bordeaux et dans le département de la Gironde*, Bordeaux, 1945; E. Dagnan, *Le Gers sous la Seconde République*, 2 vols., Auch, 1928–9; F. Dutacq, *Histoire politique de Lyon pendant la Révolution de 1848 (25 février–15 juillet)*, Paris, 1910; J. Godechot *et al.*, *La Révolution de 1848 à Toulouse et dans la Haute-Garonne*, Toulouse, 1948; R. Lacour, *La Révolution de 1848 dans le Beaujolais et la campagne lyonnaise*, Lyon, special issue of *L'Album du Crocodile*, 1954–5; G. Rocal, *1848 en Dordogne*, 2 vols. Paris, 1934; F. Rude *et al.*, eds., *La Révolution de 1848 dans le département de l'Isère*, Grenoble, 1949; P. Vigier, *La Seconde République dans la région alpine, étude politique et sociale*, 2 vols., Paris, 1963, and *La Vie quotidienne en province et à Paris pendant les journées de 1848*, Paris, 1982.

aptly describes the tone of general enthusiasm, and the meaning that the inauguration of universal suffrage had for contemporaries. We read in the first editorial: 'The Republic opens a new era for the people. Deprived of their political rights until now, the people, above all the people of the countryside, counted for nothing in the nation.'[19] Universal suffrage was not believed to be a technique of popular power so much as a kind of sacrament of social unity, as the provisional government's *Déclaration*, of 19 March 1848, made vividly clear. 'The provisional electoral law that we have drawn up is the most extensive law of any time or place to call the people to the exercise of man's highest right, his own sovereignty', it stated. 'The right of election belongs to all without exception. *From the promulgation of this law, there is no longer a proletariat in France.*'[20] This last expression is extraordinary, revealing the fundamental association between the suffrage question and the issue of social division. Universal suffrage was seen as a rite of passage, a ceremony of inclusion. As the first elections drew near, the *Bulletin de la république* noted thus, 'The Republic, which excludes none of its sons, calls you all to political life; *it will be like a new birth, a baptism, a regeneration.*'[21]

For two months, in Paris as well as in the provinces, numerous festivals celebrated the new social unity, while trees of liberty were planted everywhere. Unfortunately, there is no good synthesis of the ceremonies and national festivals of the Second Republic that would permit us to form an assessment equal to that of Mona Ozouf for the festivals of the Revolution.[22] But the accounts of the main local studies, as well as the readily available iconography, reveal a few general tendencies, most notably their diffuse religiosity. In all cases, it is clear that the essence of this religiosity lay in the celebration of social unity. Numerous engravings represent allegories of fraternity that bring together workers, peasants and intellectuals, or show parades that unite all trades and social conditions in a single procession. Some testify to extraordinary gestures: in Millery, in the Lyonnais countryside, we see bourgeois serving a table of peasants as a sign of fraternity during a democratic banquet.[23] In Avignon, the representatives of two rival groups pardon one another and embrace solemnly during a ceremony organised by the local republican

---

[19] Dated 13 March 1848.
[20] *Bulletin de la république*, no. 4 (19 March 1848). Declaration written by Lamartine. For his part, Flaubert wrote in *L'Education sentimentale*: 'After the abolition of slavery, the abolition of the proletariat. There had been the age of hate, now begins the age of love' (Paris, 1978, p. 331). (Henceforth, emphasis is original unless stated otherwise.)
[21] *Bulletin de la république*, no. 9, 30 March 1848.
[22] With the exception of a brief synthesis: G. Vauthier, 'Cérémonies et fêtes nationales sous la Seconde République', *La Révolution de 1848*, vol. 18 (June–July–August 1921).
[23] Reported by R. Lacour, *La Révolution de 1848 dans le Beaujolais*, Part II, p. 36.

committee.[24] On 20 April, an enormous festival of fraternity crowned this movement, bringing almost a million people together in Paris. No such gathering had been organised since the festival of Federation in 1790. In *La Cause du peuple*, George Sand offers an account of unbridled lyricism that shares the general enthusiasm. A rapid survey of the Paris press bears witness. *La Réforme* spoke of a 'baptism of liberty'; *Le Siècle* celebrated the unanimity that reigned; *Le National* rejoiced in the hundreds of thousands of voices joined together in a single cry proclaiming 'that there was no longer any kind of division within the great French family'. Even the austere *Constitutionnel* found warm words to speak of a 'real family delight'.

The demonstration of 20 April clearly expressed the belief that social division had been overcome by universal suffrage, that unity had been rediscovered. Far from being treated as a condition of pluralism which permitted the expression of professional differences or the diversity of social interests, the advent of universal suffrage in France was interpreted as a symbol of national concord and of entry into a new political era. Ledru-Rollin explained this in the *Bulletin de la république*, in striking terms that are worth recording:

All living forces of this multiplicitous being that is called the people joined together on the historical stage on 20 April to announce to the world that the solution of all political problems weighs no more than a grain of sand in its powerful hand. Political science is now known to us. It has not revealed itself to a single individual, but reveals itself to all, on the day that the Republic proclaims the principle of the sovereignty of all. This political science will henceforth be one of great and simple application. It will involve nothing more than convoking the people in great masses, the total sovereign, and calling upon unanimous consent to those questions about which the popular conscience speaks so eloquently and unanimously by acclamation.[25]

It is easy to mock such illusions. Since Marx, there has been no shortage of outside witnesses or historians to speak of these sentimental feelings and aspirations towards unity with disdain or condescension. While it is easy and tempting to share their judgement, we must refrain. Far from translating a passing rhetorical illusion or a simple overflowing of good feeling, the statements of a Ledru-Rollin express, on the contrary, some- thing profoundly constitutive of French political culture. In their roman- tic or utopian fashion, they express the essential illiberalism of French democracy. This aspiration to unity was founded on the idea that plural- ism was divisive. Certainly, after May 1848, economic difficulties and political confrontations removed all visible consistency from this theme.

[24] Reports by P. Vignier, *La Seconde République dans la région alpine*, vol. 1, p. 199.
[25] *Bulletin de la république*, no. 19, 22 April 1848.

But the spirit of 1848 did not lose its character of revelation: for a short time, and in its own language, it incarnated the republican utopianism which was the basis of French democracy in the post-revolutionary context. The first universal elections, which took place on 23 April 1848, strikingly illustrate this belief that the object of voting was more to celebrate social unity than to exercise a specific act of sovereignty or to arbitrate between opposing points of view.

By an accident of the calendar, election day fell on Easter Sunday. This coincidence gave rise to a multitude of images and metaphors. Crémieux, a member of the provisional government, spoke of the 'day of social regeneration', and everywhere homilies and political declarations alike associated the resurrection of Christ with the resurrection of the people. The sacramental dimension of the advent of universal suffrage was thus reinforced. Lamartine recalled this, using the words of his contemporaries:

The dawn of salvation rose over France on the day of the general election. It was Easter day, a period of pious solemnity chosen by the provisional government so that the people's work would neither distract nor offer any pretext for shirking the popular duty, and so that the religious reflections, which hover over the human spirit during these days consecrated to commemorating a great cult, make their way into public reflections and give the sanctity of religion to liberty.[26]

The unfolding of the elections themselves helped to reinforce this religious character. Balloting having been arranged to take place at county seats, voters from villages often travelled to the polls together in great processions that criss-crossed the countryside.[27] Many witnesses have described these lay processions preceded by drums and flags, led by mayors and, in some cases, accompanied by *curés*. Tocqueville gave the classic description in the celebrated pages of his *Souvenirs*. Significantly, contemporary images often represent the ballot boxes of the occasion placed upon altars that are flanked by republican symbols, as if the box were the political equivalent of the sacred altar, sign of the invisible but active spirit of the people united by the Eucharist of the ballot. This symbology struck a number of foreign travellers.[28] The calm and order that reigned over these

---

[26] Lamartine, *Histoire de la révolution de 1848*, Paris, 1849, vol. 2, p. 346.

[27] In addition to the monographs already cited, see also: 'Les Elections à la Constituante de 1848 dans le Loiret', *La Révolution de 1848*, vol. 2 (1905–6), and P. Vigier and G. Argenton, 'Les Elections dans l'Isère sous la Seconde République', in Rude *et al.*, eds., *La Révolution de 1848 dans le département de l'Isère*.

[28] Cf. for example the testimony assembled by G. Bertier de Sauvigny, *La Révolution parisienne de 1848 vue par les Américains*, Paris, Comité des travaux historiques de la ville de Paris, 1984, and the memoirs of the marquis of Normanby, at that time ambassador of Great Britain, *Une année de révolution, d'après un journal tenu à Paris en 1848*, 2 vols. Paris, 1858.

first elections can only underscore this dimension of unanimity that was associated with universal suffrage. On the day after the ballot, newspapers commented that all had gone quietly and smoothly. 'This first effort at universal suffrage', noted *La Réforme* on 24 April, 'took place everywhere with great ease, one can even say, with the greatest regularity'. Universal suffrage was immediately legitimated. 'This test is conclusive', we read in the *Bulletin de la république*, 'and if a few timid spirits still had doubts about the easy and complete application of universal suffrage, those doubts have been alleviated by the admirable spectacle just witnessed in Paris'.[29] Almost seven million electors went to the polls on 23 April, representing about 83.5% of registered voters.[30] Electoral participation had broken all records.

The images of social communion that were tied to the entry of the masses into political life extended into the association of universal suffrage with the idea of social peace. A famous engraving of the period represents a worker with a ballot paper in one hand and a rifle in the other. While putting the former into a ballot box, he pushes away the latter. 'This is for the foreign enemy', reads the legend, referring to the rifle; 'this is how we loyally fight adversaries at home', it explains, designating the ballot paper. The idea was widely shared at the time that the inclusion of everyone in political life, by the extension of the right to vote, would suppress revolutionary ferment. This theme had already appeared, albeit in a precocious fashion, at the beginning of the July monarchy. Charles de Coux, a close associate of Lamennais, had used this argument in 1831 to justify electoral reform:

Those who refuse the right of suffrage to the working classes spread a disorder throughout the country that will sweep them away. Deprived of such a right, the working classes can only make their presence felt in the city by entering it as a live force, like a devastating flood or an all-consuming fire. With this right, they will have residence there, something to lose if that residence is violated, hearths to defend, homes to plead for.[31]

At their strongest in the campaign of 1839–40, the republicans permanently took up this arithmetic of conflict; they were certain that the universal vote was the only means to truly end revolution. The central committee of Paris for the 1841 session, for example, concluded with this theme. 'Universal suffrage, far from weakening guarantees of tranquillity, will, on the contrary, have the certain effect of closing the era of revolutions

---

[29] *Bulletin de la république*, no. 20, 25 April 1848.
[30] 6,867,072 voters out of 8,220,664 registered.
[31] Charles de Coux, 'Du cens électoral dans l'intérêt des classes ouvrières', *L'Avenir*, 6 April 1831, p. 3. De Coux is one of the founders of Christian political economy.

forever.'[32] Ledru-Rollin, Armand Marrast, Etienne Arago, Lamennais: all celebrated suffrage during these years as 'eminently pacificatory'. Seen in this light, universal suffrage has an undeniably utopian aspect: it symbolised the dawning of a thoroughly homogeneous, non-exclusive society, which constituted a sort of end to history. Social divisions were conflated with geographic frontiers, and the foreigner was construed as a figure who would, from that point on, be simply outside the political community. But universal suffrage also had a cathartic function; it was a practical means of transforming politics. At the beginning of the 1870s, the founding fathers of the Third Republic would resume the struggle to defend universal suffrage and denounce the threats that called it into question. Marx is known to have ferociously denounced the 'generous drunkenness of fraternity' of the spring of 1848 and to have disdained Lamartine, who said that the provisional government had deferred 'this terrible misunderstanding between different classes'.[33] But his critique was more than a simple expression of his aversion for moderation. Marx was among those who best understood at that time that the specific character of French democracy found expression in the denial of conflict and division. On this point, he precisely distinguished between French and English political experience. 'The universal suffrage that was an expression of *general fraternisation* in 1848', he writes, 'was in England a *war cry*. In France, the immediate content of the Revolution was universal suffrage; in England, the immediate content of universal suffrage was revolution.'[34] This precisely demonstrates the particularity of the relationship between the political and the social in French politics. The political sphere was both institution and structure for the social; its sole functions were not, as in England and the United States, the guarantee of liberties and the regulation of collective life.

How to take further this singular characteristic that we have encountered since the revolutionary period? How may we understand the curious amalgam of the aspiration to unanimity and the egalitarian formalism that was associated with the idea of universal suffrage in France? What is at issue here is the manner in which pluralism is understood. All conflict seems to be a threat to social unity if it can only be associated with radical division, like that between the old and the new, between the Old Regime and the Revolution. Pluralism is unthinkable without a suspension of the original rupture; otherwise, it can only be included within the categories of misunderstanding or the outright

---

[32] Published under the title, *Réforme électorale, municipale, départementale et communale*, Paris, 1840, p. 39.
[33] Cf. his *Les Luttes des classes en France, 1848–1851*.
[34] Article that appeared on 8 June 1855 in *Neue Oder Zeitung*.

conflict of personal ambitions. Class conflict itself was, in a certain sense, interpreted in terms of the revolutionary cleavage, of the confrontation between republic and monarchy that stretched across the whole of the nineteenth century. The consequence was the permanent oscillation between the fanaticism for consensus and the menace of civil war which structured nineteenth-century political life. There was little room within this framework for a pluralist democracy of interests, just as there was little room for a reformist strategy. Universal suffrage was by no means believed to be the political instrument of a pluralist debate. Elections were not expected to effect arbitration or choice, at least not so long as the Revolution was believed to be over and the Old Regime definitively abolished. Nor were elections expected to bring social diversity into the sphere of politics. Rather, in 1848 the act of voting was understood to be a gesture of adherence, a symbolic expression of membership in the collectivity. On 23 April, there was no distinction between collective arrivals at county seats and individual voting. At that time, suffrage had a power equal to that found in contemporary one-party states.[35] Even if events quickly gave popular expression to its dimension of arbitration,[36] the utopia of *suffrage–communion* continued to constitute the limiting horizon of the French representation of politics. For this same reason, the relationship between 'formal' democracy and 'real' democracy acquired a very specific character in France. Beyond the always difficult articulation of law and practice, and the always impure coincidence of interests and good intentions – which constitute the normal field of democracy – democratic formalism played a role that was both more central and more ambiguous. More than anywhere else, formal democracy in France constituted the horizon of real democracy: it was not only its origin and juridical foundation. French democracy endlessly aspired to an abstraction as a realisable form of the political ideal: it aspired to a society without class, without personal conflict, without misunderstanding, freed of all attachment to the past, and eternally devoted to celebrating its unity. Economic competition was soundly rejected for these same reasons, and opposed with regulatory models that were based on collective organisation and centralised co-operation. Thus, the same anti-liberal threat – in the philosophically precise sense of the rejection of pluralism – runs through several dimensions of French culture. Criticism of political parties, denunciation of economic competition, suspicion of social division constituted three facets of the same political vision. In this

---

[35] On the meaning of elections in such countries, see G. Hermet, A. Rouquié and J. Linz, *Des élections pas comme les autres*, Paris, 1978, and R. Lomme, 'Le Rôle des élections en Europe de l'Est', *Problèmes politiques et sociaux*, no. 596, 1988.

[36] After 1849, elections opposed two parties with very distinct programmes.

sense, the spirit of the spring of 1848 remained faithful to the spirit of Jacobinism: only it was a pacified and sentimental version.

The connivance between the Catholic church and the republican spirit of the spring of 1848 also had its origin here. The clergy blessed liberty trees and commemorated the victims of the February days because it was in agreement with the aspirations to unanimity and union that were being expressed in society. Paradoxically, then, the church accepted in the emerging republic only that which was both its most archaic and its most utopian: its radical illiberalism. Similarly, republicans and socialists made Jesus Christ the 'first republican' or 'the brother of all proletarians' because of an exactly symmetrical ambiguity, as the iconography of the period profusely illustrates.[37] This also explains the rejection of Protestantism by all the social writers of the period. In this regard, Cabet or Pierre Leroux, Buchez or Louis Blanc shared the same point of view: they hated the individualist and rationalist character of Protestantism and saw in the Catholic spirit, taken in its broadest sense, the religious matrix of socialism and the modern republic.

In 1848, the 'utopian republic' lasted only the spring. But we cannot judge it by this fugitive appearance. In effect, it expressed, with as much candour as ardour, one of the most profound traits of French political culture: the aspiration to unity and consensus in the political transfiguration of social ties.

[37] On this critical point, see the synthesis of P. Pierrard, *1848 ... Les pauvres, l'Evangile et la révolution*, Paris, 1977; also E. Berenson, *Populist religion and left-wing politics in France, 1830–1852*, Princeton, N.J., 1984 and his article 'A new religion of the left: Christianity and social radicalism in France, 1815–1848', in F. Furet and M. Ozouf, eds., *The French Revolution and the creation of modern political culture*, vol. 3, *The transformation of political culture, 1789–1848*, Oxford, 1989.

11   The identity of the bourgeois liberal republic

John Dunn

To grasp accurately what has been involved in the invention of the modern constitutional republic it is necessary to select a relatively ample framework, both of chronology and of geography. The key practical episodes in this passage of invention may have taken place (as is conventionally agreed) in eighteenth-century north America and France. But it has required most of the twentieth century to clarify even their most essential implications; and it is a trifle sanguine to assume that all of their major implications are yet apparent even today.

At present the modern constitutional republic stands virtually unchallenged as the sole surviving candidate for a model of legitimate political authority in the modern world. It does so, to be sure, in a fairly distinct form – and in a form the merits of which were far from uncontroversial in the north America of the 1780s or the France of the early 1790s.[1] All modern constitutional republics of any longevity now profess to be democracies (as do many regimes which are far from constitutional in the sense in question). Their overt claim to legitimacy is now a direct function of their claim to be democracies. But this last pretension must be understood not as the intrinsically heady classical claim to realise ancient liberty – the claim that the sovereign political community is simply identical with the free public acts of its free citizens[2] – but rather as an instrumental precondition for enjoying (and an assertion of the popular entitlement to enjoy) the more tepid, if more dependable, charms of modern liberty. The demos of the modern constitutional republic is readily distinguishable from the republic itself. However unchallenged it may be in theory, its sovereignty is purely notional in practice:[3] virtually exhausted in a set of guarantees of non-exclusion from civil and political rights, and in no real sense a matter of *agency*.[4]

---

[1] Contrast the views of Madison with those of John Adams: Terence Ball, *Transforming political discourse*, Oxford, 1988, pp. 59–60, 173.
[2] Benjamin Constant, *Political writings*, ed. by Biancamaria Fontana, Cambridge, 1988, pp. 312–28.
[3] Cf. Mogens H. Hansen, *The Athenian democracy in the age of Demosthenes*, Oxford, 1991.
[4] Cf. Hamilton, in Ball, *Transforming political discourse*, p. 72, with Madison, *ibid.*, p. 78.

What distinguishes the modern constitutional republic most sharply from its failed competitors for modern political legitimacy (from more or less aspiringly enlightened absolute monarchy to Marxist–Leninist state socialism, fascism and so on) is less any greater scope for sovereign agency which it contrives to provide for the great majority of its citizens than it is the greater security which it furnishes them for living their lives as they please. By the same token, what distinguishes it most sharply from its ancient republican predecessors is less its far greater demographic and geographical scale, or its firm appropriation of sovereign decision-making from its own citizens, than its steady adoption of the goal, once more, of furnishing these citizens with security to live their lives as they please. In this sense the identity of the modern constitutional republic is given most decisively, both in terms of time and in terms of political alignment, by its commitment to one particular interpretation of the political requirements for modern human flourishing – for living securely and prosperously in an intensely commercialised society within a dynamic world economy. It is given, that is to say, by its full acceptance of modernity – of the human world in which, however resentfully, we all now have to live.[5]

One way of defining the particularity of this relatively modern political form is to stress its legal character and to investigate with care the distinctive political dynamics which emerge from this legal character in particular historical societies. This focus highlights representative democracy as a historically novel governmental form (first named in the late eighteenth century), constitutional rule as a systematic modern rendering of what it is to be a government not of men but of laws, and political parties as a highly institutionalised modern recipe for linking notionally sovereign demos to a practically effective modern legislature and executive. There is everything to be said, in systematic historical analysis, for working carefully through the historical cases one by one in just this perspective. But for purposes of political theory this is too weakly nominalist an approach, not merely because of the bewildering heterogeneity of examples to which terms like republic[6] or constitution have by now been applied but because of its gross lack of intellectual economy.

To see more sharply, it is first necessary to question more brusquely. If we ask why the modern constitutional republic now stands unchallenged as the sole surviving candidate for a model of legitimate political authority in the modern world the answer must be, as I have already suggested, that it and it alone at present provides a serious political recipe for how a given human community today can hope over time to combine a fair measure of security, prosperity and opportunity to live relatively

[5] John Dunn, ed., *The economic limits to modern politics*, Cambridge, 1990.
[6] Cf. already Madison, in Ball, *Transforming political discourse*, p. 76.

unmolested by the power of its rulers. The hope to live in security and to live relatively unmolested by the power of one's rulers were, as Quentin Skinner has recently shown,[7] central preoccupations of the classical republican tradition, as prominent in Niccolò Machiavelli as in a more sceptical eighteenth-century interpreter of the republican legacy like Montesquieu.[8] As Bernard Manin has made impressively clear earlier in this volume, the great eighteenth-century theorists of moderate government, Montesquieu himself and James Madison more especially, set themselves above all to resolve the problem of security for the subjects of a modern state and to do so with particular attention in relation to the dangers which they must always fear from their own rulers. It is not difficult to see in the modern constitutional republic of today clear traces of this eighteenth-century legacy. But it is apparent enough that the cosmopolitan model of today has other elements also. Montesquieu himself, for example, scarcely offers a ringing vindication of the practicability of republican rule on the scale of a modern state. For him, as Judith Shklar says,[9] the ancient or early modern city republics 'acted as contrasts, not examples to be copied'. Even Madison's carefully designed – and in some measure irrefutably practicable – model was devised with great care for a highly distinctive setting and was widely assumed to be inapplicable in the more hectic arena of European statehood. Even a genuinely cosmopolitan zealot for the modern republic like Tom Paine could still conclude, under the pressures of experience, as the nineteenth century dawned: 'I know of no republic in the world but America',[10] and attribute this lonely eminence to the new continent's immunity to Europe's slavish politics.

It was certainly still a very open question, as the nineteenth century dawned, how far a modern constitutional republic could indeed hope to provide a compelling recipe for political legitimacy of any real durability. That question has now been answered, at least for the time being. The question which remains is just what it was about this somewhat hazy formula which enabled it to provide such a recipe. One answer might be that it was its residual republicanism.[11] A second might be that it was its comparatively novel (and as yet somewhat fair-weather) constitutional-

---

[7] Quentin Skinner, 'The idea of negative liberty: philosophical and historical perspectives', in Richard Rorty, J. B. Schneewind and Quentin Skinner, eds., *Philosophy in history*, Cambridge, 1984, pp. 193–221; and his 'Machiavelli's *Discourses* and the pre-humanist origins of republican ideas', in Gisela Bock, Quentin Skinner and Maurizio Viroli, eds., *Machiavelli and republicanism*, Cambridge, 1990, pp. 121–41.

[8] Judith N. Shklar, 'Montesquieu and the new republicanism', in Bock, Skinner and Viroli, eds., *Machiavelli and republicanism*, pp. 265–79.

[9] *Ibid.*, p. 268.

[10] Gregory Claeys, *Thomas Paine: social and political thought*, London, 1989, p. 34.

[11] Cf. Madison, in Ball, *Transforming political discourse*, p. 78.

ism.[12] But a third, and in the end a strategically more compelling, answer will have to be that it was its modernity: not its detailed constructive statecraft (which was often as accident-prone as anyone else's) but its relatively steady imaginative acceptance of the economic limits to modern politics, and its continuing readiness to adjust to these limits in the face of disappointing experience. This is the judgement which I shall try to develop. But before I do so, and before I attempt to draw out some of what I see as its implications, I wish to contrast it in its entirety with the model of classical republicanism as Quentin Skinner has anatomised this.

The city republics of early modern Italy, drawing on Sallust and Cicero but also drawing more directly on their own political experience, praised their own political form for its direct contribution to the attainment of *grandezza* and for securing a free way of life. In Machiavelli's arresting reworking of their vision, the free way of life and the degree of popular commitment to a common good for which that way of life was in his view a clear necessary condition were both in the end vindicated in the last instance because of their indispensable joint contribution to expanding the power and wealth of the community. But, by the time that Montesquieu came to write, it was not necessary to emulate his sceptical sophistication to see that the classical republicans were palpably wrong, at least on this score.[13] A more interesting question, still pressed vigorously by Skinner,[14] is whether the disciplines of a shared civic pursuit of a common good still remain plausible candidates, even for the sceptical and sophisticated, for living in real security. If the answer is in the affirmative this would have two important implications. The first of these, which is acceptable enough, is that part of the explanation of the recent triumph of the modern constitutional republic (and of the astonishing debacle of its greatest historical antagonist) must lie in the former's residual republicanism: the extent to which it does still institutionalise a continuing effective responsibility of rulers to ruled which the latter has flagrantly repudiated. The second, which is less agreeable, is that since this republicanism is so devastatingly residual, the measure of real security available to any modern population must be distressingly slight.[15] (As impressionable readers of Machiavelli are likely to have noticed, however, this last

---

[12] Cf. Keith M. Baker, 'Constitution', in François Furet and Mona Ozouf, eds., *A critical dictionary of the French revolution*, Cambridge, Mass., 1989, pp. 479–93.

[13] Cf. Hont, 'Free trade and the economic limits to national politics: neo-Machiavellian political economy reconsidered', in Dunn, ed., *The economic limits to modern politics*, pp. 41–120.

[14] Quentin Skinner, 'The republican ideal of political liberty', in Bock, Skinner and Viroli, eds., *Machiavelli and republicanism*, pp. 293–309.

[15] *Ibid.*, p. 309; cf. John Dunn, 'Political obligation', in David Held, ed., *Political theory today*, Cambridge, 1991, pp. 23–47.

point scarcely involves a very decisive contrast with the predicament of the citizens of the classical republic.) What we can safely retain from these severely preliminary considerations is the simple judgement that it was always likely to prove true, and has in the end proved true, that the key dimension of practical comparison for modern models of political legitimacy is in their capacity to furnish their political clients with security. The provision of security to human populations is an inherently complicated and accident-prone endeavour; and judgements about how it is best undertaken have naturally shifted extensively over the last few centuries. It is important to register that what has brought the modern constitutional republic to its present lonely eminence as a model for modern political legitimacy is not the clarity and completeness with which it answers the question of how such security can be routinely provided, but simply the decisiveness with which all its extant competitors have now discredited their countervailing claim to be able to furnish it.

When the Chinese leader Deng Hsiao Ping appeared on television to justify his unleashing of the People's Liberation Army onto the student occupiers of Tienanmen Square, he accused his victims of seeking to establish a 'bourgeois liberal republic'. Neither observers' nor participants' testimony gives the least reason to suppose that this was a fair description of the intentions or beliefs of his youthful enemies. But, as events further west have since underlined,[16] there is better reason to accept his assessment of the prospective consequences of their actions, if they had in fact prevailed over the party gerontocracy.

True, the icon of China's student rebels, and the rallying cry which swept Eastern Europe, was the less concrete and more emotive promise of democracy. But democracy was already a nominal property of all the regimes under challenge; and its literal applicability to the regimes of the capitalist West is as open to question today as it has been throughout their history. The real threat to the crumbling edifices of Marxist–Leninist power was – and remains – not the coming of democracy but the advent of the bourgeois liberal republic. What is the bourgeois liberal republic? How and why did it come to be invented? And what do its invention and its drastic subsequent diffusion really signify for modern politics? We have considered principally so far the second of these three questions: the question of how the bourgeois liberal republic came to be invented. But I should like to concentrate most of my own comments on the first and third: on how to see the particularity of this startlingly successful political form and how to assess the significance of its remarkable success.

To capture its particularity it may help to begin with a contrast: with

---

[16] Timothy Garton Ash, *We the People: the revolution of 1989*, Harmondsworth, 1990.

the shaping of classical republicanism in medieval Italy, an intellectual and historical episode in the course of which the term *respublica* or *republica* shifts from being a general term for a lawful political regime to naming a relatively distinct subclass of non-monarchical political regimes.[17] Classical republicanism, as Skinner presents this, was essentially a conception of the special value of elective, non-monarchical, non-hereditary government, contrasted most crucially with *principalities*, as in the opening sentence of Machiavelli's *Prince*,[18] a conception derived practically from the experience of the self-governing cities of the *regnum Italicum*, from at least the twelfth century, and reinforced imaginatively by a Ciceronian (and still more a Sallustian) inheritance that tied internal peace between social forces to the effective pursuit of communal greatness and defined government as a public duty of the impartial equitable care of common interests (the *communes utilitates*) of all the citizens. The system of election to public office, in republics so understood, guaranteed an equality of all citizens before the law and uniquely enabled them to live *in libertate* (without dependence).

The most draconic and disabused statement of this viewpoint is given, classically, in Machiavelli's *Discourses*, which asserts both the unique capacity of republics to observe the *bene commune* and the special potency of a *vivere libero* to engender the *grandezza* of a given community – the expansion of its power, wealth, military viability and glory. Machiavelli's political writings are an extended dissertation on the universality of *danger* in human collective life, on the impossibility of eluding it for ever and on the consequent indispensability of attempting to meet it with energy, skill and cunning. In attempting to meet it, well conceived political institutions are a considerable aid (though not *in extremis*, as the *Prince* makes clear, a firm necessary condition). But even the best conceived of political institutions are very far from being a sufficient condition for doing so. Machiavelli took a keen interest in the causal properties of political institutions. But he also had an exceptionally acute sense of their inherent limitations. He was some way, both in social attitudes and in political expectations, from espousing the late-eighteenth-century republican doctrines of the constitutional state (the conceptions of Madison, Sieyès, Mme de Staël and Constant). Certainly, he could never have said, as Constant does, 'We must have liberty; and we shall have it.'[19]

One important dimension of difference between Machiavelli and the classic theorists of the bourgeois liberal republic lies in the close tie

---

[17] Skinner, 'Machiavelli's *Discourses*', pp. 121–41, esp. p. 133n.
[18] Cf. Madison, in Ball, *Transforming political discourse*, p. 78.
[19] Constant, *Political writings*, p. 325.

between the *ordini* favoured in the *Discourses* and a communal destiny of expansive military power, and the very apparent absence of any comparable link in the case of the republican theorists of the constitutional state, with their principled aversion to the spirit of conquest. There are many reasons for that absence in the latter case – not all of them necessarily flattering to the moderns. But one blatant and eminently consequential one is the strong link between late-eighteenth-century understandings of popular sovereignty (central to the rejection of *ancien régime* dynastic monarchy) and the belligerently universalist *Droits de l'Homme*. *Grandezza* is an inherently zero-sum concept. But it is a painful encroachment on the normative force of any universal claim of human right when it must be secured explicitly *at the expense of* the rights of other putatively equal human beings.

Machiavellian republicanism can treat the world as its oyster. Whatever its ultimate telos may be deemed to be (the protection of the security of the domestically preoccupied and mildly ignoble populace, the extraversion of the dominating energies of the ambitious *grandi*, or the collective shared grandeur of the community at large), that telos is still consistently and painlessly egocentric, whether at an individual or at a collective level. The political space of modern republicanism, by contrast, certainly from the time of the late-eighteenth-century republican theorists of the constitutional state, is very much part of the space of modern political legitimacy; and that space is cosmopolitan by conceptual compulsion. The quest for *grandezza* is no less blatant in modern political practice than it was in twelfth- or sixteenth-century Italy.[20] But no modern state even perfunctorily concerned with political legitimacy can afford to acknowledge its own quest for *grandezza* in explicitly egocentric terms. (To be truly legitimate today the pursuit of *grandezza* should ideally be conducted not by a particular people but by – or at least on behalf of – *all* peoples: not by one nation but by the United Nations.) But the bourgeois liberal republic is not just conscientiously discreet about such concern as it may have for its own relative power when set besides other states. It is not just a pure model of domestic political legitimacy which just happens to be defined with intellectually prudent parsimony. It is also a model which, implicitly or explicitly, repudiates the possibility of defining a state model in relation to foreign military danger. This brings out an important, if equivocally acknowledged, feature of the model, best captured perhaps by Immanuel Kant; a suppressed international dimension constituted by its dependence on a mutually recognising system of other sovereign states. In place of a necessarily unstable field of external

---

[20] Paul Kennedy, *The rise and fall of the great powers*, London, 1988.

power which could be lived with at ease only by dint of being dominated (brought under control), the bourgeois liberal republic conceives itself as located within, and in some measure externally secured by, a common framework of international law, sustained in the last instance by the regular efforts of other sovereign states. Not all theorists of the bourgeois liberal republic were inclined to take the existence of this framework for granted even before the French revolutionary wars began;[21] and it would have required a heroic feat of selective inattention to take it wholly for granted once these wars were in full swing. But it is fair to say, as comes out in Bianca Fontana's essay above and classically in Constant's *Spirit of conquest*, that the theorists of the bourgeois liberal republic were at their least impressive when it came to explaining how or why their favoured model of political legitimacy could hope to *win* the wars in which it found itself embroiled against the very different state forms which at intervals have happened to menace it. It is worth underlining how far from settled confidence the practice of statecraft within bourgeois liberal republics has been on this very issue virtually without interruption from 1792 to the present; and how very recently indeed the grounds for optimism in the face of their most military triumphant twentieth-century competitor have gained so dramatically in force.

International military viability (or its absence) can reasonably be treated as a theoretically extrinsic property in a model of legitimate political authority (even if that was not the way in which classical republicans happened to conceive it). But domestic political (and hence domestic military) viability cannot so readily be regarded as an extrinsic property of a legitimate political order (or rather it can be so treated only where a legitimate political order is conceived intentionally – as a formal structure of public right – and not consequentially as a concrete regime with the causal capacity to persist in the historical setting of a real society and economy over time). It is therefore imperative to bear sharply in mind, while considering the process of inventing the modern constitutional republic, the distinction between a formal normative criterion for the legitimacy of a modern political authority and a concrete recipe for establishing and sustaining institutions which meet this criterion in practice.

The late-eighteenth-century republican doctrines of the constitutional republic, as Pasquale Pasquino has insisted earlier in this volume, combine two essential elements: a rigorous insistence on the principle of the separation of powers, on the need to restrain, limit or moderate government in both its legislative and its executive elements (on the need

---

[21] Cf. Hamilton, in Isaak Kramnick, *Republicanism and bourgeois radicalism*, Ithaca, N.Y., 1990, ch. 8.

to restrict the scope of the claims of political authority and rightful coercive force), and, on the other hand, an acceptance of popular sovereignty understood both as a legal practice of authorisation to govern, and as a real causal limit on the governmental power that peremptorily excludes any countervailing authorising principles, from dynastic right to special expertise, normative or practical. (The Soviet Union had long had an extremely elaborate constitution; it was emphatically not a monarchy; and it had always fondly supposed itself to be as modern as states come. But until extremely recently it was certainly not a modern constitutional republic because of the prominence within it of the countervailing authorising principle of special expertise in the understanding of History.)

Over the last two centuries History has in fact done everything to confirm the realism of insisting on each of the two key elements of the modern constitutional republic. But it has done nothing to confirm their joint sufficiency for realising the rights or securing the interests of any set of human beings. The political world which we inhabit is saturated with the discourse of public right. But it remains an eminently Machiavellian world. What has made the bourgeois liberal republic the political victor of the late twentieth century is its thus far unique combination of coherent address to the issue of how governmental power can be justified at all, with realistic causal analysis of the methods that can hope to establish and prolong justified governmental power in practice. By the same token, what defines the limits of its sway has been and remains its lack of a causally adequate answer to the question of how justified governmental power can in fact be established, or still more frequently, how it can be prolonged for any length of time in a wide variety of historical settings. This need not be seen as an intellectual deficiency in late-eighteenth-century doctrines of the constitutional republic. (Whether it should be so seen depends principally on just what question one takes those doctrines to be attempting to answer.)[22] But it has certainly been a notable setback for modern political legitimacy.

There were probably more bourgeois liberal republics or republican constitutional states in the immediate aftermath of the collapse of European colonial rule than there had ever been before. But a good many of them have not stayed the course. There are still plenty of sites in the world where establishing a bourgeois liberal republic is less an uphill struggle than an exercise in historical levitation. It is therefore of considerable

---

[22] Cf. Biancamaria Fontana, *Rethinking the politics of commercial society: the 'Edinburgh Review', 1802–1832*, Cambridge, 1985 and her *Benjamin Constant and the post-revolutionary mind*, New Haven, Conn., and London, 1991.

importance to understand just what features of a society really are incompatible at a particular time with the bourgeois liberal republic: not just sites where the *popolo* and the *grandi* hate each other with almost as much violence as either cares for their own security (like El Salvador) or where several different political communities are ready to struggle with each other until death within what is notionally a single political community (like the Lebanon or Eretz Israel), but also the far greater variety of other settings from Brasilia and Buenos Aires to Berlin, Djakarta, Tokyo, Seoul, Manila and Beijing where the bourgeois liberal republic has been tried out for a time and gone under, or where it has required the drastic application of foreign power to give it at all a protracted chance. The Japanese and German economies are not merely by some way the most dynamic economies of the advanced world; they are also located in what at present appear especially firmly constituted bourgeois liberal republics. The manner in which a modern society comes by its constitution, it seems, perhaps somewhat against Sieyès's expectations, is not of overwhelming significance in determining the latter's eventual political prospects. Foreign bayonets, it appears, may serve just as well in the right place and at the right time as the free and externally unprompted public deliberation of the representatives of the nation.

Every actual bourgeois liberal republic is always two very distinct things. The first is a self-defining and elaborate schema of public law, allocating rights and duties across a human population and a territory and defining an immense variety of permissible and prohibited relations between them. This aspect goes back quite consciously not merely to Sieyès or Madison and their own personal intellectual heroes but also to the extraordinarily intricate heritage of European legal history for well over two millennia. But the second is wildly more complicated and dense still: the full weight and texture of a very vaguely and discontinuously bounded assemblage of human interactions. In these interactions the schema of public law is of great importance as a practical resource for human agents and agencies. But the vagueness and discontinuity of the interactive boundaries are deeply at odds with the fictive clarity and determinacy of the system of public law. The bourgeois liberal republic is a state form for a nation. But what is a nation? Sieyès defined a nation as an ensemble of the producers of goods and the providers of services. The aristocracy had no claim to special political rights – to political privilege – because they made no special contribution (Sieyès claims, in the teeth of modern professional historiography, no contribution at all) to meeting the common needs of the nation. Nobility is bad for the character and subversive of the very capacity to provide practically for others' needs. A selfish and parasitic grouping rule. Everything would go better without the aristocracy.[23]

But quite apart from its flagrant (and no doubt perfectly conscious) mystification of the nobility's contribution to the economic, political and intellectual life of France, Sieyès's portrayal has obvious difficulties as an approach to specifying the basis of modern politics. The provision of goods and services for a modern population is very far from being a domestic national achievement. The idea of a French national economy, genuinely under the charge of the French state, is, as President Mitterrand found out early in his first presidency, a tottering ideological fiction. And if a nation in modern politics is indeed a daily plebiscite, then the results of that plebiscite are always liable to come out differently on different occasions. It is neither because of the intrinsic determinacy of its territorial scope nor because of the degree of its mastery of a local economic arena that the bourgeois liberal republic has won through to such cosmopolitan political dominance. Perhaps the best clue to its triumph is still that proffered by its sternest enemies: its special relation to a structural entity which has historically no doubt always been poorly named as the bourgeoisie, but which plays essentially the role allotted by Marx to that putative class.

What the bourgeois liberal republic has the proven capacity to do (and its opponents have on the whole denied themselves the opportunity to do at all steadily) is to treat the bourgeoisie (the private possessors of capital), however flexibly, as in the last instance a public good.[24] The view that privately owned capital, viewed systemically rather than personally, is indeed a public good was common to Hume and Adam Smith,[25] to Madame de Staël,[26] to Macaulay and James Mill,[27] just as much as to Hayek or Milton Friedman. In the competitive circumstances of a modern representative democracy it can (and perhaps should) come out as a rational conclusion even on Marxist premisses for those with nothing but their own labour to sell.[28] The bourgeois liberal republic makes no overt promise to defend the bourgeoisie (or private capital) as such. But when in full working order, it does in fact defend this quite effectively even over very long periods of time.

[23] Emmanuel Joseph Sieyès, *What is the Third Estate?*, transl. M. Blondel, London, 1963, pp. 55–8, 177.

[24] Cf. Mancur Olson, *The logic of collective action*, Cambridge, Mass., 1965.

[25] Istvan Hont and Michael Ignatieff, eds., *Wealth and virtue: political economy in the Scottish enlightenment*, Cambridge, 1983; Istvan Hont, 'Property and authority: Adam Smith's critique of contractarianism', forthcoming.

[26] Fontana, ch. 6 above.

[27] Jack Lively and John Rees, eds., *Utilitarian logic and politics*, Oxford, 1978.

[28] Adam Przeworski, *Capitalism and social democracy*, Cambridge, 1985.

The late-eighteenth-century republican doctrines of the constitutional state both precede and learn from the political experience of the French revolution. It was their prior conceptions and their subsequent learning, taken together,[29] that have given them a steadier and more realistic appreciation of the political prerequisites for securing the *communes utilitates* of a modern population than the more stirring and erratic tradition of Marxist political practice. Conceived and stated very much as proposals for the politics of a commercial society, the bourgeois liberal republic has never been an exclusive candidate for the defence of these political needs; and it has never succeeded in monopolising their defence in practice.

There are at least two reasons why its standing today is so much higher than it was twenty years ago.[30] One is the very close tie between the concept of the bourgeois liberal republic and the idea of universal human rights (an idea notoriously scorned in the Marxist tradition, if perhaps in a less than ultimately coherent fashion).[31] The second is the equally close tie between an essentially market-articulated economy and reasonably efficient production within the contemporary world market. In this connection, the former is in even the medium term a necessary and not a sufficient condition for the latter. But the discovery that it really *is* (at least at present levels of human comprehension and practical skill) a necessary condition[32] has crushed the plausibility of Marxist politics at its very heart.

Both classical and modern republicanism have been deeply concerned with the design of a durable core of political institutions, allocating power amongst different social groupings and channelling its exercise towards a lasting public good. But it is fair to say that the idea of a *constitution*, conceived as a scheme for regulating the scope of a community's domestic politics, plays a far more dominant role in the self-understanding of the bourgeois liberal republic. Not merely were ancient republics, as Constant insisted,[33] obsessively and necessarily concerned with warfare (with hazard in relations outside the community); but even seventeenth-century republican theorists like Grotius were as apt to see the republic as a practical device for pursuing *grandezza* and meeting external hazards, as they were to see it as a system for regulating domestic conflicts of interest. When they judged the felicity of the fundamental institutions of a community, they did so just as much from the viewpoint of its *external* as of its

---

[29] Cf. Fontana, *Rethinking the politics of commercial society*, ch. 1.
[30] Cf. John Dunn, *Modern revolutions*, Introduction to 2nd edn, Cambridge, 1989. (First published 1972.)
[31] Steven Lukes, *Marxism and morality*, Oxford, 1985.
[32] Wlodzimierz Brus and Kasimierz Laski, *From Marx to the market*, Oxford, 1988.
[33] Constant, *Political writings*, pp. 313–28.

internal affairs. The republic of Venice might appeal to Grotius because of its masterly defence of the massive social distance between aristocracy and people. But for Algernon Sidney, 'the too great inclinations of the Venetians to peace is . . . a mortal error in their constitution'.[34] As the title of section 23 of the second chapter of his *Discourses* uncompromisingly proclaims: 'That is the best Government, which best provides for war.'[35]

Modern republican theorists may have liked to think that the spirit of conquest was deeply alien to the modern republic and to the commercial society on which it was founded (at any rate, insofar as the conquest of other civilised societies was concerned.[36] But it is better to see war as a consideration which they (unlike Sidney) felt it safe to ignore when they came to assess the merits of a constitution. And they did have very distinguished precedents for this intellectual decision. No one could accuse Hobbes of ignoring war. But it is important that he saw external dangers to a political community as lying beyond the powerfully civilising potential impact of rational thought on collective human life: 'Time, and Industry, produce every day new knowledge. And as the art of well being, is derived from Principles of Reason . . . So, long time after men have begun to constitute Common-wealths, imperfect, and apt to relapse into disorder, there may Principles of Reason be found out, by industrious meditation, to make their constitution (excepting by externall violence) everlasting.'[37] Excepting by externall violence . . .

It is History, not theoretical argument (or industrious meditation), which has vindicated the political superiority of the bourgeois liberal republic; and in that history the risks of external violence have been (and palpably remain) of overwhelming importance. It is still quite plausible, for example, that what actually broke the political plausibility of the bourgeois liberal republic's ghostly enemy, the proleterian illiberal republic, was not the lamentable living standards and odious arbitrariness to which the latter's privileged rulers subjected its alleged beneficiaries (defects which have been present in large measure since its inception) but rather the crushing competitive advantage of the American economy as a basis on which to prepare for *war*, and the single-mindedness with which that advantage was applied by President Reagan and Secretary Weinberger.

If we see, as Pasquino has suggested above, the separation of powers and an electoral interpretation of the requirements for popular sover-

[34] Jonathan Scott, *Algernon Sidney and the English republic, 1623–1677*, Cambridge, 1988, p. 32.
[35] Algernon Sidney, *Discourses concerning government*, 2nd edn, London, 1704, p. 146.
[36] Cf. John Dunn, *Interpreting political responsibility*, Cambridge, 1990, ch. 5.
[37] Thomas Hobbes, *Leviathan*, ed. by Richard Tuck, Cambridge, 1991, p. 232.

eignty as key components of the bourgeois liberal republic, and a commercial society (a society organising a huge proportion of its production, distribution and exchange through more or less doctored markets) as its initial (and thus far indispensable) base, then the conception of the bourgeois liberal republic is a precarious fusion of two very different modern idioms of ethical thought – deontological theories ascribing rights to all human beings in virtue of their humanity (or perhaps more narrowly to all human agents in virtue of their agency), and consequentialist theories assessing the distribution of utilities or preferences, or more broadly, welfare outcomes, and deeply preoccupied, accordingly, with questions of social, political and economic causation.

These two idioms are not, of course, wholly insulated from one another. But they impose very different structures on political assessment.[38] They press very different questions; and they prompt pretty different conclusions. The former idiom – deontological theories ascribing rights – is far more intimately bound up with the idea of a *constitution* than the latter is.

From a utilitarian point of view the bourgeois liberal republic at time T is a well- or ill-designed mechanism for generating desirable political consequences for a given historical society. But a *Rechtsstaat* (*Metaphysik der Sitten*), a true republic or representative system of the people, requires a constitution of some kind as a matter of legal logic and not merely of technical expediency. A *Rechtsstaat* is *constituted* as such by having a genuine constitution, and is preserved through time by that constitution's continuing to be observed. The two idioms, therefore, differ sharply over the question of what a constitution is *for*. If what a constitution is for is to specify and assign rights, then its relation to rights is internal and logical: indeed, at some level of abstraction, it is actually textual.

But to specify and assign rights is very different from delivering them. Whether a constitution holds effective authority, whether it is in fact observed, and above all whether it succeeds in guaranteeing in practice the rights which it affirms in theory, are plainly none of them textual properties of the constitution. They are emphatically causal features of the historical state whose constitution is in question, features corresponding to (or painfully discrepant from) its assignment of rights. The constitutions commended by late-eighteenth-century republican theorists of the constitutional state were commended for their assignment of rights: commended both for the superior fairness with which they allocated these rights and for the greater efficacy with which they in fact secured these rights against the arbitrary will of the ruler. The first property can be

---

[38] Cf. Stedman Jones, ch. 8 above.

equated with the intentionality of the constitutions themselves, a Dworkinian feature of them.[39] But the second certainly cannot be so equated. Even Bodin's *République* assigned some rights through its public law; but it cannot be said to have furnished them (or even perhaps to have fully *intended* to furnish them)[40] with a very powerful defence against the more or less arbitrary wills of actual rulers.

We can see the importance of this contrast if we consider the minimal value which Machiavelli's *ordini* and Montesquieu's separation of powers and Madison's contributions to the *Federalist* and Sieyès's clarion call to the Third Estate alike aspire to guarantee: the value of living in security. This extends beyond the most minimal value which modern political theorists have volunteered to serve: the value of the preservation of life itself. But it supplements that ultra-minimal goal with a psychological penumbra of assurance which goes a bit closer to capturing what might make a human life worth living. Preservation is a necessary condition for other human goods or rights to be satisfied. But security is closer to the assurance that at least some of them *will* be realised in practice. Security of life and property, as Montesquieu and Hume both argued, *can* be just as compatible with monarchy as with republican rule. Liberty and moderation are not attributes of a particular form of government. But moderate regimes do preclude the single clearest domestic threat to security – the direct sway of unmediated will: despotism. Despotism, in effect, *guarantees* insecurity, while a functional division of governmental agencies establishes the supremacy of law, creates a hierarchy of norms, and rules out government by mere will. Montesquieu's and Madison's interpretations of the separation of powers aspire to show how political power can rationally inhibit and restrict its own scope and strengthen its claim on popular allegiance by doing so through offering its subjects a measure of genuine security.

Seen in this perspective, the constitution of a moderate government is both a legal text establishing a clear hierarchy of norms (and procedures for their interpretation) and a piece of political technology calculated more or less successfully to ensure their application in practice. Here the two distinct conceptions of the mechanics through which the separation of powers acts, outlined by Bernard Manin, fit rather differently. Considered as a system for enforcing *limits* on the exercise of power, the constitution can well appear the mode for ensuring the government of laws not men; and authoritative social action can centre on (and at times almost become equated with) the defence and enforcement of rights: a true republic by the most exacting of Kantian standards. But the second

[39] Cf. Ronald Dworkin, *Law's Empire*, London, 1986.
[40] Cf. Julian H. Franklin, *Jean Bodin and the rise of absolutist theory*, Cambridge, 1973.

mechanism, stressed at greater length by Manin, the mechanism of *delay*, stands in a more obviously external relation to rights.

The retardation of wrong is better than the acceleration of wrong. It gives right a better (or at any rate, a longer) chance. But it cannot offer the (no doubt often illusory) promise to *stop* wrong in its tracks.[41] Once again, the protection of security (or rights more generally) through political technique stands in a less direct and intimate relation to constitutions than the specification of a compelling assignment of rights.

Pasquino identifies three factors as jointly responsible for the creation of the late-eighteenth-century constitutional republic: an economic process seen as irreversible and essentially positive, a crisis of the spiritual foundations and beliefs on which *ancien régime* monarchy depended, and a process of political and constitutional reflection (under fairly brisk prompting from immediate political experience) which resulted in the case of the United States and France in the installation of written constitutions. This is a convincing summary. But what exactly *is* the political entity created by the operation of these factors? Or rather, what is it when seen not just as a tissue of legal intentionality but also as a complex structure of socio-economic and political fact?

Its belated historical triumph makes this a question of very considerable historical importance. But how is it to be answered? One response would be simply to say that it is not a clear question (or perhaps even a question at all): that we can ask what Hobbes and Hume and Montesquieu and Madison and Sieyès and Constant and Hamilton and Smith and Condorcet and so on thought, and perhaps why they thought it; but we cannot coherently ask how far they were right to think what they thought or how far we would not be right in agreeing with them. But I do not myself think that this will do.[42] If we can ask what Montesquieu and Madison thought, we can certainly ask what *we* think.

Another answer (plainly with much to recommend it) is that the bourgeois liberal republic is essentially a legal instrumentation of the rights of man (human beings) and the citizen, firmly committed to the primacy of internal politics, and clearer and less deceptive than any of its predecessors or subsequent competitors on the nature of a just relation between political authority, power, and the rights of its own subjects.

I doubt, however, whether it really is this estimable aspect of the bourgeois liberal republic that has either secured its triumph or been responsible for the fairly substantial tracts of space and spans of time where it has failed to triumph over the last two centuries and the

---

[41] Cf. rights as trumps: Ronald Dworkin, *Taking rights seriously*, London, 1977.
[42] John Dunn, *Storia delle dottrine politiche*, Milan, 1992.

appreciable tracts in which it is unlikely to triumph more stably in the readily imaginable future.

These limits of its sway, I would wish to argue, have been a product of its technological limitations: its failure to specify an array of institutions and practices capable of furnishing its subjects with security of life and capable of protecting that array against internal and external threat: no security without protection. As a technical expedient for guaranteeing security of life, the bourgeois liberal republic could not endorse (and no doubt has not characteristically endorsed) the primacy of internal politics, though it has certainly taken a less voracious view than Algernon Sidney did of the comparative status both of external politics in general and of armed conflict in particular. Vulnerability to external violence remains of great practical importance. It has crushed the bourgeois liberal republic often enough in the present century, came quite close to eliminating it from the European continent within my own lifetime, and is still eminently capable of preventing its establishing in all too many settings. Constitutional order, economic organisation and the relations between social forces are still of great importance in determining a regime's capacity to withstand external violence. But it is fair to say that the bourgeois liberal republic has done as well in the face of external violence as any other type of regime of which we know, and that it has been especially effective when it confined itself to defending its own territories rather than seeking to retain control of large areas of other peoples'.

It is in its internal organisation and domestic self-understanding that both the distinctive power and the distinctive residual vulnerability of the bourgeois liberal republic resides. The last two centuries have certainly shown that the power, in the competitive circumstances prevailing, is appreciably greater than the residual vulnerability. But if we are to understand its properties clearly we must try to grasp *both*.

To do so, it helps, I think, to focus on Bernard Manin's point (Chapter 2, above) that the theoretical inheritance of the bourgeois liberal republic from its two great intellectual forebears, Montesquieu and Madison, does not include a substantive conception of a *bien commun*. Moderate government is deeply concerned with restricting the scope of governmental power; and the last two centuries have underlined the wisdom of that preoccupation with devastating thoroughness. But it approaches this task of restriction on the basis of a wary and tentative sense of practical prudence, not on behalf of a determinate schedule of goods or rights that imperatively require respect. Moderate government is a practical expedient: not a seamless exercise in the enacting of right (or, indeed, in the engendering of good). The ultimate preference for delay over limits as the mechanism for securing moderation, so emphasised by Bernard Manin, stems not from any indifference to rights on the part of its theorists (Montesquieu, for example, offers about the most resonant denunciation of slavery in the entire eighteenth century). Rather, it stems from the impossibility in a disenchanted world of designing a trustworthy endogenous political enforcer of an objective right or good. (Not that it had proved especially easy to design one even in a world still rather thoroughly enchanted.)

The bourgeois liberal republic is very much an enemy's appellation. Insofar as it is analytically apt, it is important to recognise less the imposition of an alien class truth than the product of the (no doubt often mythical) bourgeoisie's superior plausibility as a prudent and unoppressive representative of the *communes utilitates*.[43] Delay is no *guarantee* of anything at all (least of all security). But hastiness and despotic power are real human evils, and greater evils the greater the scale of power that lies in human hands.

But superior representative plausibility need not mean very great plausibility. It is in comparison with the grotesquely and flagrantly *implausible* that this superiority has recently been demonstrated so spectacularly. The bourgeois liberal republic remains acutely vulnerable not in its preference for moderate over absolute government or for responsible over despotic government, but in its purported synthesis of the legitimatory appeal of popular sovereignty with the practical articulation of interests. Here the prominence of the theme of education in the thinking of its more beleaguered defenders is acutely revealing. The legitimatory appeal of popular sovereignty is in the long run (the last instance) credibly embodied only in an exceedingly wide franchise. But it is not only in late-eighteenth-century Naples that an exceedingly wide franchise may be bad news for the *popolo civile*.[44] The uncivil people (the *popolo naturale*, or *promiscua plebs* of sixteenth-century Scotland) has remained an occasion for potential anxiety to all subsequent interpreters of the bourgeois liberal republic, up to the days of Seymour Martin Lipset and Samuel Huntington. As John Arthur Roebuck observed dolefully in the year of Queen Victoria's accession:[45] 'There is no chemical fusion to make a hundred ignorant individuals, one instructed body.'[46] The instrumental case for linking governmental choices even very distantly to the widest possible franchise can be most convincingly derived (as Bentham said that James Mill's

---

[43] Przeworski, *Capitalism and social democracy*, and his *Democracy and the market*, Cambridge, 1991.

[44] Cf. Pagden, ch. 7 above.

[45] William Thomas, *The philosophic radicals*, Oxford, 1979, p. 243.

[46] But compare the recipe of Joseph Schumpeter, *Capitalism, socialism and democracy*, London, 1950.

political creed was derived), 'less from love of the many than from hatred of the few'.[47] Machiavelli himself would hardly have demurred.[48]

The bourgeois liberal republic does a reasonably good job (perhaps, at its best, as good a job as can readily be done) at moderating modern government. But it is distinctly less convincing as a mechanism for securing the just and effective representation of interests. No one who considered the American legislative process at all closely and with minimal intellectual honesty could solemnly defend the view that it constitutes a dependable system for identifying and promoting an impartially conceived common good. (Perhaps professional participants in American national politics would be the least inclined to sustain such a claim.) Quite severe doubts have been raised over the last few decades about whether *any* modern political institutions really are well designed to locate and promote common economic interests of national populations (let alone of wider human groupings); and those institutions which look best equipped at least to *locate* such interests accurately – the OECD, for example – seem to be so essentially because of the extent to which they are extricated from immediate political pressures. The problem of motivating and instructing power is no more dependably solved in the late-twentieth-century West (or Japan)[49] than it was in fourth-century Athens.

This brings me to my final point. Insofar as the bourgeois liberal republic does succeed in institutionalising a common national interest of the governed against both their own governors (and presumably, as and where necessary, against the governors and governed of all other nations), it does so, not because the interests of its subjects coincide or because it can be trusted implicitly to serve them effectively, or even to grasp in the most rudimentary way what they in fact are. Rather, it succeeds because of its comparatively limited intrusion into a quite distinct site of power – the production and exchange of a domestic economy and a global market.[50]

In this sense a commercial society is not just a historical contribution to the genesis of the bourgeois liberal republic. It is also a precondition for the latter's major, and thus far historically decisive, merit. A society linked by market exchange (even within its own national boundaries) is not, as American political scientists in the postwar decades sometimes fondly supposed, at all a dependable instructor of power. (There *are* no dependable instructors – or even dependable systems of incentives – for

[47] Thomas, *The philosophic radicals*, p. 131.
[48] Skinner, 'The idea of negative liberty'.
[49] Kent Calder, *Crisis and compensation*, Princeton, N.J., 1988; Daniel I. Okimoto, *Between MITI and the market*, Stanford, Calif., 1989.
[50] Dunn, ed., *The economic limits to modern politics*.

the holders of power.) What can be said simply is that a society linked by market exchange has a capacity of its own to promote many human interests; and that such capacity does not depend on either the initiative or the intelligence of the holders of political power, and is certainly more dependable than any comprehensive alternative society or economy devised in its entirety by those holders. To live in a society dominated by market exchange is often humanly very ugly. But it has everything to be said for it in comparison with living for any length of time under a poorly informed and self-righteous despotism.

Bibliography

The purpose of this bibliography is to suggest some introductory reading on the history and theory of classical and modern republicanism. It includes only secondary sources and does not list all the works cited in this volume.

Appleby, Joyce, *Liberalism and republicanism in the historical imagination*, Cambridge, Mass., 1992.

Aylmer, G. E., *The Levellers in the English revolution*, London, 1975.

Baczko, Bronislaw, *Comment sortir de la Terreur – Thermidor et la Révolution*, Paris, 1989.

Bailyn, Bernard, *The ideological origins of the American revolution*, Cambridge, Mass., 1967.

Baker, K. M., 'Constitution', in F. Furet and M. Ozouf, eds., *A critical dictionary of the French revolution*, Cambridge, Mass., 1989, pp. 479–93.

Ball, Terence, and Pocock, J. G. A., eds., *Conceptual change and the constitution*, Lawrence, Kans., and London, 1988.

Baron, Hans, *The crisis of the early Italian Renaissance: civic humanism and republican liberty in the age of classicism and tyranny*, Princeton, N.J. (1955), rev. edn, 1966.

Bock, Gisela, Skinner, Quentin, and Viroli, Maurizio, eds., *Machiavelli and republicanism*, Cambridge, 1990.

Bouwsma, William J., *Venice and the defense of republican liberty*, Berkeley, Calif., 1968.

Buel, Richard, Jr, 'Democracy and the American revolution: a frame of reference', *William and Mary Quarterly*, 3rd ser., vol. 21 (1964), pp. 165–90.

Burns, J. H., and Goldie, Mark, eds., *The Cambridge history of political thought, 1450–1700*, Cambridge, 1991.

Burrow, John W., *Whigs and Liberals: continuity and change in English political thought*, Oxford, 1988.

Campbell, R. H., and Skinner, Andrew, eds., *The origins and nature of the Scottish Enlightenment*, Edinburgh, 1982.

Dunn, John, *Interpreting political responsibility*, Cambridge, 1990.

   Modern revolutions, Cambridge (1972), 2nd edn, 1989.

   Storia del Pensiero Politico, Jaca Book, Milan, 1992.

Dunn, John, ed., *The economic limits to modern politics*, Cambridge, 1990.

   Democracy, the unfinished journey: 508 BC to AD 1993, Oxford, 1992.

Fink, Zero S., *The classical republicans*, 2nd edn, Evanston, Ill., 1962.

Finley, Moses, *Politics in the ancient world*, Cambridge, 1983.

Fontana, Biancamaria, *Rethinking the politics of commercial society; the 'Edinburgh Review', 1802–1832*, Cambridge, 1985.
  Benjamin Constant and the post-revolutionary mind, New Haven, Conn., and London, 1991.
Forbes, Duncan, *Hume's philosophical politics*, Cambridge, 1975.
Forsyth, Murray, *Reason and revolution. The political thought of the abbé Sieyès*, Leicester, 1987.
Fritz, Kurt von, *The mixed constitution in antiquity*, New York, 1948.
Furet, François, *Interpreting the French revolution*, Cambridge, 1981.
Gauchet, Marcel, *La révolution des droits de l'homme*, Paris, 1989.
Gueniffey, Patrice, 'Les Assemblées et la représentation', in K. Baker, C. Lucas and F. Furet, eds., *The French revolution and the creation of modern political culture*, 3 vols., Oxford, 1987, vol. 2, pp. 233–57.
Gwyn, W. B., *The meaning of the separation of powers. An analysis of the doctrine from its origins to the adoption in the United States constitution*, New Orleans, La., 1965.
Haitsma Mulier, Eco O. G., *The Myth of Venice and Dutch republican thought in the seventeenth century*, Assen, 1980.
Halévi, Ran, 'The constituent revolution: the political ambiguities', in K. Baker, C. Lucas and F. Furet, eds., *The French revolution and the creation of modern political culture*, 3 vols., Oxford, 1987, vol. 2, pp. 69–85.
Hampson, Norman, *Prelude to Terror: the Constituent Assembly and the failure of consensus, 1789–91*, Oxford, 1988.
Hansen, Mogens H., *The Athenian democracy in the age of Demosthenes*, Oxford, 1991.
Herman, Arthur, 'The Huguenot Republic', *Journal of the History of Ideas*, vol. 53 (April–June 1992), pp. 249–69.
Higonnet, Patrice, *Sister republics: the origins of French and American republicanism*, Cambridge, Mass., and London, 1988.
Hill, Christopher, *The world turned upside down*, 2nd edn, Harmonsworth, 1975.
Hont, Istvan, and Ignatieff, Michael, eds., *Wealth and virtue: political economy in the Scottish Enlightenment*, Cambridge, 1983.
Houston, Alan Craig, *Algernon Sidney and the republican heritage in England and America*, Princeton, N.J., 1991.
Keohane, Nannerl O., *Philosophy and the state in France: the Renaissance to the Enlightenment*, Princeton, N.J., 1980.
Keonigsberger, H. G., ed., *Republiken und Republikanismus im Europa der Frühen Neuzeit*, Munich, 1988.
Koselleck, Reinhart, *Critique and crisis*, Oxford, 1988.
Kramnick, Isaak, *Republicanism and bourgeois radicalism*, Ithaca, N.Y., 1990.
Lively, Jack, and Rees, John, eds., *Utilitarian logic and politics*, Oxford, 1978.
McCoy, Drew R., *The last of the Fathers*, Cambridge, 1989.
MacPherson, C. B., *The political theory of possessive individualism*, Oxford, 1962.
Mager, W., 'Republik', in O. Brunner *et al.*, eds., *Geschichtliche Grundbegriffe*, vol. 5, Stuttgart, 1984, pp. 549–651.
Mandler, Peter, *Aristocratic government in the age of reform, 1830–1852*, Oxford, 1990.

Manin, Bernard, *Elective aristocracy: an essay on the character of modern democracy*, Cambridge, 1993.

Nedelsky, Jennifer, *Private property and the limits of modern constitutionalism: the Madisonian framework and its legacy*, Chicago, Ill., 1990.

Nicolet, Claude, *L'Idée républicaine en France. Essai d'histoire critique*, Paris, 1982.

Palmer, R. R., *The age of democratic revolution: a political history of England and America, 1760–1800*, Princeton, N.J. (1939), 1964.

Pangle, Thomas L., *The spirit of modern republicanism: the moral vision of the American founders and the philosophy of John Locke*, Chicago, Ill., 1988.

Pasquino, Pasquale, 'Emmanuel Sieyès, Benjamin Constant et le gouvernement des modernes', *Revue française de science politique*, vol. 37 (1987), pp. 214–29.

'Le Concept de nation et les fondements du droit public de la révolution: Emmanuel Sieyès', in F. Furet, ed., *L'Héritage de la révolution française*, Paris, 1989, pp. 309–33.

Patrick, Alison, *The men of the first French republic: political alignments in the National Convention of 1792*, Baltimore, Md., 1972.

Pitkin, Hanna F., 'Republicanism', in D. Miller, ed., *The Blackwell encyclopaedia of political thought*, Oxford, 1987, pp. 433–6.

Pocock, J. G. A., *The Machiavellian moment. Florentine political thought and the Atlantic republican tradition*, Princeton, N.J., 1975.

Virtue, commerce and history, Cambridge, 1985.

Pocock, J. G. A., ed., *Three British revolutions: 1641, 1688, 1776*, Princeton, N.J., 1980.

Pole, J. R., *Political representation in England and the origins of the American republic*, London, 1966.

Przeworski, Adam, *Capitalism and social democracy*, Cambridge, 1985.

Democracy and the market, Cambridge, 1991.

Raynaud, Philippe, 'La Déclaration des droits de l'homme', in K. Baker, C. Lucas and F. Furet, eds., *The French revolution and the creation of modern political culture*, 3 vols., Oxford, 1987, vol. 2, pp. 139–59.

Richter, Melvin, *The political theory of Montesquieu*, Cambridge, 1977.

Rosanvallon, Pierre, *Le Moment Guizot*, Paris, 1985.

'L'Utilitarisme français et les ambiguïtés de la culture politique prérévolutionnaire', in K. Baker, F. Furet and C. Lucas, eds., *The French revolution and the creation of modern political culture*, 3 vols., Oxford, 1987, vol. 1, pp. 435–40.

Schmitt, Charles, and Skinner, Quentin, eds., *The Cambridge history of Renaissance philosophy*, Cambridge, 1988.

Scott, Jonathan, *Algernon Sidney and the English republic, 1623–1677*, Cambridge, 1988.

Shalhope, Robert E., 'Toward a republican synthesis: the emergence of an understanding of republicanism in American historiography', *William and Mary Quarterly*, 3rd ser., vol. 29 (1972), pp. 49–80.

'Republicanism and early American historiography', *ibid.*, vol. 39 (1982), pp. 334–56.

Shama, Simon, *Patriots and liberators: revolution in the Netherlands*, London, 1977.

Shklar, Judith, *Men and citizens: a study of Rousseau's social theory*, Cambridge, 1969.

Montesquieu, Oxford, 1987.

Skinner, Quentin, *The foundations of modern political thought*, 2 vols., Cambridge, 1978, vol. 1, *The Renaissance*; vol. 2, *The age of reformation*.

Tackett, Timothy, 'Nobles and Third Estate in the revolutionary dynamic of the National Assembly, 1789–1790', *The American Historical Review*, vol. 94 (April 1989), pp. 271–301.

Thomas, William, *The philosophic radicals*, Oxford, 1979.

Tuck, Richard, *Natural rights theories. Their origin and development*, Cambridge, 1979.

Valensise, Marina, 'The French constitution', in K. Baker, C. Lucas and F. Furet, eds., *The French revolution and the creation of modern political culture*, 3 vols., Oxford, 1987, vol. 1, pp. 441–67.

Venturi, Franco, *The end of the Old Regime in Europe, 1768–1776*, Princeton, N.J., 1989. [Vol. 3 of *Il settecento riformatore*, Turin, 1979.]

Vile, M. J. C., *Constitutionalism and the separation of powers*, Oxford, 1967.

Waley, Denis, *The Italian city-republics*, 3rd edn, London, 1988.

Woloch, Isser, 'Republican institutions, 1797–1799', in K. Baker, C. Lucas and F. Furet, eds., *The French revolution and the creation of modern political culture*, 3 vols., Oxford, 1987, vol. 2, pp. 371–87.

Wood, Gordon S., *The creation of the American republic, 1776–1787*, Chapel Hill, N.C., 1969.

The radicalism of the American revolution, New York, 1992.

Woronoff, Denis, *La République bourgeoise de Thermidor à Brumaire, 1794–1799*, Paris, 1972 (Nouvelle histoire de la France contemporaine, vol. 3).

Index